DRIVERLESS

DRIVERLESS

Intelligent Cars and the Road Ahead

Hod Lipson and Melba Kurman

The MIT Press
Cambridge, Massachusetts
London, England

This book was set in Century Schoolbook and Gotham by Toppan Best-set Premedia Limited. Printed and bound in the United States of America.

Library of Congress Cataloging-in-Publication Data

Names: Lipson, Hod, author. | Kurman, Melba, author.
Title: Driverless : intelligent cars and the road ahead / Hod Lipson and
    Melba Kurman.
Description: Cambridge, MA : The MIT Press, [2016] | Includes bibliographical
    references and index.
Identifiers: LCCN 2016012608 | ISBN 9780262035224 (hardcover : alk. paper)
Subjects: LCSH: Automobiles--Automatic control. | Autonomous vehicles. |
    Autonomous vehicles--Social aspects. | Autonomous vehicles--Environmental
    aspects. | Traffic safety--Technological innovations.
Classification: LCC TL152.8 .L57 2016 | DDC 388.3/42--dc23 LC record
    available at https://lccn.loc.gov/2016012608

10   9   8   7   6   5   4   3   2   1

Contents

Preface   vii
Acknowledgments   ix

1   The Robotic Chauffeur   1
2   A Driverless World   23
3   The Ultimate Mobility Device   45
4   A Mind of Its Own   65
5   Creating Artificial Perception   85
6   First There Were Electronic Highways   107
7   Build Smart Cars, not Smart Highways   127
8   Rise of the Robots   149
9   Anatomy of a Driverless Car   171
10   Deep Learning: The Final Piece of the Puzzle   197
11   Fueled by Data   237
12   The Ripple Effects   255

Afterword: The Cambrian Explosion   279
Notes   291
Index   307

Preface

The mundane automobile is about to disrupt your life. Thanks to rapid advances in mobile robotics, cars are poised to morph into the first mainstream autonomous robots that we will entrust with our lives. After almost a century of failed attempts to automate driving, modern hardware technology, and a new generation of artificial-intelligence software called *deep learning*, are giving cars human-level ability to safely guide themselves through unpredictable environments.

We wrote this book to tell the story of this revolution. We found ourselves drawn to driverless cars for two reasons. First, we keep a close eye on potentially disruptive new technologies, and driverless cars promise to be one of the most game-changing new machines we'll encounter in our lifetimes. The second reason was more personal. Like most people, we drive an hour or two a day in all kinds of weather, frequently with precious cargo—kids, friends, and pets—on board. Yet, if it were possible, we would prefer to drive, but without having to sit behind the steering wheel ourselves. When Google's driverless cars started making real progress a few years ago, needless to say, we paid close attention.

In the coming decades, driverless cars will gradually replace human-driven vehicles. As transportation evolves into an automated, on-demand service, the result will be a major paradigm shift in the way cars move people and goods around the physical world. Driverless cars will change our perception of time and space, how we commute to work, where we live, and how we shop.

We believe that many changes will be positive, as driverless cars will save millions of lives, smooth congestion, and help clear the air. Parents will no longer spend several hours in traffic each day chauffeuring their kids to school and activities; the elderly and disabled will gain new mobility.

Every disruptive technology has a dark side, however, and driverless cars are no exception. Millions of truck drivers and taxi drivers will lose their jobs. Public transportation will languish as people are drawn to the unbeatable convenience of on-demand, driverless pods that can pick anyone up, anywhere, at any time, for less than it costs to buy a bus ticket. Unless stringent privacy protections are put into place, driverless-car passengers might find themselves sacrificing privacy for safety and convenience as the software that guides their driverless car tracks and logs their every move.

In the following pages, we explain how cars will be transformed into intelligent transportation robots. We assess the impact that driverless cars will have on the automotive industry. We describe how cities will be affected as driverless cars transform everyday driving, a tedious and dangerous activity, into friction-free personal mobility. We explore the nearly sixty-year-long history of failed attempts to automate driving. Finally, we guide the reader through a clear and engaging explanation of the hardware and software technologies that enable the modern driverless car.

Our goal is to give readers the insight they need to make sense of the new world that lies ahead, when driverless cars outnumber those with human drivers. We hope you will enjoy the journey.

Acknowledgments

This book grew organically over the years from inspiring and illuminating discussions we've had with numerous people. We owe special thanks to all those who helped shape this text one way or another.

We'd like to thank two long-standing luminaries of the field of autonomous vehicle research, Brad Templeton of Singularity University and Alain Kornhauser of Princeton University. It is difficult to find independent experts on the topic who are deeply knowledgeable about robotics and embedded in the automotive field, yet able (and willing) to freely share their insights and opinions. We have gained tremendously from conversing with Brad and Alain in person and from reading their blogs and regular email digests.

We would also like to thank Carnegie Mellon University's NREC staff, and in particular Brian Zajac, who spent hours giving us a grand tour of their facilities and all things autonomous. We'd like to thank Dr. Amnon Shashua, founder of Mobileye, for sharing his insights on machine vision with us.

We owe an intellectual debt to the current and former students of the Creative Machines research lab at Cornell University and at Columbia University for their research on autonomous systems and AI. In particular, thanks to Jason Yosinski for being one of the first to recognize the value of deep learning. We are grateful for Jason's insistence that we develop deep-learning software applications in the lab years before deep artificial neural networks gained the wide acceptance they enjoy today.

We appreciate the hard work and dedication of the team at MIT Press, particularly Marie Lufkin Lee, Michael Sims, and Kathleen Hensley, for their enthusiastic support of the book.

Finally, no book on driverless cars would be possible without the inspiration and genius of the creative and bold innovators out there, the engineers, developers, inventors, artists, and entrepreneurs, both past and present. Thanks to you, soon the streets, parking lots, and highways of the world will be a better and safer place.

1

THE ROBOTIC CHAUFFEUR

In the not-so-distant future, automotive museums will host exhibits of highly polished cars from the early twenty-first century. Like history buffs ducking through the doorway of a carefully preserved medieval hovel on a historic estate, museumgoers will squeeze themselves into the car's front seat. People will sit behind the steering wheel, poke at the screen of the built-in GPS, and playfully pump the brake with their foot, marveling that, not so long ago, everyone used such an inconvenient and dangerous mode of transportation.

Today's cars are brainless. The standard automotive "platform" of the modern car (four wheels, a metal body, and a gasoline-powered engine) has not changed significantly since its introduction nearly 100 years ago. Meanwhile, the rest of the world has been shaken to its foundations by increasingly intelligent software, nearly ubiquitous communication networks, and robust and accurate hardware sensors that shrink in size and price each year. Thanks to recent advances in robotics technology and artificial-intelligence software, the era of unintelligent cars is finally coming to an end. The everyday car is about to evolve into a self-guided, mobile robot.

For nearly a century, human-driven cars have shaped our lives. The introduction of horseless carriages rearranged the layout of "walking cities," lives of small meandering alleyways and homes intermingled with shops and public squares, into "driving cities," tidy grids of wide streets and parking lots. Cars gave people freedom, as well as access to new work and social opportunities. Cars gave businesses the ability to rapidly deliver their products to entirely new markets.

Precious personal mobility, however, has come at a high price. Over the course of nearly one hundred years, traffic accidents have stolen millions of lives. While cars give people the freedom to drive long distances to work, their use has also catalyzed the development of a new evil: traffic-choked cities and suburbs. Today, as people in cities all over the world embark on their daily, solo commute to work and freight trucks haul goods to their final destination, urban air has degenerated into an oily cloak of yellowish smog.

Roughly one billion human-driven cars roam the Earth. Our reliance on cars is costly on many levels. Yet, for most of the world's population, car travel remains the speediest, cheapest, and most comfortable form of personal mobility available. For better or worse, cars will remain an integral part of modern life.

The best way to solve the problems caused by cars is to make them smarter. When human drivers let intelligent software take the wheel, driverless cars will offer billions of people all over the world a safer, cleaner, and even more convenient mode of transportation. In the next decade, self-driving cars will hit the streets, once again rearranging where we live and how we work and play.

Skeptical? We don't blame you. For nearly a century now, various experts have predicted the demise of human beings at the hands of intelligent machines.

So far, these predictions have come true only in highly specific industrial jobs, or in activities confined to the virtual world. For example, mechanical robotic arms flawlessly do work once performed by human factory workers. In the virtual realm, artificial-intelligence software has bypassed our human ability to play board games, make rapid stock market trades, or plan optimal routes for complex, mass transit systems.

It's true that modern software boasts a lot of intellectual horse-power and advanced robots are capable of performing skilled work. Yet, even the most advanced artificial-intelligence software programs falter when they're tasked with managing the movements of a robotic body that's not bolted down, but equipped with mechanical limbs so it can move about and interact with its environment. For several reasons we will explore in later chapters, mobile robots today are about as physically nimble and perceptive as a cockroach or, on a good day, a toad.

While roboticists continue to struggle to build capable mobile robots, building a reliable driverless car is a feat of engineering that's technologically well within reach. When it comes to writing code to manage physical movement, cars enjoy a major advantage over other forms of mobile robots: it's easier to roll than to walk or climb.

Software that guides the movements of a multilimbed artificial creature rapidly balloons in volume and complexity because multiple limbs can assume a nearly infinite number of different types of movements and positions. In contrast, a car's four wheels, brakes, and steering wheel behave in a fairly predictable manner. The software that guides the physical movements of a driverless car must manage a relatively small set of actions, such as turning the car's wheels in the right direction and overseeing the car's stopping and acceleration.

The second reason the task of driving lends itself to automation is that guiding a car is a relatively repetitive and reactive activity. Humans of all levels of intelligence are able to obtain a driver's license. A driverless car needs to be only aware enough to respond immediately to clear physical hazards such as an approaching pothole or slow-moving herd of schoolchildren, to plan a route along clearly delineated roads and highways, and to obey relatively clear traffic rules.

At this point, a skeptic would (correctly) point out that there must be more to the story. If building a driverless car were as simple as programming a four-wheeled robot to follow the rules of the road, driverless cars would have become commonplace decades ago. There are two reasons why cars are only now becoming capable of guiding themselves. The first is practical: the bar is high. Cars are two-ton metal boxes that run on public streets. If something were to go wrong with the software that guides a driverless car, the results would be gruesome and tragic.

The high cost of human life explains why the first autonomous vehicles are in use today in places where human casualties would be minimal if a vehicle were to malfunction and veer unexpectedly off course. In remote Northern Australia, for example, mining companies use gigantic autonomous trucks to haul gravel. In North America, farmers use self-driving tractors to seed, plow, and spray vast, unpopulated agricultural fields. In distribution centers and factories, specialized automated vehicles move boxes from one side of the room to the other. At resorts and airports, driverless shuttles carry passengers back and forth on set tracks at speeds of fifteen miles per hour.

The second and more formidable challenge that has delayed the development of driverless cars is purely technological. Although 99 percent of the time driving is mind-numbingly dull and predictable, 1 percent of the time it suddenly becomes exciting. Biological life forms rely on so-called "simple" instincts to deal with the unexpected events that life throws at us. The instincts that enable humans to drive through rush-hour traffic actually cloak a formidable amount of intelligence.

Roboticists have given a name to the unexpected rare events that take place 1 percent of the time: *corner cases*. Corner cases are unusual situations that are difficult to anticipate but can have potentially catastrophic results. How effectively a robot's artificial "instincts" handle corner cases ultimately determines that particular robot's reliability, and hence its usefulness. If a robot's software is unable to handle each and every one of the corner cases it encounters, the best-case scenario would be that the robot is unreliable; the worst-case scenario would be that the robot would fail miserably at its assigned mission and wreak havoc.

Driving might be mostly repetitive, but it's fraught with an endless supply of potentially deadly corner cases. The software that guides a driverless car must be able to instinctively react to a deer that leaps onto the hood of a car, or know how to handle the aggressive panhandlers who swarm cars with spray bottles, hoping that passengers will pay them for cleaning the windshield. Despite decades of effort, automotive engineers and roboticists have failed to write software capable of handling the infinite variety of situations a driverless car will encounter on the road.

One of the basic rules of robotics is that the simpler and more predictable the environment (i.e., the lower the number of corner cases), the easier it is to build software to enable a robot to navigate that environment. Robots thrive in industry because the typical factory is a *closed world,* a highly structured environment in which corner cases have been anticipated and carefully removed by industrial engineers. In a closed-world environment, a robot's work setting is carefully designed around a particular task. Robots in industrial settings know what's coming. They run on software that that guides the robot through a series of unchanging activities such as stamping metal parts, attaching bolts, or lugging boxes from one place to another.

While it's possible to set up a tidy closed-world environment in a factory setting, in the real world, streets and highways are chaotic and unpredictable. Anyone behind the wheel of a car must not only deal with novel situations, but with another related challenge that's difficult for software programs to address: interactions that are guided by rules of conduct that are either vague or highly situation-specific. In particular, artificial-intelligence software stumbles over two activities that are critical for safe driving: complex nonverbal communication and the ability to consistently recognize the same object in a wide range of settings.

Driving demands complex social communication between other drivers and pedestrians. Human drivers routinely engage in a nonverbal "social ballet" when they're behind the wheel, nodding, waving, and making eye contact to announce their intentions. Waving and smiling may be simple activities for humans but it's extraordinarily difficult to write software that can read people's facial expressions and body language and respond appropriately.

Not only do mobile robots struggle to engage in complex non-verbal communications, their computer-guided intelligence falters when faced with an unexpected event. Both of these shortcomings are caused by a deficiency of perception, the ability to make sense of what one sees and to react accordingly. Ideally, computer scientists would solve this problem by writing a program to provide cars with consistent, accurate artificial awareness and situational understanding. The problem has been that until very recently, such software has not existed.

Since the founding of the field of artificial intelligence more than half a century ago, computer scientists and roboticists have unsuccessfully searched for ways to automate the mysterious art of perception. One aspect of perception involves cognition, a person or animal's ability to get a "read" on a complex situation, and to know how to respond appropriately. Another involves processing visual data. Living things have highly developed visual systems capable of recognizing an object even when viewing it from different angles, in different lights or in unusual settings.

Humans process visual data instinctively and nearly flawlessly. Yet, our capacity for making sense of what we see has resisted automation. For decades, researchers in the field of *machine vision* have tried and failed to create software that, like us, is capable of rapidly and accurately "understanding" the visual environment. The lack of such software has been a major technological barrier in the field of mobile robotics research.

For most of their history, robots have struggled to process visual information. Industrial robots deal with this shortcoming by toiling blindly in closed-world environments in dark, unlit factories. For robots whose work involves some kind of visual activity, their workday is set up in such a way that they are never asked to classify or inspect objects that are unfamiliar to them.

One of the barriers to the development of machine vison software has been insufficient computing power. Since processing images is a data-intensive activity, the first machine-vision systems streamlined the process by using a structured approach that used a set of rules to parse visual information. These early machine-vision systems worked by attempting to match perceived objects against a robot's small template library of known objects, a slow, inaccurate, and inflexible process.

One of the biggest weaknesses of early machine-vision software was that it proved unreliable when presented with a novel object or situation. As a result, any robot (or vehicle) guided by such software would be frequently unable to recognize even familiar objects if they appeared in a slightly unfamiliar setting. Since the ability to correctly identify nearby objects is key to safe driving, underperforming machine vision software has held back the development of driverless cars for decades. A recent breakthrough in artificial intelligence, however, promises to change everything.

After years of languishing in the fringes of academic artificial-intelligence research, in 2012 a new type of software called *deep learning* has attained human-level accuracy in correctly classifying random objects in thousands of digital images. While the ability to classify random objects in images accurately may sound trivial, that ability provides a foundation for artificial perception. Once an object can be correctly identified, it can be "handed off" to other types of artificial-intelligence software that can do what software traditionally does best: calculate the optimal response using either statistical reasoning or a logical, rule-based approach.

One of the reasons deep-learning software is so effective for driverless cars is that it's ideal for use in unstructured environments such as the open road. Deep learning belongs to a category of artificial-intelligence software called *machine learning* that breaks tradition by not being designed by a human programmer. Rather than attempting to build a model of the world and address it using formal logic and rules, machine-learning software is "trained" to do its job by being fed huge amounts of *training data*. To develop deep-learning software for a driverless car, for example, programmers "feed" the software program a daily feast of gigabytes of raw visual data gathered by driving around with a camera on board.

The fact that deep-learning software "learns" by looking at the world gives it another major advantage: it's not rule-bound. In the same way a human toddler learns to recognize objects according to their distinctive, identifying features, deep-learning software classifies objects according to their visual features. A software program using a traditional rule-based approach would falter in confusion if presented with an image of a cat riding a bicycle. In contrast, deep-learning software would focus on the cat's identifying visual features—perhaps its pointy ears and tail—and would quickly (and correctly) surmise that although the cat appears in an unusual setting, it's still a cat.

Deep learning has transformed the study of artificial perception and is being applied with great success to speech recognition and other activities that require software to deal with information that presents itself in quirky and imperfect ways. In the past few years, in search of deep-learning expertise, entire divisions of automotive companies have migrated to Silicon Valley. Deep learning is why software giants like Google and Baidu, already armed with expertise in managing huge banks of data and building intelligent software, are giving the once-invincible automotive giants a run for their money.

Deep learning has been so revolutionary to the AI community that its reverberations are still unfolding as we write this book and will likely continue to unfold in the years ahead. Cars won't be the only technology that's transformed by deep learning. We predict that deep learning will change the developmental trajectory of mobile robotics in general. As robots gain the ability to visually understand their environment, the development of artificial life forms will follow a path similar to that already trod by biological life forms more than 500 million years ago.

The fossil record indicates that roughly before the Cambrian Era, all biological life forms were blind. As the Cambrian Era dawned roughly 500 million years ago, nearly blind organisms whose "eyes" consisted of primitive clusters of light-sensitive cells suddenly and mysteriously evolved complex new visual systems. Once they could see, these simple organisms also evolved complex physical body shapes capable of rapid response and locomotion. New physical capabilities, in turn, demanded the development of a bigger brain to oversee the coordination of these new limbs and fins. Armed with a visual system, a responsive body, and a bigger brain, what were once blobs of cells evolved into a diverse set of complex creatures that crawled out of the primordial ooze and adapted to thrive in a particular niche on land.

One intriguing hypotheses for the Cambrian Explosion—the burst of rapid evolution that took place during the Cambrian Era—is the Light Switch theory. This theory, developed by Andrew Parker, holds that the evolution of eyes initiated an evolutionary arms race among living things, and those with the best vision became the most likely to survive. Perhaps the Light Switch theory will apply to robots, too.

As once-blind machines gain the gift of perception, they, too, will crawl out of their primordial confinement in the structured and unlit industrial environments where they dwell today. Robust machine vision will enable robots to make use of new physical configurations of wheels, limbs, or treads that will grant them new levels of agility. To guide their complex new mechanical "limbs," their robotic brains will also expand. We will witness a Cambrian explosion of robotic diversity of form and function as sighted robots master new skills and find productive new niches in which to work.

GETTING TO DRIVERLESS

A school of tropical fish is a beautiful sight to behold. Their brightly colored bodies wiggle through the water in an evenly spaced tight formation. This collective of dozens of individual fish can pivot and change direction in a split second, moving with the tight precision of a single body. If an obstacle suddenly appears in the school's path, individual fish swarm past the obstacle and swiftly reestablish themselves in their original formation. Fish never collide with one another, nor do they ever collide with unexpected objects—branches, rocks, a coral reef—that the sea throws into their path.

In an ideal future, our streets and highways will glisten with schools of tightly packed driverless cars. Like fish, swarms of driverless cars will demonstrate extraordinary anti-collision abilities, navigating intelligently and instinctively through urban streets full of pedestrians and falling gracefully into fuel-efficient formations on long, empty stretches of highway. Some cars will carry a passenger or two. Others will be empty, on their way to drop off a pizza or to pick up a child from daycare.

How do we get from now, from today's clumsy human-guided traffic formations, to this ideal future where driverless cars of all shapes and sizes smoothly and safely swarm the streets? In Ernest Hemingway's 1926 novel *The Sun Also Rises,* character Bill asks another character Mike, "How do you go bankrupt?" "Two ways," Mike responds. "Gradually and then suddenly."

The technology will develop suddenly. By now, most people reading this book are familiar with Moore's Law. Moore's Law is the observation that as the performance of computer chips continues to improve at an exponential rate, the price and size of the chips drop at a corresponding asymptotic rate. As reflected by Moore's Law, the technologies that enable driverless cars—sensors, lots of data, and computing power to process it all—have become reliable, robust, and affordable.

The exact configurations vary, but most driverless cars use several digital cameras, a radar sensor, and a laser-radar (lidar) device to "see" where they're going (for an in-depth exploration of these enabling technologies see chapter 9). Digital cars pair a *global positioning system* (GPS) device with another location device called an *inertial measurement unit* (IMU) that compensates for GPS inaccuracies. An on-board computer takes the information streaming in from the sensors and GPS, folds that data onto a high-definition digital map that contains information on intersections and stop lights, and processes it all together into a digital model of the world outside the car called an *occupancy grid*.

Driverless-car technology is nearly mature. Elon Musk, CEO of car company Tesla and an advocate of fully autonomous vehicles, sums up the situation. "It's a much easier problem than people think it is. ... But it's not a one-guy-three-months problem. It's more like, thousands of people for two years."[2] While the technology may be nearly ready, the society that's wrapped around that particular technology may not be.

Several social factors will delay the deployment of driverless cars. One of the lessons that software developers reluctantly learn is the *people problem*. When new software programs are introduced into an organization, the biggest barrier to adoption is usually not the performance of the technology; it's the fact that the organization's culture and workflow are built on previous software products, and changing people's work habits stirs up resistance. As their workflow changes, some people lose turf, others are forced to rethink how they get things done, and so on. The people problem is frequently the iceberg hidden underneath the surface that can foil an organization's successful adoption of a new technology that would otherwise save the organization time and money and improve productivity.

In the adoption of driverless cars, one aspect of the people problem might be resistance from consumers, but we predict otherwise. Although the executives of automotive companies gamely insist that people love the experience of driving, and will continue to prefer it, we believe that consumer acceptance will not be an obstacle. Research by the accounting firm KPMG indicates that many consumers would happily ride in a driverless car, assuming the technology was mature and there were no risks to their personal safety. When researchers asked people what the likelihood was on a scale of one to ten that they would ride in a self-driving car for everyday use, the focus group respondents rated their willingness at an average level of six out of ten. If a driverless car reduced their travel time by 50 percent and could get them to their destination at a guaranteed time, respondents' willingness increased to nearly eight.[3]

Research by Boston Consulting Group revealed a similar enthusiasm. A survey of more than 1,500 U.S. drivers revealed that 55 percent of respondents said they would likely, or very likely, buy a partially automated car within five years, and 44 percent said they would be very likely to buy a fully self-driving car within ten years should they become commercially available.[4] The report predicted that the first autonomous vehicles would be available for purchase in the year 2025, and that by 2035, roughly 10 percent of new vehicles sold will be fully autonomous, representing a global market worth $38 billion.

The younger the consumer, on average, the greater his or her enthusiasm for driverless cars. A survey by Harris Poll queried four age groups, millennials (ages 18–37), generation X (38–49), baby boomers (50–68), and matures (69+) on their attitudes on self-driving vehicles.[5] More than half of the "matures" vehemently responded, "I will never consider buying or leasing a self-driving vehicle," compared to only 20 percent of millennials. Nearly 25 percent of surveyed millennials said they would buy a driverless car when they believed the "bugs" had been worked out, and when their cost dropped to a reasonable price. We suspect the adoption would be even higher once cars are proven to drive more safely than a human.

Younger drivers are just not that into driving and, unlike their grandparents, would be happy to let a robot take the wheel. In a talk we watched at an autonomous vehicle conference in 2014, an executive of the consulting firm JD Powers described a generational shift his firm observed when studying attitudes toward cars and driving.[6] People under age thirty, a demographic some call *generation Y*, view time spent driving as a hindrance, forced dead-time away from social media and the internet. The executive summed up the situation, saying that "the young folks, the Gen Y ... tend to be less engaged with the idea that driving is something we should cherish. ... Their main motivation is to get to where they're going. ... They're looking for having that time to be useful to them in their own personal way."

The more significant people problem that will delay the widespread adoption of driverless cars will be government oversight and regulation, in particular, state and federal traffic regulations, liability laws, and insurance coverage. Thus far, the most significant force behind the development of driverless cars has come from industry. Federal oversight of autonomous driving has gotten off to a slow start. In 2016, however, the U.S. Department of Transportation began to show signs it might be warming up to the potential benefits of driverless cars by announcing plans to provide guidance to state Departments of Motor Vehicles on driverless-car regulation. At the time of this writing, in the United States, four states—California, Nevada, Florida, and Michigan—offered an official autonomous car license and several states are considering one.

A driverless license is a good start, but a significant amount more research and exploration of regulatory oversight is needed. Ideally, the highest levels of the government should adopt a proactive, rather than reactive, approach. For example, legal experts need to examine and possibly revamp liability laws to clarify who, exactly, is at fault in a driverless accident. Car insurance will need to be similarly restructured. Legislators will need to decide how safe is safe enough for a car to drive without a human at all, and how safety should be tested. Although these challenges of governance are entirely solvable, as they remain unaddressed, human-driven cars will continue to reap their grisly harvest in the form of lives lost, time wasted, and polluting fuel burned.

As driverless-car technology matures and the people problem rears its ugly head, the cost of delay can be directly tallied in the number of human lives lost. According to the World Health Organization, car accidents are the leading cause of death worldwide among people aged 15 to 29, and the second leading cause of death for all age groups. Most of these traffic tragedies are caused not by vehicular malfunction, but by preventable human error, or the "4 Ds," drunk, drugged, drowsy, or distracted drivers.

As long as humans are still behind the wheel, the number of deaths from car accidents is likely to grow. People in emerging economies have eagerly embraced car ownership; in developing nations such as China, India, Brazil, and Russia, as more cars crowd the roads, the number of people injured and killed will also increase. Another hazard is that distracted driving is on the rise: in the year 2013, 424,000 people in the United States alone were injured in car crashes caused by a distracted driver, an almost 10 percent increase from the year 2011.[7]

A CURE FOR THE DEADLIEST DISEASE

One peculiar irony of the automobile is that while cars have killed millions of people since their invention, our society has a blind spot—perhaps grim acceptance—of the resulting death toll. Each year, cars kill about 1.2 million people around the world.[8] To put things in perspective, an annual 1.2 million fatality rate is equivalent to having ten Hiroshima-scale atomic bombs go off each and every year.

Cars are nearly as deadly as war, violence, and drugs combined. Homicide, suicide, and war are responsible for the death of an estimated 1.6 million people each year.[9] An estimated 183,000 people die annually from drug-related causes.[10] Yet, despite the high global death toll from preventable car accidents, there's no federally funded "war on cars" or calls to ban people from driving. In the aftermath of yet another massive freeway pile-up that sends dozens of people to the hospital, there's rarely lasting public outrage against car companies.

What if there were a solution to reduce the number of people who die each year in a car crash? If such a solution existed, federal, state, and city governments would band together to put it into widespread use. Reducing the death toll from car accidents would become a top governmental priority, backed by public opinion. Advocates of this solution would host fund-raisers and hand out badges boasting a highly recognizable symbol of the effort, similar to the iconic pink ribbon for breast cancer research. Federal agencies would dole out generous research grants to universities.

The reality is that such a solution will soon exist. The solution is to remove human drivers from the equation and replace them with intelligent software and sensors. If our society were to pull together to make the development of driverless cars our next cultural "Apollo moment," we could save millions of lives. A study by the Eno Center for Transportation estimates that in the United States alone, if 90 percent of the cars on the roads were autonomous vehicles, the number of driving-related deaths would fall from 32,400 a year to 11,300.[11]

It would be irresponsible, however, at this point to not mention that replacing human drivers with robots would not solve everything. Humans might simply find new ways to misbehave. Some analysts point out that while autonomous vehicles offer some safety benefits, they could introduce new risks, such as hacking. Passengers could take on new risks because they feel safe, for example, not wearing their seat belts or weaving in and out of platoons of self-driving vehicles for sport.[12]

Even if we factor in the possibility that in the future, new forms of poor human judgment will no doubt appear, driverless cars will still make road travel safer. Safer roads and highways won't be their only benefit, though. Driverless cars will make more efficient use of the roads, reducing traffic jams and air pollution. As people gain access to safe and convenient personal transportation, they will also gain new opportunities in their choice of where they live, work, and play.

Losing the burden of a tedious commute would be one direct benefit of driverless cars. Another benefit would be that more people could enjoy the benefits of convenient personal mobility. According to the U.S. transportation data, each day 586 older drivers are injured in car accidents.[13] Unfortunately, the decision to stop driving is usually one that people resist for as long as possible. Driverless cars would give the elderly and the impaired the ability to move around the world on their own.

SEVEN DELAYING MYTHS

The cost of not aggressively embracing driverless cars can be counted in lives, time, pollution, and lost opportunities. Yet not everyone is convinced of their value. While writing this book, we discovered a few pieces of misinformation that stubbornly remain in wide circulation and are used by opponents of driverless cars when arguing against policy that would favor their adoption. We distilled these bits of misinformation into seven myths. These myths are:

1) Autonomous driving technology will evolve out of today's driver-assist technology. Some believe that the transition to autonomous vehicles should take place in stages, by gradually expanding the use of driver-assist features like adaptive cruise control and lane keeping. In reality, a staged transition is not only technologically challenging, it is unsafe. Research indicates that when humans and machines share the wheel, humans respond by ceasing to pay attention, making them less capable if suddenly forced to grab the wheel in case of an emergency.

2) Technological progress is linear. When predicting the readiness of driverless-car technology, some people believe that the rate of progress made by robotic technologies over the past ten years will be maintained at the same rate into the future. The development of driverless cars will actually progress much more rapidly, since they make use of enabling technologies that follow Moore's Law trajectories of performance and price. As a result, the performance of driverless cars will continue to improve rapidly as the price of components drops in tandem. Another accelerating force in the development of driverless cars is *fleet learning*. As cars pool their driving "experience" in the form of data, each car will benefit from the combined experiences of all other cars. Within a few years, the operating system that guides a driverless car will accumulate a driving experience equivalent to more than a thousand human lifetimes.

3) The public is resistant. The advertising departments of big car companies like to tell us that people love to drive. In reality, most people's driving experience consists of a few tedious hours each day commuting to work or running mundane errands, inching along on crowded roads. Most people would eagerly trade in the time they spend driving in order to do something else. Once the technology matures and driverless cars are usable and safe, consumers will eagerly embrace them.

4) Driverless cars require extensive investment in infrastructure. The software that guides driverless cars relies on clear lane marks, but beyond that, driverless cars require no special infrastructure. One reason for this misperception could be that for decades, the U.S. Department of Transportation has focused its resources on promoting its vision of a *connected car*, a scenario in which cars and roadside infrastructure are equipped with expensive wireless transmitters to share data. In contrast, driverless cars will use robotic machine-vision technologies and stored digital map data that place the intelligence into the car, not into the road.

5) Driverless cars represent an ethical dilemma. A driverless car is no more or less ethical than a human. Arguments claiming that driverless cars pose an ethical challenge stem from the uncomfortable fact that intelligent software guiding the car must at some point quantify the value of human and animal life in order to decide what the car's response should be in an impending accident. For whatever reason, we humans would prefer that a human, not a machine, conduct the rapid and informal cost/benefit analysis in the split seconds before a crash. Yet, human drivers already instinctively calculate "who they can kill" when faced with split-second driving decisions. Insurance companies already quantify the potential costs of many aspects of our lives.

6) Driverless cars need to have a nearly perfect driving record to be safe enough. The benefits of driverless cars will begin as soon as they have a safety record that exceeds the average human driver. Waiting until driverless cars have a flawless safety record will unnecessarily maintain our society's high death toll from car accidents. Driverless cars should be made legal not when they're perfect, but when they're twice as safe as an average human driver.

7) The adoption of driverless cars will be abrupt. Some people like to ask for the "year" when driverless cars will take over the roads. In practice, driverless cars will follow a gradual adoption curve. Autonomous cars will first be used in confined regions such as resorts, university campuses, and closed city centers. On public roads, the encroachment of driverless cars will be gradual, increasing a few percentage points each year as old human-driven cars are gradually retired.

THE TIMELINE

The timeline for the adoption of driverless cars is not a simple, linear one. Instead, the transition to a world of driverless vehicles will happen gradually. It's impossible to select a specific year when cars will become driverless, for two reasons. The first is that adoption of driverless cars will take place in some environments and countries before others. The second is that car companies are currently promoting a staged approach to autonomy; if they succeed, humans might drive just part of the time, making it impossible to pin down an exact transition point.

The first autonomous vehicles will appear in special environments before they appear on mainstream roads. Mines and farms already use autonomous vehicles. Freight trucking will likely also be an early adopter

In cities, at first, driverless-car adoption will be cautious, taking the form of low-speed shuttles that drive slowly in enclosed and structured environments such as airports or resorts. In the United Kingdom, for example, the town of Milton Keynes is testing two-seater, electric, autonomous taxi pods that will drive people on pavements and footpaths. As time passes and these driverless shuttles perform well and prove their safety, the speeds at which they operate and their driving range will gradually increase. We predict that Google's first sales of driverless cars will be not to consumers for everyday driving, but more likely to corporations and some municipalities as a niche transportation solution. At some point there will be a quiet crossing over, and the autonomous vehicles will venture outside their enclosed territories and onto city highways.

Another aspect of the transition to driverless cars is location, that is, where the first driverless cars will come into everyday use. Some countries will adopt driverless cars sooner than others. Within countries, some states or provinces will agree to legalize driverless cars before others

One way to define "completion" would be to insist that complete autonomy will have been achieved only when 100 percent of the cars on the road are fully autonomous, 100 percent of the time. Complete autonomy defined this way means that achievement of full autonomy could take as long as a century. Because of the several ways in which adoption of driverless cars could take place, there's little consensus on the timeline.

Some of this wide variance on an adoption timeline stems from practical considerations. Since cars must meet strict safety and emissions requirements, new vehicle technology tends to be implemented more slowly than technologies used for other applications. In addition, cars are expensive, and therefore people hang onto them for several years. The fact that people buy and discard cars at a slower rate than they do their smart phones will result in a transition phase from human-driven to driverless that will span several decades.

In general, car companies and transportation officials take a longer view, estimating that driverless cars will be a mainstay on public roads sometime after the year 2025. According to the automotive market research firm IHS, the first sales of autonomous vehicles will begin around the year 2025.[14] IHS analysts estimate that by the year 2035, roughly 10 percent of new cars sold will be autonomous, a total number of 11.8 million cars each year. After 2050, IHS predicts that almost all new vehicles sold will be autonomous.

Car companies have preferred a staged, gradual approach to autonomous driving, another factor that makes it impossible to pin down an exact date for the adoption of driverless cars. A typical headline for a press release from a car company promoting its driver-assist technology will trumpet, "Company X to launch its driverless-car product by 2020." A closer read, however, reveals that the product Company X is discussing is actually a feature that will enable a car to guide itself through a specific task, for example, parking itself under controlled conditions, or perhaps some kind of glorified cruise control and lane keeping combination.

Tech companies are a bit more optimistic about the day when cars will be capable of fully driving themselves in all environments. Google and Tesla are firm in their conviction that the future of driving lies in fully autonomous vehicles, although the exact date and details are to be determined. In October 2014, Tesla's Elon Musk told Bloomberg Television that "five or six years from now we will be able to achieve true autonomous driving where you could literally get in the car, go to sleep and wake up at your destination." But he cautioned, "it will then take another two to three years for regulatory approval."

Analyst Tod Litman predicts that without a federal mandate to speed along adoption, deployment will follow the pattern of the adoption of automatic transmissions, a process that took nearly five decades. Litman calculates that even if driverless cars are made legal by the year 2020, the gradual replacement of human-driven cars with driverless ones will take decades. He estimates that by the year 2050, driverless cars will make up 80–100 percent of new car sales. Yet, since it takes several years for the average car to reach the end of its lifespan, 40–60 percent of the cars on the roads will still be those driven by humans.[15]

Turning over the world's population of human-driven cars will be no small matter. In the United States there are roughly 250 million active cars on the roads, a group analysts call "the active car park."[16] Every year, 13–14 million of the cars in the active car park are retired and consigned to the scrap heap. Even if it were possible to purchase a well-tested and legal autonomous vehicle immediately, because of the 10–15-ear average life span of a modern automobile it would take nearly twenty years for all of the old, human-driven cars to be taken off the road.

No matter whose predictions turn out to be correct, one thing is clear. The transition to fully self-driving cars will be one that will take decades to complete. While the details of who drives what, when, and where remain to be worked out, humans and robots will share the road for decades ahead.

In the following chapters we'll explore driverless cars from several angles, debunking the myths that limit their development along the way. We lay out new cityscapes where parking lots are repurposed as human-friendly space and commutes are no longer painful. We delve into the robotics technologies that give modern driverless cars the ability to "see," "react," and "think." We explore what will happen to the auto, media, and retail industries. We explore the long, rich history of previous efforts to liberate cars from human drivers, culminating in today's autonomous vehicles that are the fruit of decades of academic research in artificial intelligence and machine learning

2

A DRIVERLESS WORLD

If the billion cars that roam the world's roads were magically transformed into reliable, driverless vehicles, the first thing you would notice would be the silence. After all, wailing sirens and honking car horns are effective only when humans are behind the wheel. In this future world the streets will swarm with small vehicles shaped like golf carts, some containing a passenger or two and some completely empty. Every now and then an RV-sized vehicle—perhaps a commuter's well-appointed mobile office—rolls grandly by. On rare occasions, a car bearing a human driver appears. Warned of the presence of a nearby biological being behind the wheel, other cars react with caution, giving the human-driven car an extra-wide berth.

To summon a taxi, you press a button on your phone. A few minutes later, a driverless taxi sidles up next to you. Since you agreed to ride-share, your pod already contains a passenger or two headed in your general direction, a minor annoyance that will substantially reduce the cost of your fare.

Like the inside of an elevator, your pod's interior is bare bones, utilitarian, with hard, easy-to-clean surfaces and minimal moving parts. Similar to a battered old subway car after rush hour, the floor of the driverless taxi is littered with food wrappers and cigarette butts. The seats are stuck with used pieces of chewing gum and covered with amateurish graffiti. The taxi's security video camera has observed nothing of the littering and vandalism

Figure 2.1
A depiction of customized autonomous mobile office pods (concept).
Source: Courtesy of IDEO

since it has been blind all day, its lens covered by a cheap polyester knit cap.

In this new era, anonymous taxi rides of yore in which passengers paid a human driver in cash are a relic of the low-tech past. Your pod knows who you are from the moment you hop inside. Since you agreed to be recognized, your pod rapidly examines your online browsing and shopping histories and recent whereabouts and reminds you that the route to your destination goes past two of your favorite stores.

You climb into your taxi and close your eyes. Aside from the annoying patter of the pod's marketainment system, the ride is relaxing, impersonal. As if they're in the subway, the other pod passengers avoid making eye contact. There's no pressure to chitchat with a human driver. Since you trust the pod's software is taking you on the shortest path to your destination, you don't surreptitiously compare the route against the map on your cell phone.

When you arrive at your destination, the fare is automatically deducted from your account. There's no tip, since there's no driver. Because you shared the pod with other people and endured the stream of advertisements, the ride is even cheaper. Although the trip wasn't particularly clean or comfortable, given the taxi's utilitarian interior, it was easy, like taking an elevator.

FRICTION-FREE PERSONAL MOBILITY

One of the great unknowns about driverless cars is whether their convenience will worsen traffic congestion and its accompanying evils. An optimistic scenario would be that driverless cars will improve the efficiency of urban transportation systems, and hence reduce private vehicle ownership, thereby reducing congestion and therefore reducing the size of a city's carbon footprint that's related to transportation. Another, less environmentally friendly scenario is that as people embrace the convenience of friction-free mobility, driverless cars will wind up actually logging more vehicle-miles per year on average, leaving a larger carbon footprint.

Convenience can be a double-edged sword. People are drawn to convenience like iron filings to a magnet. Sometimes, however, convenience carries with it a price: unexpected and negative consequences. The friction-free personal mobility offered by driverless cars might solve the worst excesses already inflicted on us by automotive technology. Or, the hidden cost of convenient personal mobility might be that an ever-growing number of people casually rack up their number of miles driven.

Economists call the unforeseen reduction of expected gains from new technologies owing to increased usage the *rebound effect*. It's not clear whether driverless cars will have a rebound effect on traffic, increasing the number of miles that people travel each year, and the number of cars on the roads. Some research paints an optimistic picture, in which city streets will be emptier of vehicles in a few decades. In an interview with the *Economist*, Luis Martinez of the International Transport Forum, a think tank dedicated to transportation policy, predicted that fleets of self-driving vehicles could replace all vehicular public transportation taxi and bus trips in a city, providing as much mobility but with far fewer vehicles.[1]

To test this theory, Martinez created an agent-based model to simulate daily travel patterns in a medium-sized European city. Using several years of actual data from previous transportation surveys, he calculated that if city inhabitants used fleets of shared autonomous taxis rather than privately owned cars and public transportation, the number of vehicles on the city's roads could be reduced by 90 percent.[2] While fleets of autonomous taxis would drastically reduce the number of cars on the streets, the simulation also predicted that the overall number of vehicle-miles traveled per car would increase slightly because the self-driving taxis would shuttle back and forth more frequently to pick up passengers.

A report from the University of Michigan Transportation Research Institute supports these findings. The report concludes that the adoption of autonomous vehicles would reduce the number of cars owned by the average U.S. household from just over two to one vehicle per household.[3] According to the report, one-vehicle households will be made possible because self-driving vehicles will use a "return-to-home" mode after they drop one household member at work so other household members can use the family self-driving car to be shuttled to errands and activities.

There's a catch, however. Although a family's driverless car can transport family members efficiently back and forth, the fact that one car is supporting more people would result in higher per-vehicle mileage. Although the average household of the future might own fewer cars, the remaining driverless car will be used 75 percent more frequently, accumulating an average of 20,406 annual miles per vehicle per year. The upside of this finding is that even if a single driverless vehicle were to rack up 75 percent more miles on average, the mileage for the entire household would still be lower than if two human-driven cars were in use.

One potential risk of having a single driverless car support an entire household is that the increase in per-vehicle mileage ends up being more than the predicted 75 percent. There's no doubt that summoning a driverless car to pick you up and drop you off would be a great convenience. However, an unintended negative consequence of more efficient transportation could be that a driverless vehicle will drive significantly more miles than would the equivalent human-driven vehicle.

Ideally, an empty self-guided car would find a safe place out of the way of traffic to sit and await its next summons. If that safe place were several miles away, however, the car would be forced to drive itself back and forth a great distance rather than just parking nearby. Its mileage would increase, and its wasteful shuttling would make traffic congestion and air pollution even worse.

If the availability of too-convenient transportation creates a rebound effect on traffic and dramatically increases the number of road miles that people travel each year, driverless cars could have a devastating environmental impact. Today the transportation sector is already one of the largest contributors to air pollution. In the United States alone, exhaust from cars and trucks causes an estimated 29 percent of the greenhouse gas emissions that human activities generate each year.[4] If driverless cars were to increase the number of vehicle miles traveled per capita, densely populated "megacities" in developing nations would be hit particularly hard.

. While the United States has a nearly 100-year-old relationship with the car, other nations are enthusiastically catching up. China is following in the footsteps of the United States, gaining its own car culture. As a growing and newly affluent Chinese middle class embraces the convenience of car travel, cities such as Beijing and Zhengzhou are suffering from spectacular eight-lane traffic jams and worsening smog levels.

Today, the ratio of cars per person is still lower in China than in the United States or Europe, averaging 85 vehicles per 1,000 people (compared to 797 vehicles per 1,000 people in the United States.)[5] However, the rate at which the Chinese auto industry manufactures and sells new cars continues to skyrocket, increasing at an annual rate of 7 percent since 2013.[6] Perhaps Chinese car culture will sidestep some of the worst excesses of car culture by adopting driverless cars sooner, rather than later. To tame the traffic beast, Baidu, the Chinese search engine company some describe as the Google of China, is working together with BMW to develop autonomous vehicles that are familiar with Chinese roads.

In both developing and developed nations, traffic jams are a major source of air pollution. In the United States alone, as commuters inch forward in traffic jams, their idling cars waste 2.9 billion gallons of gasoline each year, enough to fill four football stadiums.[7] Only time will reveal whether driverless cars will produce less pollution, or whether their use will entice people to log an ever-growing number of miles each year, further degrading air quality and making urban traffic jams even worse.

Another environmental side of effect of driverless cars could be shorter vehicular lifespans. A car's longevity is indicated by its odometer. According to *Consumer Reports* magazine, today the typical life span for a personal vehicle is about 150,000 miles which means that on average, over the course of eight years, that car will be driven about 18,750 miles per year. In comparison, since it drives roughly 70,000 miles a year, the lifespan of the average New York taxi cab is only 3.3 years.[8]

It remains to be seen whether the introduction of driverless cars will ease the negative effects inflicted on us by the modern automobile. If the University of Michigan research is correct and a driverless car racks up 20,406 miles each year, the average family car would be "used up" more quickly, reaching its lifetime expectancy of 150,000 miles in just over seven years of use. One worst-case scenario would be a future in which used-up driverless cars litter the landscape, filling junkyards and backyards with decommissioned auto bodies and worn-out engines. History has taught us, however, that new technologies do not merely extend a former status quo. Driverless cars have several characteristics that could change their potentially gloomy and environmentally devastating trajectory.

If the internet of the 1990s were suddenly forced to absorb today's data traffic, it would buckle under the load. Over the years, several enhancements have enabled the modern internet to absorb new users and handle an increasing amount of data, including better compression technologies, fiber-optic cable, and more intelligent routers. Similarly, improvements in technology could also ease the potentially negative rebound effect caused by driverless cars. Several research studies support such an optimistic view.

First, let's address the issue of vehicular lifespan. A report from McKinsey calculates that driverless cars will be able to brake and accelerate more gradually, resulting in fuel savings of 15 to 20 percent and a reduction of CO_2 emissions of 20 million to 100 million tons per year.[9] If McKinsey's research is correct, then smoother driving would increase a driverless vehicle's longevity.

Not only would driverless cars last longer, they could be built specifically to achieve longevity. There's nothing sacred about a lifespan of 150,000 miles. If there were a market for it, car companies could design driverless cars that could drive for several hundred thousand miles. City transit operators expect their buses to have a useful lifespan of at least twelve years and 250,000 miles.[10] Semitrailers are designed to operate for 1,000,000 miles and their engines are designed to run virtually nonstop.[11] Rail cars last even longer: some of the original BART cars in San Francisco, built in 1968, are still in operation today.

Even if their lifespan remained the same as today's human-driven cars, driverless cars could milk more capacity out of existing roads. To decrease their wind resistance, cyclists ride behind one another in a closely spaced line, an energy-saving strategy known as *drafting*. Fleets of driverless cars and trucks could use a similar approach and save energy by driving behind one another in tight formation, a fuel-saving strategy known as *platooning.*

Platooning saves fuel both by reducing wind resistance and using road "real estate" more efficiently. Human-driven cars don't use the space on the road very efficiently. People have to drive several hundred feet apart for safety and we aren't very adept at smoothly changing lanes. In contrast, platoons of driverless cars would use road space more effectively, resulting in less congestion at the places where traffic jams regularly form, such as highway on-ramps and off-ramps, before lane changes, and at intersections.

A study by researchers at the University of Texas estimates that if 90 percent of the cars on the road in the United States were self-driving, it would be equivalent to doubling road capacity. Texas researchers predict that tightly spaced platoons could reduce congestion-related delays by 60 percent on highways and by 15 percent on suburban roads.[12] Trucks, because of wind resistance, are particularly prone to fuel inefficiency. Platoons of autonomous trucks spaced fewer than three feet apart while driving would reduce fuel consumption by 15 to 20 percent per truck.[13]

Another potential environmental benefit lies in rethinking car design. If driverless cars become substantially safer than those driven by humans, automotive designers could dramatically improve upon a mechanical body whose shape and size is the compounded result of a century's worth of incremental improvements and creeping crash-safety requirements. As accident rates drop significantly, driverless cars could be lighter and smaller, and therefore more fuel efficient.

Driverless taxis would not be the only vehicles to shrink in size. The delivery of packages and food orders could be handled by tiny, lightweight autonomous delivery drones on wheels. On college campuses, pizza, the perennial U.S. favorite, would be delivered in plastic, wheeled autonomous "pizza drones," baked to just

Figure 2.2
A depiction of a revitalized city where autonomous taxis have brought an end to traffic jams.
Source: Granstudio

the right consistency during the ten-minute journey. Contrast that with the nearly one-ton vehicle required to deliver a one-pound pizza today. Most of that ton of weight is for the benefit of the human driver, not for the pizza.

One core characteristic of cars that could be improved upon is how they're powered. Driverless cars will likely have electric engines. One of the barriers to the adoption of electric-only cars has been a lack of widely available methods for charging the car's battery. Tesla has overcome this limitation by building its own recharging infrastructure. As cars become intelligent enough to plan their journeys to include pit stops at charging stations, much of the uncertainty associated with an engine that needs regular recharging will be reduced.

A combination of energy-saving benefits, including platooning, lightweight car bodies, efficient driving, and rechargeable batteries will minimize some of the negative effects of driverless cars. Another environmentally degrading activity that most of us participate in on a daily basis is parking. Driverless cars will improve city life by reducing cruising, the tedious circling that drivers do when in search of a parking space, and by doing away with the need for parking lots altogether.

PARKING

It's difficult to pinpoint why, exactly, a particular city is considered charming. Similar to the debate about what constitutes art, a city's appeal is a factor that people can't easily explain, but they recognize it with certainty when they experience it. In our experience, cities that are appealing places to visit, live in, and work in are those that enjoy a vibrant pedestrian culture. The more people walking the streets, the more enjoyable a city's sense of hustle and bustle, as well as the more money that will exchange hands in the streets' stores and restaurants.

The shape of a city's parking lots has a surprisingly powerful effect on its personality. Older east-coast cities in the United States, as well as many cities in Europe, were designed and developed before the widespread use of cars. Those older cities have a significantly different vibe than newer cities that developed after cars became ubiquitous. This feeling of old city charm is often called walkability. Needless to say, parking lots don't increase a city's walkability, nor its charm.

Parking guru Donald Shoup describes the high hidden cost of searching for on-street parking as an activity that "congests traffic, causes accidents, wastes fuel, pollutes the air, and degrades the pedestrian environment."[14] Although estimates vary, people spend anywhere between 3.5 and 14 minutes circling in search of free curbside parking, contributing significantly to the congestion of downtown traffic. Shoup's recommendation for curing downtowns of the negative side effects of cruising is to raise the price of curbside parking. An even more effective way to reduce cruising would be to eliminate downtown parking altogether.

Like plaque clogging arteries, parked cars clog our streets. The typical parked car consumes on average, 14 square meters of pavement.[15] It eats up even more space if you factor in the access road leading up to the parking spot, which makes the total footprint for a single parked car 100 square meters large. On average, cars remain parked 95 percent of the time.[16] That's a lot of wasted space.

Cars are greedy. Most require multiple parking spots: one at home, one at work, and, sometimes, an additional parking place after work if the car's owner goes to the mall or the gym. These parking spots are rarely in use simultaneously: the one at home remains vacant while the car is parked at work.

Even more space is lost to parking when time is factored into the equation. In their classic text *The Urban Transportation Problem* (1965),[17] authors John Meyer, John Kain, and Martin Wohl calculate that over its lifetime, the average car takes up twice as much space parked than when it is being driven. At first this conclusion doesn't sound right; after some analysis, however, it makes sense.

Core to Meyer's, Kain's, and Wohl's calculation is the idea of *area hours*, the notion that the land needed by cars is not just a matter of space, but a function of both space and time. Cars spend most of their time parked, on average, about twenty-three hours a day. As a result, parked cars consume significantly more area hours than do cars in use.

How did so much precious downtown real estate end up getting allocated to the inglorious purpose of storing cars? When it comes to designing cities, parking lots are widely accepted as a necessary evil. Although we might analyze and debate the construction of every new highway or public building, few dispute the need for parking lots.

Another reason for the prevalence of parking lots is that many cities mandate they be there. Most cities have strict zoning ordinances with minimum parking requirements. Zoning ordinances kick in when someone wants to build a new restaurant or apartment building and applies to the city for approval. To get the city's permission to proceed, most municipalities require that a minimum number of new parking spaces are also constructed to accommodate the people using the new building or business.

Zoning ordinances requiring parking were originally well intended. After all, nobody enjoys circling around for parking. Yet, the unintended consequence of decades of mandated minimum parking requirements has been that modern towns and cities are riddled with dead space devoted to storing cars.

Another way to assess the staggering impact of car parking on the look and feel of modern towns and cities is to calculate a city's total parking coverage rate, or the total amount of space dedicated to urban parking garages. In cities, many parking garages have multiple levels stacked on one another. Imagine how much area would be revealed if all the different levels of a city's parking garages were "unrolled" and laid out flat.

The newer the city, the greater its slavishness to parking space. Downtown Los Angeles boasts 107,441 parking spots; if these spots were laid out in a two-dimensional plane they would add up to a surface area of 331 hectares, or 81 percent of the city's entire downtown area of 408 hectares. Another city heavily dedicated to parking space is Melbourne, Australia, where parking spaces represent 76 percent of the total area of its downtown. In Houston, Texas, parking space represents 57 percent of its total downtown space. In older cities such as London and New York, parking eats up less of the downtown, about 18 percent.[18] Cities with the least space dedicated to parking lots and structures were Bangkok (8 percent), Tokyo (7 percent), and Manila (2 percent).

If cars suddenly no longer needed to park downtown, city planners would find themselves with a huge blank canvas of unused space that could be constructively repurposed. Municipal codes, the local laws that dictate what sort of structures can be built where, could drop their requirement that each new business venture or residence be accompanied by the addition of a minimum number of new parking spaces. City planners could busy themselves with the more gratifying task of repurposing parking lots into human-friendly space. The result would be a new urban utopia. Or not.

At first glance, erasing parking lots from downtown areas sounds like a guaranteed cure for the evening doldrums that characterize many urban areas. Reforming parking lot space into parks, playgrounds, and sidewalk cafés would inject charm into dreary, sprawling downtowns, and perhaps create many new jobs. As people no longer cruised for a parking space, there would also be less traffic congestion.

Imagine how clean and beautiful cities could become. Without parking lanes, streets would instantly broaden into stately boulevards. With fewer cars circling in search of an elusive parking spot, the air would be fresher and cleaner. An optimist would conclude that driverless cars will enable all cities, even Los Angeles, to acquire some charm.

A more rational observer, however, would point out that the process of recouping large chunks of land formerly dedicated to parking space carries some risk. City dwellers and planners alike must figure out how to turn former downtown parking space into the equivalent of urban gold. The cities that will fare best in their liberation from parking will be those whose strategies are based on a broad and holistic view of the impact of driverless cars on the urban landscape.

The health of a city's downtown depends on a number of variables. One key question is how much of a city's budget inflow comes from revenue earned from parking tickets and parking fees. If that money were to disappear, what condition would the municipal budget be in?

Other variables that demand exploration include the density and composition of the local population. If downtown parking lots were turned into appealing new housing units and businesses, would enough people be willing to live in these new homes? Would these residents spend enough money to keep the new businesses afloat? Finally, what would prevent the emptying suburbs outside the city from becoming ghost towns?

Transforming parking space into usable residential and commercial space will be one challenge cities must resolve. Another unintended consequence of friction-free personal mobility is that vibrant city centers might spiral into a slow decline. In his gargantuan tome of parking lore, *The High Cost of Free Parking*,[19] Donald Shoup tells a cautionary tale of the unintended impact of a new six-story parking garage built directly underneath a concert hall in downtown Los Angeles.

During the years between 1987 and 2003 while Disney Hall and its parking structure were under construction, the city ran into financial hardship. The hall's new parking lot contained spaces for 2,188 parked cars and cost the city $110 million to build, a cost that averaged out to roughly $50,000 per parking spot. Convinced that convenient parking was critical to the hall's success, as construction costs exceeded the original budget, the city was forced to sell bonds to fund the enormous underground structure.

Los Angeles city planners argued that the high cost of Disney Hall's parking garage would be quickly paid back by parking revenues earned once the garage was up and running. This assumption was based on the understanding that in order for the new underground parking lot to pay for its construction costs, the new concert hall would host at least 128 full-house performances a year. The irony that the concert hall ended up in service to the parking lot rather than the other way around was not the only cautionary tale associated with the project, however.

Another lesson that Los Angeles city planners learned from building a costly and super-convenient parking structure directly underneath a prime downtown attraction was that too-efficient parking can be as deadly for the health of a downtown as extremely inefficient parking. Since the parking garage was located directly under the hall, concert-goers stepped out of their cars and went right into the concert. As a result, they never set foot onto the streets outside the symphony hall. They emerged from the underground parking lot on escalators that deposited them grandly, like minor royalty, in an internal entrance near their seats.

The new concert hall may have drawn people to downtown Los Angeles, but these people didn't stick around to dine in a nearby restaurant or patronize the local shops. Shoup describes the unintended consequence of a too-convenient underground parking lot. "Almost everyone prefers downtown San Francisco to downtown Los Angeles. ... In Los Angeles the sidewalks are empty and threatening at night. Even a spectacular new concert hall does not help to create a vibrant downtown if every concertgoer drives straight into its underground garage."[20]

If Shoup is correct, the streets near San Francisco's Davies Symphony Hall enjoy lively pedestrian traffic in part because the hall's parking lot is small (at 618 spaces) and is located a slight distance away. As a result of this slightly inconvenient transportation situation, people going to see a concert in San Francisco are forced to spend a little bit of time on the streets downtown. Regardless of whether concert-goers arrive via public transportation or walk a few blocks from where they parked, their presence adds vitality and energy to the streets outside the hall.

The lesson of the Los Angeles symphony hall is that every convenient new technology has hidden costs. Driverless cars will reduce the need for urban parking lots (a good thing), but their convenience could also reduce the enforced mingling that gives life (and revenue) to downtown shops and restaurants (a bad thing). If driverless pods dropped off pedestrians right outside their downtown destination with the punctuality and surgical precision of a military strike, the unintended hidden cost of such appealing efficiency could be the loss of lively and lucrative pedestrian foot traffic on downtown sidewalks.

Parking spaces are intimately interwoven into the geography of the modern urban downtown. In the coming decades, driverless cars will render parking lots obsolete, rearranging the shape of modern cities. Another side-effect of convenient personal mobility will be that people will go in search of new places to live.

COMMUTING

The greater metropolitan areas of cities such as Mumbai, Mexico City, and Shanghai are each home to more than 20 million people. By the year 2050, the size of the global urban population will nearly double, from today's figure of 3.3 billion people to a projected 6.4 billion.[21] These megacities will stretch for miles and their streets will be stuffed with cars as their citizens are forced to engage in a daily and potentially deadly attempt to get around.

As urban populations grow, cities will need to use their space wisely. When driverless cars become commercially available, forward-thinking city planners can repurpose urban parking lots as parks and affordable housing. Another way to improve the quality of urban life would be to make commuting to work easier.

People spend a large chunk of their day driving themselves to work. In the United States, the average commute time is roughly 30 minutes each way, an hour each day.[22] On average, most people's hour-long journey to work and back is usually made alone.

New forms of transportation change the way people perceive distance. In the 1950s, cars made it possible for people to conveniently commute into the city to work. Along with millions of other newly affluent New Yorkers, my grandparents joyously moved out of Manhattan to a suburb in Queens. To accompany their brand new home, they bought themselves an Oldsmobile, a car with the weighty appeal of a military tank that could barely squeeze into their one-car garage.

My grandparents left the city for several reasons. While a realtor might tell you that buying and selling a house is all about "location, location, location," there are several additional factors that people weigh when deciding where to live. Most people choose their home according to its price and its proximity to their jobs (i.e., commute time) and the quality of the local schools. Even though people may try to settle somewhere near work, in order to find a home they can afford that meets their other criteria, they often wind up with a long and stressful commute to work.

TABLE 2.1

In the U.S., the average commute to work is roughly half an hour.

New York-Northern New Jersey-Long Island	18,919,649	34.6
Los Angeles-Long Beach-Santa Ana	12,844,371	28.1
Chicago-Joliet-Naperville	9,472,584	30.7
Dallas-Fort Worth-Arlington	6,400,511	26.5
Houston-Sugar Land-Baytown	5,976,470	27.7
Philadelphia-Camden-Wilmington	5,971,589	28.6
Washington-Arlington-Alexandria	5,609,150	33.9
Miami-Fort Lauderdale-Pomano Beach	5,578,080	27.0
Atlanta-Sandy Springs-Marietta	5,286,296	30.3
Boston-Cambridge-Quincy	4,559,372	28.8
San Francisco-Oakland-Fremont	4,343,381	28.7
Detroit-Warren-Livonia	4,290,722	26.1
Riverside-San Bernardino-Ontario	4,245,005	30.6
Phoenix-Mesa-Glendale	4,209,070	25.8
Seattle-Tacoma-Bellevue	3,447,886	26.9
Minneapolis-St. Paul-Bloomington	3,285,913	24.8
San Diego-Carlsbad-San Marcos	3,105,115	24.1
St. Louis	2,814,722	24.8
Tampa-St. Petersburg-Clearwater	2,788,151	24.1
Baltimore-Townson	2,714,546	30.0
Denver-Aurora-Broomfield	2,554,569	26.5
Pittsburgh	2,357,951	25.9
Portland-Vancouver-Hillsboro	2,232,896	24.9
Sacramento-Arden Arcade-Roseville	2,154,583	26.2
San Antonio-New Fraunfels	2,153,891	24.6
Orlando-Kissimmee-Sanford	2,139,615	26.3
Cincinnati-Middletown	2,132,415	24.2
Cleveland-Elyria-Mentor	2,075,540	24.5
Kansas City	2,039,766	22.5

http://oldurbanist.blogspot.com/2012/07/commutes-tradeoffs-and-limits-of-urban.html

Driverless cars will make it easier to commute, giving people more choice in where they buy their home. As future city streets become less congested and the number of residential spaces increases, more people will move into newly appealing downtowns. Those who don't like city life will have the option to move into the once too-distant surrounding countryside, now a reasonable commute. The least appealing neighborhoods will be those located in the ring of traditional commuting centers, or "bedroom communities," outside the city center.

Another way driverless cars will change where people live is by reducing the average cost of transportation for both city dwellers and people living in smaller towns. Research from Columbia University's Earth Science Institute modeled the cost of transportation if fleets of driverless purpose-built shared vehicles were to be made available in Manhattan, Ann Arbor, and a small town in Florida. Columbia's research concluded that the combined effect of on-demand autonomous vehicles, lightweight car bodies, and freedom from the overhead costs of car ownership would significantly reduce the cost of personal transportation. The study revealed that Ann Arbor residents would pay 75 percent less, per mile, if they gave up their cars and used fleets of driverless taxis. New Yorkers would enjoy cab rides that cost 50 cents a mile, rather than the estimated $4 a mile for today's human-driven yellow cabs. Small-town inhabitants could ride around at an estimated cost of 46 cents per mile.[23]

TAKE THE POD—MEET PEOPLE

Although conveniences are hard to resist, sometimes life's inefficiencies can have a positive effect, that they foster social interactions. One side effect of cheap and efficient personal mobility could be loneliness. According to the U.S. Census Bureau, one in four Americans lives alone, and the number of people who report that they're lonely increases each year. Several theories explain why self-reported loneliness is on the rise, from changes in family structures, to work demands, to the isolating effect of television and the internet, to the false friendships formed on social media.

One reason people feel lonely is that they don't have a *third space*, a place that is neither work nor home, but where they go to hang out. In the old days, professors used to enjoy the perks of a faculty club or tearoom, where faculty would meet spontaneously, without a specific agenda, and chat about their research. Outside of work, people used to go to church, a bowling alley, or their local pub. One of the sad realities of modern life is that it doesn't offer people very many options for third spaces.

In North America, the lives of many middle-class people follow a pattern something like this: After college, by expectation or by necessity, we move to the next phase of life: adulthood. Once we can afford it, we purchase a home with a large, private yard that requires a lengthy and solitary commute to work.

For many people, at the end of a long work day there's little time left over for spontaneous social activities. Weekends are dedicated to improving the house and yard or catching up on "family time" that could not take place during the busy workweek. Perhaps because of this busy, yet isolated lifestyle, many middle-class professional people don't have many friends.

Three factors are critical for making friends: physical proximity, repeated unplanned social interactions, and an atmosphere where people can let their guard down.[24] Work involves physical proximity and repeated social interactions, but it does not provide a good place to let down one's guard. That's why many people have friends from their college years, but not many from later in their lives. The informal camaraderie of college dorm rooms provides physical proximity, repeated exposure, and an environment where people can be themselves.

Like other technologies of convenience, driverless cars will improve the quality of people's lives by easing the pain of commuting and giving people more options for where to live. Yet, the cost of more convenient transportation will be the loss of another traditional third space, that of public transit. City dwellers of the future could find themselves missing the enforced human contact of the old and inefficient modes of public transportation on subways, buses, and trains.

The other day we saw an ad in the local newspaper that read: "Take the bus—meet people." What a brilliant way to advertise public transportation! The ad wryly conceded what most people already know, that public transportation is usually not faster or easier than driving. Yet, rather than trying to convince people of what they wouldn't believe anyway, the ad cleverly focused on another undeniable benefit of taking the bus: the time spent waiting for the bus and rattling around town on inefficient routes will help you make new friends.

Time we "waste" in the car has hidden value. Cars serve as a mobile third space for parents and their children. A recent study of 2,000 parents found that parents spend an average of six hours and forty-three minutes per week chauffeuring their kids to school and to after-school and social activities.[25] At that rate, parents and kids wind up experiencing nearly thirty hours every month of enforced togetherness in the car.

As any parent/chauffeur would tell you, much of this driving is sheer drudgery. Many busy parents (ourselves included) would eagerly pop their children into a driverless car and wave them off if such a vehicle were a safe and widely accepted form of transportation. If such a convenience existed, however, its hidden cost would be the loss of precious time in which parents and children mingle on a regular basis. Like the emotional thievery of a smartphone at the dinner table, driverless cars will erase another of the few remaining technology-free zones where we can interact with our children.

I experienced the value of enforced "car time" when I used to drive my then-teenage son to early morning crew practice six days a week. On one hand, I dreaded the 5 am trips, having my deepest sleep rudely interrupted by the alarm clock's cheerful tune of steel drums. If I had been presented with the option to hand my chauffeuring duties over to a driverless car, I would probably have eagerly embraced it. The driverless car would have been a safer driver than I was and I could have gotten a few extra hours of precious sleep.

In hindsight, the cost of such a convenient solution would have been the loss of the intimacy my son and I enjoyed in those precious early morning car trips. Those trips to crew practice were our chance to spend time together, just the two of us in close physical proximity with no agenda or distractions. As we drove together my son shared his music with me. He shared his thoughts, usually wry analyses of the state of the world. The convenience of a driverless car would have robbed me of memories of the two of us cruising around the banks of the local lake in search of the designated meeting place, embraced by the predawn chill of a hushed and sleeping world.

Friction-free physical mobility could make us lonelier. Or, on the other hand, if going out becomes no more difficult than pressing a button on your cell phone, opportunities for in-person mingling could someday be as easy as mingling online. Another social catalyst will be that driverless cars will be intelligent and data-literate. Passengers could pay a little extra for the "Meet People" option next time they take a driverless pod so they could be matched up with other passengers of the same age, or with similar patterns of web browsing and Facebook "likes." Someday, when people open up their web browser, they'll see an advertisement for a driverless pod: "Take a pod. Make a friend."

3

THE ULTIMATE MOBILITY DEVICE

In the year 2014, Google fired a shot heard all the way to Detroit. Google's newest driverless car prototype had no steering wheel and no brakes. The message was clear: cars of the future will be born fully autonomous, with no human driver needed or desired.

Even more jarring, rather than retrofit a Prius or a Lexus as Google did to build its previous two generations of driverless cars, the company custom-built the body of its youngest driverless car with a team of subcontracted automotive suppliers. Best of all, the car emerged from the womb already an expert driver, with roughly 700,000 miles of experience culled from the brains of previous prototypes. Now that Google's self-driving cars have had another few more years of practice, the fleet's collective drive-time equals more than 1.3 million miles, the equivalent of a human logging 15,000 miles a year behind the wheel for 90 years.[1]

Car manufacturing is a changing playing field. For decades, the automotive industry has operated inside protective walls, sheltered from external competition by high barriers to entry and exclusive relationships with preferred suppliers. As the appeal and value of a new car becomes increasingly dictated by its software, for the first time, traditional automotive companies will face competition from companies outside the industry. Google (or its parent company, Alphabet, Inc.) is the front-runner, but Apple is rumored to be hiring automotive engineers and software developers to build its own autonomous vehicle. Adding to the speculation, in a recent speech at a tech conference, Apple vice president Jeff Williams cryptically described cars as "the ultimate mobile device."[2]

In response, car companies are pouring billions of dollars into software development and the epicenter of automotive innovation has moved from Detroit to Silicon Valley. At the time this book was written, Mercedes-Benz's Silicon Valley Division employed nearly 300 people working on advanced engineering projects and user experience design. Volkswagen had 140 engineers, social scientists, and product designers integrating Google Earth maps into Audi's navigation system and developing new infotainment systems.[3] Toyota announced that it would invest $1 billion over the next several years in artificial-intelligence research, with a laboratory near Stanford and another in Massachusetts, near MIT.

Four trends are forcing car companies to rethink their business models: electric cars, ubiquitous wireless, car-sharing, and autonomous vehicles. As driverless-car technology matures, these four trends will be folded into one: autonomy. To survive, car companies will have to reenvision their product as an autonomous transportation robot, a shift that will demand major changes in their workforce and product development process. Car companies have two options: they can scramble to develop their own in-house software expertise, or they can form a go-to-market partnership with a company that will provide the car's operating system while the car company builds the car's body.

CARS AND CODE

But wait! Modern cars are already automated. Even a budget sedan is loaded with sensing capabilities that a decade ago would have been found only on a custom-built fighter jet. Today, a typical car has as many as 100 microprocessors that manage the brakes, cruise control, and transmission.[4] Other software modules warn drivers of the presence of a pedestrian, or that the car is weaving out of its lane. In fact, a new car contains a respectable 5–10 million lines of code.[5]

While the average car may be loaded with software, the problem is that it's the wrong kind of code. Automotive software systems are modular, meaning they act as mostly independent silos with only a few exchanges or *handshakes*, between them. A more formidable barrier, however, is the fact that today's cars lack the right kind of artificial intelligence.

As long as a human driver is in charge, the software on-board a modern car works very well. Take the human out of the equation, however, and the car is nearly paralyzed. Today's human-dependent cars lack a robust robotic operating system that contains the necessary artificial intelligence to capably respond to novel situations and is capable of "learning" from previous experience.

To drive as well as or better than a human, a driverless car's software must be intelligent enough to know where it is located, understand what's around it, anticipate what's going to happen next, and plan how to respond. But that's not all. In addition to making good decisions about where to turn, when to wait, when to hit the brakes, or when to change lanes, an autonomous car's operating system must also oversee the car's low-level physical activities, such as telling the car's synthetic "muscles" (called *actuators*) to press the brakes, or to turn the steering wheel just a tiny bit to the right.

The big unanswered question that will determine the future of car companies is which industry—automotive or software—will be the first to develop an intelligent operating system, complete with the crown jewel of artificial-intelligence research: consistently accurate artificial perception. One fear that keeps car company executives up at night is that vehicle "hardware"—the car's metal frame (chassis), engine, and interior—will follow the path already trod by computer hardware and become a secondary feature to the car's software. If a vehicle's software becomes its most distinguishing marketable feature in the eyes of consumers, car companies will lose control of the automotive market.

To learn more, we ventured out to Burlingame, California, to attend the Automated Vehicles Symposium, a conference put together by the Association for Unmanned Vehicle Systems International (AUVSI). All the big players in the car industry were there, showcasing their company's latest and greatest autonomous vehicle technology. The atmosphere of the conference was reminiscent of a poker game at an exclusive men's club: lots of cheerful bonhomie among the players cloaking the fact that no one knew the content of one another's poker hands.

Our first lesson was that players in the autonomous vehicle industry keep their cards close to their chests. Of the employees we contacted at half a dozen car companies, not a single one responded to our email requests for an interview. When we reached out to Google X, the division of the company developing the driverless car, after several repeated queries, an administrative assistant politely pointed us to an exhibit on the history of driverless cars taking place in the Computer History Museum in nearby Palo Alto.

Our second lesson was that cars can be deadly overlords. For three days, we scurried back and forth from the conference hotel to where were staying, a harrowing pedestrian experience involving crossing several ten-lane highways that slice apart the parched landscape outside Silicon Valley. We arrived each morning at the conference hall, sweaty and shaken, but grateful to have survived the gauntlet of restless or distracted human drivers, each wielding his own potentially lethal two-ton weapon.

Our third lesson was that car companies and automotive suppliers are just getting their feet wet when it comes to creating robotic operating systems. Speaker after speaker shared beautifully designed and compelling presentations about their company's research into autonomous parking software or machine-vision technology capable of ... identifying street signs. Despite a healthy dose of hype about driverless cars, the so-called "autonomous vehicle" projects presented by the big car companies were essentially driver-assist systems on steroids.

Ironically, car companies are experts in robotics, but of another sort. The automotive industry is the leading employer of robots, whose arms tirelessly help assemble, paint, and build cars. A measure of an industry's or nation's reliance on robotic labor is *robotic density*, or the ratio of robotic workers to human workers. The robotic density of the U.S. automotive industry is higher than that of any other industry, roughly 1,100 robots per 10,000 human employees.[6] Each year, automotive companies hire more robots as the robotic density of the global automotive industry continues to grow at a rapid clip, a rate of 27 percent each year.

While the car-making process might be heavily robotized, however, driverless cars would not recognize their brawny, simple-minded cousins on the assembly lines as fellow robots. Hard-working manufacturing, assembly line, and warehouse robots are neither mobile nor autonomous They're bolted into place, and carefully programmed by human technicians to do a specific task in a highly structured setting. If their environment throws them a curve ball, they can't deviate from the script, nor are they capable of learning from previous experience.

THE SHAKE-UP

If car companies had the power to define the transition to driver-less cars, they'd likely favor a very gradual process. Their pre-ferred stage 1 would involve refining driver-assist technologies. Stage 2 would involve implementing a few high-end models with limited autonomous capability in specific situations, most likely on highways. In stage 3, limited autonomous capacity would trickle down to cheaper car models.

Consulting firm Deloitte describes such a gradual approach as one that's incremental, "in which automakers invest in new technologies—e.g., antilock brakes, electronic stability control, backup cameras, and telematics—across higher-end vehicle lines and then move down market as scale economics take hold."[7] Such a cautious approach, although appealing to an industry incum-bent, may actually be unwise. For car companies, inching closer toward autonomy by gradually adding computer-guided safety technologies to help human drivers steer, brake, and accelerate could prove to be an unsafe strategy in the long run, both in terms of human life and for car industry bottom lines.

One reason car companies favor an incremental approach is that it prolongs their control over the automotive industry.

Driverless cars need an intelligent on-board operating system that can perceive the car's surroundings, make sense of the data that's flowing in, and then act appropriately. Software capable of artificial intelligence—especially artificial perception—requires skilled personnel and a certain depth of intellectual capital to create. Car companies, while extraordinarily adept at creating complex mechanical systems, lack the staff, culture, and operational experience to effectively delve into the thorny thickets of artificial-intelligence research.

Driverless cars introduce uncertainty into the automotive industry. For the past century, selling cars directly to consumers has been a good business. However, if driverless cars enable consumers to pay per ride rather than buy their own car, the business of selling generic car bodies to transportation companies that lease out driverless taxis might not be as lucrative. If car companies are someday forced to partner with a software company to build driverless cars, such a partnership could result in car companies taking home a smaller slice of the final profits.

Like a growing kitty in the middle of an all-night poker game, there's a lot of money sitting on the table. Former University of Michigan professor and GM executive Larry Burns explains that there's a gold mine tucked into the three trillion miles a year that people drive each year (in the United States). He said, "If a first-mover captures a 10 percent share of the three trillion miles per year and makes 10 cents per mile, then the annual profit is $30 billion which is on par with Apple and ExxonMobil in good years."[8]

The auto industry's dogged attachment to human-led driving may be partly a strategic ploy, but there's more to the story. Car companies bear a tremendous responsibility for consumer safety. Over the past several decades, they have been forced to become preoccupied with product safety in the face of engineering tragedies such as the Ford Pinto affair and, more recently, GM's auto-ignition malfunction. Safety is an onerous responsibility that can cost a car company billions of dollars in product recalls, negative PR, and class action lawsuits.

In addition to safety, car companies bear responsibility for the health of a sizeable chunk of the world's economy. In the United States alone, the automotive industry and its extended value chain—e.g., rental cars, oil companies, car dealers, insurance, media, and medical—adds up to a $2 trillion industry; in 2014, it totaled 11.5 percent of the U.S. gross domestic product (GDP).[9] Any major misstep on the part of the big automakers can cost the entire value chain a lot of money and damage all the players' reputations.

In 1979, the CEO of Chrysler, Lee Iacocca, made history when he asked Congress for a $1.5 billion loan to save his ailing company, at that time the tenth largest corporation in the world. In his testimony to Congress, when asked why he, a long-time advocate of a free market system, was asking for help from the government, Iacocca replied, "I do not speak alone here today. I speak for the hundreds of thousands of people whose livelihood depends on Chrysler remaining in business. It is that simple. Our one hundred forty thousand employees and their dependents, our forty-seven hundred dealers and their one hundred fifty thousand employees who sell and service our products, our nineteen thousand suppliers, and the two hundred fifty thousand people on their payrolls."[10]

As the size of Chrysler's economic footprint indicates, car companies have enjoyed a position of economic incumbency for decades. However, as insular as the automotive industry may be, making and selling safe, affordable, and reliable cars is still a tough business. In a series of interviews, a group of auto executives argued that "outsiders simply do not appreciate the sheer complexity of developing a vehicle today, the challenge of introducing new advanced technologies into a vehicle's architecture, or the rigor and inertia of the regulatory environment."[11]

The act of building even a simple car is a formidable undertaking that involves advanced logistics, technology, and manufacturing, the culmination of a century of hard-won experience. Each automotive company has global relationships with thousands of individual suppliers who provide raw materials and parts. A single car has about 30,000 components, including the big parts, such as door panels, and the little parts, such as the screws that bolt the car together.[12] To assemble these parts takes about 17–18 hours per car.[13]

Ironically, the auto industry's emphasis on building great hardware might eventually end up being what keeps them in business. Tech companies such as Google have zero experience in assuming responsibility for the physical safety of the general public on a large scale. Driverless cars will still require a safe, fuel-efficient automotive body that meets exacting regulations. When driverless cars become commercially viable, we predict that the new automotive industry will consist of a series of corporate marriages between software companies and car companies, each contributing what they do best. At the time of this writing, a few tentative unions have already formed between Google and Ford, Volvo and Microsoft, and GM and Lyft.

Intimate partnerships between different car companies are already a time-tested business model in the automotive industry. Car-making takes place in a multitiered network of suppliers and entanglements between different car companies. It's not unusual for one car company to make a portion of a car that will later be sold bundled into another company's vehicle.

We recently rented an RV for a week-long trip, and during that trip, got familiar with the RV's dashboard. A week later, while riding in an airport shuttle, we found ourselves staring at an identical dashboard. We later looked up the RV and shuttle companies and learned that both were using Ford's "E-Series" platform, a standard chassis and dashboard that Ford sells to downstream companies who build a custom body on top.

One day, partnerships between software and car companies will be commonplace in the automotive industry. The most likely scenario is that car companies will sell "building block" platforms to downstream technology companies who transform them into autonomous vehicles. Such an industry model could wind up being a win-win for everyone involved What remains to be seen is how such go-to-market pairings pan out for car companies.

The situation is reminiscent of an earlier race between hardware and software providers that took place in the personal computer market. When I bought my first computer in the early 1980s, the most important factor in the decision was the computer's hardware. I had the choice of several dozen personal computers, each with its own operating system, dedicated software, and mutually incompatible peripherals. Some of my friends chose the Commodore 64, but I chose the "BBC Micro."

As time went on, Microsoft restructured the market for personal computer hardware. Microsoft created the DOS operating system and then later Windows to be hardware-agnostic, meaning they would run on any IBM-compatible PC. Microsoft further enriched the value of its operating system by opening up the Windows application program interface (API) and encouraging third-party software vendors to build applications for both desktop and server platforms.

Today, the software has become the more valuable portion of the personal computer and the hardware is a commodity. In a 180-degree turnaround from my youth, I now select my laptops first according to what operating system they run. The identity of the hardware vendor matters very little.

The exception to the "software-first" paradigm is Apple. As Microsoft fitted its operating system onto the bodies of several different OEM platforms, Apple maintained tight control over both its hardware platform and operating system. Some people believe that Apple's end-to-end ownership of its products is what enabled the bold leap forward in product design that resulted in the breakthrough designs of the iPhone, iPod, and iPad.

Today, car companies and Google are like gigantic tankers on a collision course, both slowly cruising toward a common destination: to wring the most profits from the next generation of automated cars. Car companies favor an evolutionary approach, to develop driver-assist modules to the point where they can take over the wheel for extended periods of time. In contrast, Google's strategy aims to dive directly into full autonomy.

If Google gets there first, its fully autonomous vehicles will become commercially available in a few select environments. As these early driverless cars prove their reliability, they'll eventually creep into mainstream use on regular streets and the revolution will begin. As today's teenagers mature into tomorrow's consumers, a car's software will become its most salient feature and the car's mechanical body will be an afterthought. The Microsoft paradigm will prevail.

In the Microsoft paradigm, car companies will make cost-effective car bodies and their go-to-market partner, Google or another software company, will outfit the "naked" cars with an intelligent operating system. The software company will also serve as a production hub, installing and testing the operating system and managing the hardware vendors that provide the car's various sensors. The role of the car companies will be demoted to mere original equipment manufacturers (OEMs), nearly invisible and interchangeable.

The Microsoft paradigm would also apply if the automotive industry shifts to mostly fleet sales. Should the market for personal car ownership shrink as predicted, the intervention of transportation companies who manage fleets of driverless taxis could further diminish the role of the carmaker. If most new cars are sold to fleets, not to consumers, the software company will still remain the sales lead and production hub. Since cost will be key, the car's hardware body will be sold to fleet owners as a generic commodity and fleet sales will result in an even smaller profit margin.

A happier outcome for car companies would be the Apple paradigm, that car companies remain in control of the car's product development and sales process. Not all consumers of the future will want an efficient and generic transport pod. Some consumers will still want to buy their own car, an expensive specialty model that's designed for a specific purpose, perhaps an office on wheels, or a mini, autonomous "home away from home," boasting a bright and recognizable logo.

Consumers who purchase these costly specialty models will be a desirable demographic: high-net-worth individuals, the same people who own a second home for vacations, or who prefer to charter a private jet to go on vacation rather than flying commercial. While a partnership with a software company will still be required, the focus of the sale will be on the quality of the entire car, both hardware and software. If the Apple paradigm prevails, automotive OEMs will remain in charge of at least a slice of the automotive industry of the future.

HUMAN IN THE LOOP

Car companies aren't the only ones that prefer a gradual approach. The U.S. Department of Transportation (USDOT) and the Society of Automotive Engineers have each sketched out their own maps of the road to full autonomy.[14] While their stages differ slightly, what they have in common is the assumption that the best way forward is via a series of gradual and linear stages in which the car's "driver assist" software temporarily takes over the driving, but quickly gives control of the car back to the human driver should a sticky situation occur.

We disagree with the notion that a gradual transition is the best way to proceed. For many reasons, humans and robots should not take turns at the wheel. Many experts, however, believe that the optimal model is to have human and software share control of the wheel, that the human driver should remain the master and the software the servant.

MIT roboticist David Mindell points out that "the most challenging problem for a driverless car will be the transfer of control between automation and driver."[15] In the delicate dance between human and automation, Mindell believes the best artificial-intelligence software is that which remains subordinate to a human pilot or driver. The right combination of the human and the mechanical, Mindell argues, enables robot designers to sidestep a potentially fruitless struggle with the process of developing software capable of responding appropriately to the environment. In Mindell's paradigm, the result of pairing human with software is a machine that performs better than either human or machine alone.

Software that's based on a paradigm in which humans and machines are partners is known to engineers as *human in the loop* software. In many situations, pairing up a human and a computer does indeed yield excellent results. Skilled human surgeons use robotic arms to achieve inhuman precision during surgery. Today commercial airplanes use human in the loop software, as do many industrial and military applications.

Arguments in favor of keeping humans in the loop have their appeal. It's an enticing thought experiment to dream of meticulously wiring together the best of human ability with the best of machine ability, similar to the intoxicating optimization puzzle of hand-picking professional football players for a fantasy football team. Machines are precise, tireless, and analytical. Machines excel at detecting patterns, performing calculations, and taking measurements. In contrast, humans excel at drawing conclusions, making associations between apparently random objects or events, and learning from past experience.

Mindell is an eloquent writer and an expert, thoughtful commentator on the state of modern robotics. In theory, at least, if you combine a human with an intelligent machine, the result should be an alert, responsive, and extremely skilled driver. After all, the advantage of human in the loop approaches to automation is that it's possible to harvest the strengths of what humans and machines do best.

In reality, human in the loop software could work in the case of a driverless car only if each party (human and software) maintained a clear and consistent set of responsibilities. Unfortunately, maintaining clear and consistent sets of responsibilities between human and software is not the model that's being proposed by the automotive industry and federal transportation officials. Instead, their proposed approach keeps the human in the loop, but with unclear and shifting responsibilities.

At the core of this strategy of gradual transition is the assumption that should something unexpected occur, a beep or vibration will signal the human driver that she needs to hastily climb back into the driver's seat to deal with the situation. A gradual and linear path toward full automation may sound sensible and safe. In practice, however, a staged transition from partial to full autonomous driving would be unsafe.

Machines and humans can work together well in some situations, but driving is not one of them. Driving is not an activity suitable for a human in the loop approach for one major reason: driving is tedious. When an activity is tedious, humans are all too happy to let machines take over, so they eagerly cede responsibility.

When I was in officer training in the navy, I learned that one of the core tenets of good management was to never divide a mission-critical task between two people, a classic management blunder known as *split responsibility*. The problem with split responsibility is that, ultimately, both people involved in completing the task may feel it's safe to drop the ball, assuming the other person will pick up the slack. If neither party dives in to the rescue, the result is mission failure. If humans and machines are given split responsibility for driving, the results could be disastrous.

Even as he champions machine and human partnerships, Mindell himself describes a harrowing example of split responsibility between man and machine in the plight of air France Flight 447, which, in 2009, plunged into the Atlantic Ocean, tragically killing all 228 people on board. Later analysis of the plane's black box revealed that the cause of the crash was not terrorism or a mechanical malfunction. What went wrong was the handoff from automated flight mode to the team of human pilots.

While in flight, the plane's auto-pilot software became covered in ice and unexpectedly shut down. The team of human pilots, befuddled and out of practice, were suddenly called to the controls on what they expected would be a routine flight. When thrust into an unexpected position of responsibility, the human pilots made a series of disastrous errors that caused the plane to nosedive into the sea.

Mindell calls the case of Flight 447 an example of a "failed handoff." Google calls the problem of humans relying too heavily on auto-pilot software simply "silly behavior." In its monthly report from October 2015, the company described the behavior of humans in an earlier version of its driverless car a few years before.

In the fall of 2012, several Google employees were allowed to use one of the autonomous Lexuses for the freeway portion of their commute to work. The idea was that the human driver would guide the Lexus to the freeway, merge, and, once settled into a single lane, turn on the self-driving feature. Every employee was warned that this was early stage technology and they should be paying attention to the driving 100 percent of the time. Each car was equipped with a video camera inside that would film the passenger and car for the entire journey.

Employee response to the self-driving car was overwhelmingly positive. All described the benefits of not having to tussle with freeway rush-hour traffic, of arriving home refreshed to spend quality time with their families. Problems arose, however, when the engineering team watched the videos from these drives home. One employee turned completely away from the driver's seat to search his back seat for a cell-phone charger. Other people took their attention away from the wheel and simply relaxed, relieved to have a few peaceful moments of free time.

The Google report described the situation of split responsibility, or what engineers call *automation bias*. "We saw human nature at work: people trust technology very quickly once they see it works. As a result, it's difficult for them to dip in and out of the task of driving when they are encouraged to switch off and relax."[16]

Google's conviction that there's no middle ground—that humans and machines should not share the wheel—sounds risky, but is actually the most prudent path forward when it comes to consumer safety. Automation can impair a driver in two ways: first, by inviting him to engage in secondary task engagements, activities such as reading or watching a video that directly distract him from watching the road; second, by disrupting his situational awareness, or his ability to perceive critical factors in the driving environment and to react rapidly and appropriately. Put the two together—a distracted driver who has no idea of what's happening outside the car—and it's clear why splitting the responsibility for driving is such a dangerous idea.

Research at Virginia Tech University sponsored by GM and the U.S. Department of Transportation Federal Highway Administration put some numbers around the temptation humans face when a capable technology offers to unload a tedious task. Virginia Tech researchers evaluated twelve human drivers on a test track. Each test vehicle was equipped with two forms of driver-assist software: one that managed lane centering, and another that handled the car's braking and steering, called *adaptive cruise control*. The goal of the study was to measure how humans reacted when presented with driving technologies that took over the car's lane keeping, maintained the car's speed, and handled its braking. To measure the human driver's activities during the study, each vehicle was equipped with data collection and recording devices.

Researchers recruited twelve individuals, twenty-five to thirty-four years old, from the general population of Detroit, Michigan, and offered $80 for their participation. Recruited drivers were asked to pretend they were taking a long trip and were not only encouraged to bring their cell phones with them on their test drive, but were provided with ready access to reading material, food, drinks, and entertainment media. As participants showed up for the study, researchers explained to them that someone from the research team would be joining them inside the vehicle. Each driver was told that their fellow passenger had a homework assignment he needed to complete during the trip, so he would be watching a DVD on his laptop for most of the drive.

The twelve human subjects were placed into common freeway driving scenarios on the test track and their responses and activities were measured and recorded. The researcher's goal was two-fold: one, to gauge the temptation to engage in secondary tasks such as eating, reading, or watching a video; two, to measure the degree to which driver attention would wander if software were to handle most of the driving. In other words, researchers were testing whether automated driving technologies would encourage humans to engage in unsafe misbehaviors such as mentally tuning out, engaging in inappropriate behavior while behind the wheel, or losing their situational awareness, including their ability to perceive critical factors in the driving environment.

It turned out that most human drivers, when presented with technology that will drive for them, eagerly become guilty of all three bad driving behaviors. The "fake homework" strategy of the researcher, combined with the competence of the adaptive cruise control and lane centering software, lulled the participants into feeling secure enough to stop paying attention behind the wheel. Over the course of approximately three hours of test driving time, during which different automated driving technologies were used, most drivers engaged in some form of secondary task, most frequently eating, reaching for an item in the back seat, talking on the cell phone and texting, and sending emails.

The lane-keeping software especially invited the human drivers to engage in secondary activities. When the lane-keeping software was switched on, a whopping 58 percent of the drivers watched a DVD for some time during the trip. Twenty-five percent of the drivers enjoyed the free time to get some reading done, increasing their risk of a car crash by 3.4 times.[17]

The human drivers' visual attention was not much better. Once again, when the lane-centering software took the wheel, driver attention wandered. Overall, drivers were estimated to be looking away from the road about 33 percent of the time during the course of the three-hour trip. More dangerously, the drivers engaged in long and potentially dangerous "off-road glances" lasting more than two seconds an estimated 3,325 times over the course of the study. The good news, however, was that these deadly long off-road looks occurred only 8 percent of the time.

Clearly, this particular study is just a starting point. Twelve people is a fairly small control group and more research on driver inattention is needed. One interesting finding that emerged was that although most drivers were eager to read, eat, watch movies, or send email while at the wheel, some were able to resist the temptation to tune out. For reasons that deserve additional research, the study revealed that not all human drivers were so quick to give up their responsibilities at the wheel. As researchers concluded, "this study found large individual differences in regard to the nature and frequency of secondary task interactions suggesting that the impact of an autonomous system is not likely to be uniformly applied across all drivers."

Clearly there's a tipping point at which autonomous driving technologies will actually create more danger for human drivers rather than less. Imagine if the twelve human drivers in Virginia Tech's research project were given a seat in a fully autonomous vehicle for a three-hour drive. It is highly likely that the intensity of their secondary activities would increase to the point where the human driver would fall asleep or become deeply absorbed in sending email. Full autonomy would make it nearly impossible for a deeply distracted or sleepy human driver to effectively take over the wheel in a challenging situation if control were abruptly handed over.

In another study, at the University of Pennsylvania, researchers sat down with thirty teens for a frank discussion of teen drivers' cell-phone usage while at the wheel.[18] Two central points emerged. While teens said they understood the dangers of texting while driving, they still did it. Even teens who initially claimed they did not use their cell phones while driving, revealed reluctantly when pressed that they would wait until they were at a red light to send a text. Also, teens used their own classification system to define what constituted "texting while driving" and what didn't. For example, they said that checking Twitter while driving did not constitute texting; nor did taking a passenger's picture.

Wandering human attention is one risk. Another risk of having humans and software share the wheel lies in the fact that if not used regularly, human skills will degrade. Like the pilots of Flight 447, human drivers, if offered the chance to relax behind the wheel, will take it. If a human hasn't driven in weeks, months, or years, and then is suddenly asked to take the wheel in an emergency situation, not only will the human not know what's going on outside the car, but her driving skills may have gotten rusty as well.

The temptation to engage in secondary tasks and the so-called *handoff problem* of split responsibility between human and machine are such significant dangers in human/machine interactions that Google has opted to skip the notion of a gradual transition to autonomy. Google's October 2015 monthly activity report for its driverless-car project concludes with a bombshell: based on early experiments with partial autonomy, the company's strategy path forward will focus on achieving only full automation. The report states, "In the end, our tests led us to our decision to develop vehicles that could drive themselves from point A to B, with no human intervention. ... Everyone thinks getting a car to drive itself is hard. It is. But we suspect it's probably just as hard to get people to pay attention when they're bored or tired and the technology is saying 'don't worry, I've got this ... for now.'"[19]

At the time this book was written, Google's driverless cars had a total of seventeen minor fender benders and one low-speed collision with a bus. In the seventeen fender benders, the culprit was not the not driverless car, but the other human drivers. On February 14, 2016, however, Google's car had its first significant accident when it "made contact" with the side of a city bus. Unlike the previous seventeen minor collisions, this accident was the fault of the car's software because it erroneously predicted that if the car rolled forward, the bus would stop.[20]

With the exception of the run-in with the bus, the rest of Google's accidents have happened because, ironically, Google's cars drive too well. A well-programmed autonomous vehicle follows driving rules to the letter, confusing human drivers who tend to be less meticulous behind the wheel, and not always so law-abiding. The typical accident scenario involves one of Google's obedient driverless cars trying to merge onto a highway or turn right at a busy intersection on a red light. Impatient human drivers, not understanding the car's precise adherence to speed limits or lane-keeping laws, accidently run into the driverless car.

So far, fortunately, none of Google's accidents have resulted in any injuries. In the near-term future, the best way to avoid collisions will be to teach driverless cars to drive more like people, carelessly and illegally. In the longer term future, the best way to solve the problem of human drivers will be to replace them with patient software that never stops paying attention to the road.

As car and tech companies gather at the table to play their high-stakes, global game of automotive poker, it remains to be seen who will have the winning hand. If federal officials pass laws that mandate a "human in the loop" approach, the winner will be car companies, who will retain control over the automotive industry. On the other hand, if eventually the law permits, or—for safety reasons—even requires full autonomy for driverless cars, then software companies will take the lead.

Google retains some major advantages as the undisputed industry leader in digital maps and deep-learning software. From the perspective of business strategy, Google's lack of a toehold in the automotive industry could actually be one of its key strengths. Analyst Kevin Root writes that "Unlike OEMs, they [Google] are not encumbered by ... lost revenue from bypassing the new feature trickle down approach, they are developing for the end state of fully autonomous driverless cars and appear to have a sizeable lead."[21] Add to that Google's eagerness to create a new revenue stream that's not reliant on selling internet ads, currently its primary source of revenue.

One thing is clear. Regardless of how the transition to driverless cars unfolds, the automotive industry will be forced to develop new core competencies. In order to remain a player in the new industry of selling driverless cars, car companies will have to master the difficult art of building artificial-intelligence software, a challenge that has eluded the world's best roboticists for decades.

4

A MIND OF ITS OWN

There's an old joke that made the rounds on the internet back in the 1990s. One version of the joke has Bill Gates (at that time the CEO of Microsoft), boasting that if Microsoft were to build operating systems for cars instead of computers, cars would be transformed into high-tech miracles that, among other things, would get 1,000 miles to the gallon.[1] The joke continues with the CEO of GM angrily firing off a detailed, multipoint rebuttal in response, laying out several reasons why Microsoft should stick to building operating systems for computers, not cars.

According to the joke, if Microsoft built operating systems for cars:

1. Automobiles would frequently crash for no apparent reason. This would be so common that motorists would simply accept it, restart their car, and continue driving.

2. Occasionally all the car's doors would lock, and motorists could enter their vehicle only by simultaneously lifting the door handle, turning the key, and holding the radio antenna.

3. Vehicles would occasionally shut down completely and refuse to restart, requiring motorists to reinstall their engine.

4. Every time a car company introduced a new model, car buyers would have to relearn to drive because all controls would operate in a new manner.

5. Whenever roadway lines were repainted motorists would need to purchase a new car that could accommodate the new "operating system."

6. Cars could carry only one passenger unless the driver paid extra for a multipassenger license.

7. Oil, water temperature, and alternator warning lights would be replaced by a single, all-purpose "general car fault" warning light.

8. Airbags would ask, "Are you sure?" before deployment.

Of course, the Windows of today is much more robust than the Windows of the 1990s. Nonetheless, I still like this old joke because it demonstrates how much advanced engineering is involved in building an operating system for a driverless car. The software must faultlessly guide a large, metal machine carrying precious human cargo from point A to point B, all the while avoiding other cars and navigating thickets of unpredictable pedestrians and bicyclists.

Tech companies are veterans in the art of building intelligent software. Car companies are masters of manufacturing, logistics, and political lobbying. Despite their respective strengths, both tech companies and car companies have their work cut out for them in creating an intelligent operating system that's capable of driving a car.

ROBOTIC OPERATING SYSTEMS

The *Oxford English Dictionary* defines an operating system as "the software that supports a computer's basic functions, such as scheduling tasks, executing applications, and controlling peripherals." The operating system of a driverless car has a similar set of responsibilities, to *support the car's basic and advanced functions in response to real-time data*. But that's not all. The operating system for a driverless car must also be super-reliable and secure, and it must contain artificial intelligence deep in its digital DNA.

Similar to the services performed by a person's brain and senses, a car's operating system must know where the vehicle is located, understand what's nearby, anticipate what's going to happen next, and plan how to respond. Given these weighty responsibilities, the robotic operating system that guides a driverless car dwarfs those that run a computer or a smart phone, both in complexity and in scope. For many reasons, the state of development for robotic operating systems is in its infancy.

To date, no robotic operating system can claim to have fully mastered three crucial capabilities: real-time reaction speed, 99.999% reliability, and better than human-level perception. Industrial robots operate with real-time precision, yet they are not capable of human-level perception. The operating systems that guide commercial airplanes are robust and reliable, but they also lack the ability to respond to novel situations. Autonomous airplanes have proven to be a safe mode of transport because the skies present fewer perplexing corner cases than does a busy urban intersection. Finally, intelligent software—for example, Facebook's facial recognition software or applications such as Siri—emulate human-level perception, but they don't operate in real time, nor are they particularly robust.

The cost of sub-par performance in the operating system for a driverless car will be counted not in lost productivity, but in human lives. Real-time reaction speed is not just the ability to react quickly, but to react at precisely the right time. The operating system that runs a driverless car must time a car's responses with microsecond punctuality. When a desktop computer stalls for half a second while its operating system spins up the hard drive, the brief delay might be annoying, yet the operating system is still providing an acceptable level of performance. In contrast, if a driverless car executes a left turn half a second too late or too early, the result could be a serious accident.

The bar for reliability is similarly higher. The operating system for a driverless car must not only be hack-proof, it must also be redundant, designed and built so it can immediately recover fully after a hardware or software failure. Finally, as we covered in previous chapters, a robotic operating system must be intelligent enough to understand and react appropriately to its surroundings.

THE ART OF BUILDING ROBOTS

To gain insight into the work of building intelligent, mobile robots, we journeyed to the robotic mecca, Carnegie Mellon University (CMU) in Pittsburgh, Pennsylvania. CMU has been at the fore-front of robotics and autonomous vehicle research for decades. Led by legendary robotics professor William "Red" Whittaker, CMU's Tartan racing team dominated the series of three government-sponsored races between autonomous vehicles that some people credit with catalyzing the development of the modern driverless car—the DARPA Challenges of 2004, 2005, and 2007 (DARPA is the research arm of the U.S. Department of Defense). In February 2015, the ride-sharing company Uber, eager to jump-start the development of its own autonomous vehicle, also gravitated to Pittsburgh and hired away some forty staff members from CMU's robotics and computer science departments.

Our goal was to spend a day visiting a legendary off-campus division of CMU's formidable robotics department, the university's National Robotics Engineering Center, or NREC. At the time of our visit, the Uber raid on Carnegie Mellon's roboticists had not yet taken place. Fortunately for our research for this book, one of my former students, Brian Zajac, was a hardware developer at NREC and graciously agreed to give us a tour of the facility.

NREC's mission is to build working robotic prototypes based off of the academic research generated by CMU's computer scientists and roboticists. Many of the robots and robotic vehicles NREC builds are intended for military application, in particular, for disaster recovery work, although a sizeable number ultimately wind up in industry. On the morning of our visit, as we drove into NREC's parking lot, we noticed that our surroundings had an industrial flavor, a refreshing reminder that we'd left the ivory towers of academe.

NREC was housed in a former train-repair facility made of weathered red brick that sat on the shores of the Allegheny River.

Traces of Pittsburgh's manufacturing past were everywhere. Crumbling loading docks lined the riverbank. As we walked through the parking lot, we noticed a few rusty abandoned tractors resting next to stacks of discarded tractor tires.

After greeting Brian in the building's sunny lobby, we admired exhibits of previous NREC projects. One of the first things visitors see when they enter the building is Workhorse, a disaster-recovery robot built by Red Whittaker and other CMU researchers in 1979 to help clean up a meltdown at the Three Mile Island Nuclear Power Station. Now retired and standing proudly next to the reception desk, Workhorse was a tangle of stainless steel tubes and parts mounted on a six-wheeled cart.

As our tour began, Brian led us through a door behind the reception desk and into NREC's warren of offices and labs. We followed Brian up a spiral staircase, and finally to a large, well-lit, two-story-high central atrium that's the heart of the facility. In the old days, when NREC used to be a train-repair shop, engineers pulled ailing trains into this space to fix them. Today, this is where the robots are built.

Several retired robots were suspended from the atrium's ceiling and walls where they watched over the development of the next generation. In its heyday, one of the retirees, an eight-legged robot named Dante, used to boldly venture into the underworld of active volcanos in Alaska. SensaBot, another retired robot, designed to inspect and monitor hazardous oil fields, was attached to a set of tracks on the wall. At random intervals during our visit, SensaBot zipped up and down the wall high over our heads, displaying the ease of an athlete leaping up and down a flight of stairs.

Our first stop in this robotic wonderland was to meet one of NREC's star creations, a strapping 443-pound, five-foot-tall red metallic disaster recovery robot named CHIMP (or CMU Highly Intelligent Mobile Platform). It took twenty-five hardware and software engineers more than a year to build CHIMP. Our guide Brian, one of the project's lead hardware developers and at the time a new father, joked to us that CHIMP had actually been his other firstborn.

Brian explained that DARPA funded the development of CHIMP as part of an ongoing initiative to develop disaster response robots that can work independently in unsafe or toxic conditions that would sicken or kill a human being. For three years running, DARPA sponsored several such projects at different universities and research labs. To see its funded robots in action, between the years 2012 and 2015 DARPA hosted three competitions called the DARPA Robotics Challenges. The challenges gave teams from all over the world the opportunity to demonstrate their robot's prowess.

The Robotics Challenge competitions took place in specially designed arenas that resembled the site of a natural disaster, complete with fallen chunks of concrete and doorways blocked by toppled steel beams. CHIMP and other competing robots had to work without direct human oversight to complete a series of assigned disaster recovery-related tasks, such as closing a metal valve, cutting a hole into a wall, clearing debris, climbing stairs, and using a power tool. While the average human being could carry out these activities without too much trouble, for a robot, these tasks are a formidable assignment.

In the 2013 DARPA disaster-response competition, none of the competing robots (including CHIMP), were able to complete all of the assigned tasks. Thanks to the same technological advances that are accelerating the maturation of driverless cars—faster, smaller, hardware sensors and computers and better artificial-intelligence software—by the 2015 DARPA competition CHIMP and two other robots completed the course in less than an hour. CHIMP placed third out of twenty-five of the world's most advanced robots, earning his proud creators at NREC a cash prize of half a million dollars.

Brian explained that on today's tour of NREC, we would see CHIMP in action, but in only a brief and simple demonstration. To prepare for the demo, CHIMP's team of human trainers and handlers bustled around, booting up the robot's operating system software. Several other engineers huddled together in front of a nearby monitor, poring over a complicated user interface. Meanwhile, CHIMP sat hunched and inert on the floor, his unassuming air belying the complexity of the advanced engineering that would guide and coordinate his physical movements, software virtually gluing together his magnificent mechanical body.

While CHIMP warmed up, we admired his mechanical limbs. CHIMP had two powerful ape-like arms, robotic legs that could transform into tank treads and back into limbs, and delicate pincer-like fingers that could extend and retract at will. A suite of sensors on the robot's body streamed data from the environment that was rapidly processed by his robotic operating system.

Finally, after ten minutes, CHIMP's operating system finished booting. Suddenly, he began to move. Like a human athlete warming up, his black mechanical hands flexed in anticipation. In slow stages, CHIMP came to life.

CHIMP's team of expert human roboticists closely monitored his movements and typed rapid-fire commands into the keyboard. As CHIMP's sensors studied the environment, his team of operators gave him a simple command: "Move ten feet forward." In response, CHIMP created a mental 3-D digital model of his surroundings from sensor data and then calculated his next move.

Computation complete, CHIMP's stubby legs morphed elegantly into tank treads and he rolled smoothly several feet across the floor. He turned in a circle, raised an arm, and then, in an even, dignified glide, returned to his original location. As his body returned to its resting position, CHIMP's tank treads morphed back into inert limbs. The demo complete, he shut down, resting quietly on his red, metallic haunches.

ARTIFICIAL INTELLIGENCE IN MOTION

CHIMP is an extraordinary mobile robot, the equivalent of an Olympic-level athlete. Ironically, advanced disaster response robots—even masterfully designed robots such as CHIMP—

unwittingly demonstrate one of the great challenges of artificial-intelligence research: it's easier to teach a computer to play chess at the Grand Master level than to teach a robot to pick through a pile of rubble. Roboticist Hans Moravec succinctly summed up the challenge of automating seemingly simple tasks in what would come to be known as *Moravec's paradox*. Moravec observed that "it is comparatively easy to make computers exhibit adult-level performance on intelligence tests or playing checkers, and difficult or impossible to give them the skills of a one-year-old when it comes to perception and mobility."[2]

Moravec's paradox illuminates a long-standing breach between AI researchers and roboticists. For decades, AI research sought to emulate human intelligence by creating software that could perform tasks most people would consider intellectually elevated, such as playing chess, solving puzzles, or performing mathematical calculations. Roboticists, meanwhile, pursued another goal: to create artificial life forms that had the capacity to see and make sense of their environment with the same level of skill and grace exhibited by the average human toddler.

Activities we humans experience to be simple—for example, to close a valve, pick up a power tool, and cut a hole in the wall—actually require a tremendous amount of sensor data and computational power. Like a duck that appears to swim smoothly while its legs paddle furiously under the surface of the water, robotic software is constantly running through an intricate series of calculations to guide one smooth glide of a robotic limb. The result is that disaster-recovery robots such as CHIMP and his brethren can tolerate physical conditions that would sicken or kill a human, yet their response times are magnitudes slower than the lightening-quick reflexes of even a low biological life-form.

In videos of DARPA competitions, the footage shows robots moving through their tasks at a slow and unnatural pace. Their limbs seem to operate in slow motion because the software code that guides a simple physical action—for example, crossing the room and grabbing a wrench—can take a robotic operating system a minute or more to run. Another seemingly simple activity, that of looking around the room to check for obstacles and to plan a path through, is also resource-intensive. To "perceive" its surroundings, a robot's visual system scans the environment and processes bulky streams of data to look for patterns and meaningful information. When the robotic operating system identifies what's nearby and settles on an appropriate response, the resulting movements of each limb demand additional analysis, and hence more time.

Brazilian scientist Suzana Herculano-Houzel provides some insight into why software that guides movement, perception, and response is so resource intensive and difficult to design. Dr. Herculano-Houzel's research on the human brain reveals an unexpected insight that sheds light on Moravec's paradox: our ability to perceive and respond to our immediate environment actually demands a lot of brainpower. Over the course of millions of years of evolution, our brains have adapted by investing huge amounts of cognitive real estate to oversee the seemingly straightforward activity of reacting to what's around us.

To map brain function, Dr. Herculano-Houzel devised a technique to count the number of neurons in the mammalian brain. After years of painstaking research, she discovered that the human brain contains roughly 86 billion neurons. Contrary to what brain researchers previously believed, far more neurons are dedicated to overseeing basic bodily functions and reflexes than to enabling so-called "higher" acts of cognition.

It turns out that the average human cerebellum dedicates a whopping 69 billion "back brain" neurons to orchestrating basic bodily function and movement. Dr. Herculano-Houzel's research revealed that a paltry 16 billion neurons are located in the cerebral cortex, the part of the brain that governs self-awareness, problem solving, and abstract thought.[3] Herculano-Houzel's research demonstrates why robotic brains also need to devote a significant amount of their artificial "neurons" to overseeing the robot's perception and physical movement.

On the day we visited NREC, we walked away from CHIMP's demo with new insight into robotic operating systems. Given

Moravec's paradox and the computational power required to automate simple physical movements, it would not be unreasonable to wonder whether it may simply not be possible to build a robotic operating system that's fast enough, reliable enough, and smart enough to guide a car, particularly considering the high bar that driverless cars will have to clear when it comes to their safety and reliability.

Our next and final stop at NREC, however, refueled our confidence. Hope appeared in the form of a bright green John Deere tractor. We were introduced to Carl Wellington, another NREC researcher, whose work focuses on helping agricultural companies automate farming equipment.

Modern agricultural practices are technologically sophisticated, using an approach called *precision agriculture.* Carl explained that farmers have used partially autonomous vehicles for more than a decade. In the early stages of automation, farmers equipped their tractors with highly accurate GPS systems and used farm management software to map out their fields.

In the early days of precision agriculture, a human driver was still required. The first generation of autonomous agricultural vehicles, while capable of handling the straightaways, still needed a human driver to steer the tractor around the curves at the end of each field. A few years later, however, commercial software capable of guiding an autonomous tractor around curves became available.

As autonomous tractors have proven to be safe and capable drivers, the notion of full autonomy has gained acceptance. Farmers are all too happy to have a robot help them with the tedious, yet critical, work of plowing, planting, and spraying fields. "With automated steering on the tractor, the human operator can focus on other tasks," Carl explained.

Today companies such as John Deere and its competitors sell a wide variety of different types of self-driving modules for their tractors that have proven to be safe and capable drivers. As young people in rural areas migrate away to cities in search of work, self-guided tractors have become standard equipment on many modern farms. Given their punishing schedules, hard-working farmers are all too happy to have a robot help them with the time-consuming, yet critical, work of plowing, planting, and spraying their fields. As we wrapped up our interview with Carl, he summed up the appeal of any sort of self-guided equipment in today's time-starved world: "With automated steering, the human operator can focus on other tasks."

CONTROLS: THE AI MASHUP

On the spectrum of engineering challenges, creating an operating system to guide driverless cars lies somewhere between that of writing code for CHIMP and programming an autonomous tractor. The operating system for a driverless car spans two large and diverse research areas. One is *controls engineering,* a field of engineering that deals with the regulation of the performance of mechanical parts. The second is the study of artificial intelligence.

Controls engineering deals with complex systems (for example, mechanical systems such as robots) that interact in some way with their surrounding environment via inputs and outputs. To impose some order onto a complex system, roboticists organize activities into *low-level* controls and *high-level* controls. In a driverless car, low-level controls govern the way the car regulates its internal systems, such as brakes, acceleration, and steering. High-level controls govern the car's longer-term strategic plans, for example, its navigation and route-planning activities.

While controls engineering focuses on applying software to manage complex systems, researchers in the closely related field of artificial intelligence strive to build computer software that is capable of intelligent behavior, a broad and vague definition that reflects the field's staggering breadth and diversity. AI research uses theory borrowed from several other fields, ranging from psychology to linguistics to statistics. Although the quest to create software that exhibits so-called general intelligence is still among the field's long-term goals, much of modern AI research homes in on a particular problem space, for example, making industrial processes more efficient, or enabling cars to safely guide themselves.

An in-depth examination of artificial-intelligence techniques is beyond the scope of this book. To simplify matters, we divide the rich diversity of AI techniques into two major groups: rule-based, or *symbolic* AI, and bottom up, or *data-driven* AI, also increasingly known as *machine learning*. Symbolic AI involves breaking down a complex situation or task into a formal set of rules that a human programmer writes into software code. In contrast, data-driven AI (or machine learning) involves the application of algorithms to large amounts of data and uses statistical techniques to classify, rank, or otherwise parse that data.

No form of artificial intelligence is innately superior to another. What matters is applying the best AI for the particular task at hand. What all AI programs attempt to do is to break the complicated and ultimately unknowable "real world" into a finite number of logical "chunks" that can then be processed by software. Each chunk, or distinct situation, is called a *state*. A state can be a particular configuration of chess pieces on a board, or it can be a split second in which physical objects are frozen in a particular configuration. The set of all possible situations in a particular problem space is called a *state space*.

Symbolic AI techniques work best in smaller state spaces, situations in which all possible outcomes can be anticipated and then addressed with formal rules. For example, a factory assembly line has a smaller number of possible state spaces than does a busy city street. Therefore, rule-based artificial intelligence would be an effective technique for the software that guides a factory robot through a finite number of possible actions and reactions.

Symbolic AI has been the ruling paradigm for decades. At the end of the twentieth century, however, as computing power has improved and sensors increased the amount of available data from a trickle to a deluge, machine learning emerged from research margins to gain wide acceptance. One of the great advantages of machine-learning is that it doesn't require a human programmer to anticipate every possible outcome of a situation, as is required by traditional symbolic AI techniques. A programmer armed with lots of computation power and a large amount of training data can create a machine-learning software program that "learns" to react to the situation at hand and, in some cases, becomes capable of reacting to novel and unfamiliar situations.

A car's operating system is threaded through with different types of artificial-intelligence software that manages all of its various control functions. The autonomous equivalent of modern *Homo sapiens,* Google's wide-eyed little autonomous buggy, did not burst fully formed from the well-guarded labs of ingenious Google researchers. Instead, Google's modern robotic car is the beneficiary of nearly a century of AI and robotics research and contains traces of robotic DNA from several long-extinct research projects, each contributing a key concept here, or a breakthrough technology there.

In the popular imagination, there's a long-cherished but inaccurate belief that *Homo sapiens,* thanks to their innate superiority, managed to remain viable while earlier, more primitive *Homo* species went extinct. Modern DNA analysis is proving that this notion is flawed. Neanderthals, once thought to have been driven to extinction by their superior cousins, still lurk among us. DNA analysis reveals that people of European and Asian origin carry bits and pieces of Neanderthal genetic material, suggesting that the process of human evolution is not as staged and linear as once believed.

The origin of the software that guides the modern autonomous vehicle is similarly murky, debatable, and complex. Google's low-level controls, the software that oversees its system of brakes, steering, and speed control, are the intellectual offspring of a primitive military robot, the Dog of War built in 1912. To guide the car along the optimal route, Google's high-level control software uses decades-old search algorithms. Some of Google's car's ability to learn by comparing current driving scenarios to past experiences evolved from machine-learning techniques that were initially developed in the 1950s.

ACCELERATING, BRAKING, AND TURNING

Let's begin with low-level controls. The function of low-level controls is to pull a system back to an optimal set point. Modern feedback control devices are an unheralded but ubiquitous army of referees, constantly adjusting an engine's fuel injection, regulating the voltage in manufacturing machines, even keeping the temperature in your home exactly at the degree to which you set the thermostat. These feedback controls strive to maintain a system's balance: any system—be it mechanical or electrical or biological—needs to be constantly dragged back to a state of equilibrium.

Automotive engineers have been using low-level controls in antilock brakes and cruise controls since the 1980s. On a driverless car, low-level controls manage the car's major hardware subsystems, making sure the car drives precisely along a calculated trajectory, and ensuring that its braking and acceleration are smooth. Low-level controls make split-second decisions by running signals to the car's computer via the controller area network (CAN) bus. If low-level controls are operating correctly, a passenger on board a driverless car wouldn't even notice; she would be aware only that the car was "handling" itself smoothly.

It has taken industrial engineers more than a century of trial and error to perfect the art of low-level feedback controls. The earliest control technologies were crude by today's standards. In the steam-engine era in the eighteenth century, a metal gadget called a *governor* was used to regulate the pressure feeding from the engine's boiler, thereby maintaining a constant operating speed for the steam engine despite varying load. An old-fashioned mechanical governor was a simple spinning metal contraption weighted with two steel balls. It did not contain much in the form of artificial intelligence, but what it did provide to the engine in which it was installed was critical: self-regulation.

In 1912, in what was arguably the world's first autonomous vehicle, inventors John Hammond Jr. and Benjamin Miessner

Figure 4.1
The "electric dog" (circa 1912).
Source: *Scientific American,* supp. 2267, June 14, 1919, pp. 376–377.

rigged up a simple self-guided go-cart with an electric circuit and a pair of light-sensitive selenium cells. When the light-sensitive cells on the go-cart were exposed to light, a system of low-level controls would tug the car's "steering wheel" in order to bring the two light sources into equilibrium, and the cart would spin in the direction of the source of the light. This crude autonomous vehicle, given the fierce name Dog of War by its inventors, was built with military application in mind to help the United States win World War I.

The idea behind the Dog was straightforward. The Dog would be released near enemy lines where it would continue its mission of destruction on its own, without a human minder. As Miessner described it, as "the enemy turns their search light on it, it will immediately be guided toward that enemy automatically," carrying an explosive payload right into the hands of an unsuspecting night watchman.[4]

Primitive as it was by today's standards, the Dog of War was an early working example of the same science that guides every driverless car. The Dog was also the predecessor of more sinister modern devices like heat-seeking missiles. Today, automotive cruise control uses essentially the same algorithm to make sure that if the speed of the car is too low, more gasoline is injected to increase the car's speed. If the car's speed picks up too much, the controller injects less gasoline until the difference between the desired speed and actual speed is brought close to zero.

As time has passed, primitive low-level regulators such as those used in the Dog have fallen by the wayside, and electronic circuits that regulate actuators using data from sensors have taken their place. Modern low-level controls are an exercise in advanced math. Low-level controls use a large and diverse family of algorithms to keep a single component or an entire system humming smoothly. Other names for the family of commonly used low-level control algorithms are *control schemes* or *filters;* sometimes they're called *reactive controls.*

Now that data is abundant, advanced machine-learning techniques have found their way into low-level controls. Predictive algorithms are commonly used in low-level controls to keep a robot smoothly on course. Predictive algorithms facilitate a car's situational awareness while also keeping an eye on its digital map in order to calculate how much fuel should be injected into the engine so that it can smoothly crest the big hill that's approaching. Some fuel-injection systems make use of data from several different sensor streams, factoring in multiple variables such as engine load, air humidity, and even ambient oxygen levels to inject just the right amount of fuel to maintain the engine's steady speed.

One of the most challenging aspects of keeping a gasoline-powered engine running smoothly is that of time delay, or *lag time.* Lag time is one of those seemingly trivial quirks of an engine or system that thwarts even the best feedback controllers. Because injecting fuel into a gasoline engine remains at its heart a mechanical and chemical (not an electrical) activity, gasoline engines are notorious for their unpredictable lag times. This delay means that it is challenging to get a car to start, accelerate, and stop with precise timing.

There are at least two ways to reduce the problem of lag time in an autonomous vehicle. One is to throw more computing power into the low-level controls. A rapid computer can reduce and compensate for lag time in a fuel injector and can offer more accuracy in maintaining the delicate balance that goes into moving a gasoline engine forward at a steady rate and precise timing. The second way to do away with the problem is to switch from gas-powered to electric engines.

Electric engines are easier to regulate one of the reasons they're preferred by Google and Tesla for their driverless-car prototypes. If a specific voltage is applied to an electric engine, the engine consistently and immediately yields a certain known *torque*, or thrust forward. Although several decades of bright minds have applied their talents to the problems of regulating gasoline powered engines, this rich intellectual heritage might become irrelevant should electric engines become the gold standard for driverless cars.

ROUTE PLANNING AND ROAD NAVIGATION

While low-level controls require only a split second to do their work, high-level controls are engaged over an extended period of time, perhaps for as long as the length of the car trip. If low-level controls are like reflexes, high-level controls are akin to the sort of higher mental activities that were traditionally considered "intelligent." High-level controls include route-planning and navigation, both activities that are addressed with the search algorithms.

Search algorithms are a classic example of traditional, rule-based symbolic AI. To successfully apply a search algorithm to a high-level control problem, it's crucial that the algorithm have sufficient computing power available to rapidly complete its work. Search algorithms consume a lot of system resources since most problems have lots of possible paths, and to determine the best one, it's necessary to assess them all.

Search algorithms are a versatile breed. Today they're used in a variety of different applications ranging from chess (searching and then ranking best to worst outcomes from possible chess moves) to navigation. To plan its route, a driverless car uses search algorithms to make a list of all the available route options between here and there, and rank the options from best to worst.

One commonly used search algorithm is the A* algorithm (pronounced A-Star), invented in 1968 by Nils Nilsson and his colleagues. The A* algorithm has become the tool of choice for almost any problem whose solution involves ranking outcomes and choosing the best option. The A* algorithm provides the intelligence behind GPS-navigation devices the world over and is used by many different types of software applications today, including chess playing and factory job scheduling.

Like the old joke about dancing the Argentinian tango, what the A* algorithm does is simple but not easy. Before the A* algorithm was invented, early AI researchers puzzled over how to make search more efficient. The answer lay in applying a clever cost-function to the process. The A* algorithm speeds up the search process by using a cost-function that combines the cost of the paths examined so far with the optimistically estimated remaining cost to the target destination. The A* cost function cleverly eliminates most of the long paths early in the search, and is mathematically guaranteed to zero-in on the shortest path.

Although A* is a general purpose search algorithm, it is particularly useful for high-level driving-related functions. If a software developer adjusts the algorithm's cost function and reruns the algorithm, it can be used to tackle a wide variety of costs. Possible costs might include a traffic delay, road congestion, road works, traffic lights, and even the number of left turns.

Nilsson and his colleagues open-sourced the A* algorithm when they invented it, an act of generosity that has accelerated the development of digital-navigation software. Since then, the A* has become one of the most influential algorithms in all of artificial-intelligence research. I met Nilsson a few years ago in Switzerland at a small workshop celebrating the fiftieth anniversary of artificial-intelligence research. Nilsson, wryly observing the modern tendency to patent every little piece of new AI research, told me, "If I got one cent every time someone uses a GPS, I'd be a rich man today.'

Today, both high- and low-level controls are mature and time-tested technologies in widespread use in the automotive industry. Their very maturity, however, raises an interesting question: why aren't driverless cars already available? The answer lies in Moravec's paradox, the fact that seemingly straightforward acts of mobility and perception have proven to be difficult to automate. To drive safely on public streets and roads, driverless cars require more than just automotive controls. They also need an intelligent operating system that can visually understand the environment and know how to react appropriately.

5

CREATING ARTIFICIAL PERCEPTION

The technological last mile in driverless-car design is the development of software that can provide reliable artificial perception. If history is any guide, this last mile could prove to be a long haul. Consider the case of hacker George Hotz, who in 2015 claimed he spent a month putting together his own driverless car in his garage.

Hotz rigged up a 2016 Acura ILX with the usual equipment: lidar, a camera, and a glove compartment packed with a computer, a networking switch, and GPS sensors. According to Hotz, his driverless car worked well. The tension started to build when Hotz boasted that with just a few more months of improvements and practice, the software guiding his do-it-yourself (DIY) Acura could drive better than the autodrive module of a Tesla Model S.

Tesla's CEO, Elon Musk, was not amused by Hotz's public challenge. In a response posted on Tesla's website, Musk deflated Hotz's claims, pointing out that

> the true problem of autonomy: getting a machine learning system to be 99% correct is relatively easy, but getting it to be 99.9999% correct, which is where it ultimately needs to be, is vastly more difficult. One can see this with the annual machine vision competitions, where the computer will properly identify

something as a dog more than 99% of the time, but might occasionally call it a potted plant. Making such mistakes at 70 mph would be highly problematic.[1]

The debate between Hotz and Musk demonstrates the significance of the critical missing piece—artificial perception software—and how important its development will be for the maturation of a commercially viable driverless car. George Hotz's home-built Acura is evidence that today a skilled developer can build a pretty good driverless car in a fairly short period of time. However, as Musk points out, when it comes to software you will trust with your life, the leap from 99 percent to 99.9999 percent accuracy is a big one.

In the past few years, mobile robots have gotten better at finding their way around their environment. It helps that the performance of computer vision software has improved dramatically, aided by the advent of big data, high resolution digital cameras, and faster processors. Another catalyst has been the successful application of machine-learning software to solve thorny problems of machine vision, sparking a mini-renaissance in the study of artificial perception.

The last mile for driverless-car technology remains the development of software to oversee the car's perception and response. While writing this book, we found ourselves confounded when faced with the question of what to call this emerging bundle of various software tools that do not fall neatly under either high- or low-level controls. After some thought, we wound up naming this software the *mid-level controls*.

In this chapter, we use the phrase *mid-level control software* to describe the collection of different software tools that provide the car with artificial vision. Mid-level control software enables the car's operating system to make sense of sensor data, understand the physical layout of the nearby environment, and to select the best reaction to nearby objects and events. The average duration, or what roboticists call an *event horizon*, of a mid-level activity ranges from a few seconds to a few minutes. In contrast, low-level controls operate within a time horizon of a fraction of a second and high-level controls plan hours ahead.

For a human, an example of a mid-level activity might be the act of selecting a dirty coffee cup from the sink and placing it into the dishwasher. In a disaster response robot such as CHIMP, the robot's mid-level controls would note that its visual sensors have identified the presence of a round dark object on the floor. CHIMP's mid-level control software would classify the viewed object as a rock (rather than a shadow, for example) and would guide the robot's tank treads safely around it. In a driverless car, mid-level controls make critical life-and-death decisions based on data from the car's visual sensors, for example, identifying a shape at a crosswalk as a man on a bicycle and then making the decision to wait and let him pass.

THE CHALLENGE OF OBJECT RECOGNITION

Mid-level control software guides a driverless car through complex, real-world situations where there are a nearly infinite number of possible responses. To demonstrate the challenges that developers face, imagine you've been tasked with writing software to guide a car through a busy intersection. Your software will be held to the same standard as a human driver, so it must obey the rules of the road as laid out in any standard-issue DMV handbook.[2]

> Slow down and be ready to stop. Yield to traffic and pedestrians already in the intersection or just entering the intersection. Also, yield to the vehicle or bicycle that arrives first, or to the vehicle or bicycle on your right if it reaches the intersection at the same time as you.

Easy, right? The subtle complexities begin to emerge when you break down the process into functional steps. Your first task is to write code to enable the car to recognize that the intersection is approaching, so that it can "Slow down and be ready to stop." Any good developer could engineer this response by using using GPS location points and a detailed digital map that contains information on intersections. The visual cue of a stop sign or stop light helps too. So far, so good.

Now on to the next task, to "Yield to traffic and pedestrians already in the intersection or just entering the intersection." At this point, the project starts getting trickier. First, what counts as "traffic"? How does software know to recognize a category of object called "pedestrian?"

To perform as well as a human driver, your mid-level control software must somehow correctly classify the categories of things that are traffic, pedestrian, or bicycle. One way to tackle this problem could be to write an artificial-intelligence program that uses a rule-based approach. You could attempt to classify each pedestrian, vehicle, and specific traffic situation the car might encounter by writing an exhaustive list of what programmers call *if-then statements*.

Now on to the next problem: you must somehow describe all the things in these various categories so the software can identify them. One way to identify objects belonging to categories such as "traffic" or "pedestrian" could be according to what these objects are likely to look like. For example, traffic = rectangular boxy object between ten and twenty feet long. Pedestrian = two-legged object less than two feet wide and between two and seven feet high.

As artificial-intelligence researchers have learned over the past several decades, the problem with this approach is that category definitions don't hold true for every situation. Inevitably, an exception will appear in the form of a corner case or two that brings the most carefully constructed set of if-then statements to its knees. In the example of the intersection, one pedestrian might be on crutches and another carrying a bulky package that increases his total girth to wider than two feet. Perhaps a motorcycle that's seven feet long (i.e., too short to count as a vehicle) will roar through the intersection and your software will fail to recognize it as traffic.

The problem that plagues rule-based AI software is that without a robust method to classify every object a car might encounter, it's impossible to write rules to guide the car's response. Since your software can't always be 99.999% certain that what it encounters is indeed truly a vehicle or a bicycle, it can't advise the car how to react appropriately as instructed by the rules of the road. This is why if life were completely logical, writing mid-level control software would be a straightforward task. Instead, on any given busy street corner in any given city, a rich and steady stream of novel corner cases will elude definition. Clearly, although we take it for granted, we humans have mastered the art of perception.

In his landmark book *On Intelligence*, Palm founder Jeff Hawkins describes a long-standing puzzle that has confounded philosophers and machine vision researchers alike: *invariant representation*. We humans are equipped with a mental model that enables us to consistently recognize objects, even when they appear to us in an unfamiliar context, or that we view from a new angle. For example, most people can consistently recognize a friend's face in a split second, even if she has changed her hair color from blond to brunette. Exactly how the human brain learns invariant representations, however, remains a mystery.

Human eyes stream data to our brain so smoothly we don't have to consciously pick apart the visual scene to make sense of it. In contrast, software that reads streams of data from visual sensors has to do more work. A stream of visual data is at heart a numerical array. Machine-vision software processes these numerical arrays with aplomb, but is incapable of understanding the visual scene the numbers depict, a conundrum that cuts to the heart of artificial-intelligence research.

The mystery of how humans achieve nearly flawless *scene understanding* has puzzled philosophers and scientists for centuries. Since the first computers were developed, AI researchers have tried to crack the mystery of scene understanding and its close kin, *object recognition*, using a wide variety of techniques. Some techniques used logic ("If the object has three sharp corners, then it must be..."). Other techniques used brute force, storing as many images as possible of objects the robot might encounter and having the software check new visual information against that database, using some comparison metric. Both of these approaches worked some of the time but were too slow and still didn't provide the software with a crucial skill, the ability to consistently recognize objects in unfamiliar settings.

To automate the process of object recognition, it's necessary to have software that can extract visual information from raw data in order to identify the objects depicted. Over the years, researchers have attempted to do this in several different ways. One of the earliest forms of computer vision software developed in the 1960s worked by distilling digital images into simple line drawings.

A famous example of this approach was a robot named Shakey, described somewhat optimistically by his creator, Stanford researcher Charles Rosen, as "the first electronic person." Shakey's "body" consisted of a stack of heavy boxes containing electronic equipment stacked onto a cart. On top of the

Figure 5.1

Time-lapse image of Shakey in action (circa 1970).
Source: SRI International

boxes perched Shakey's "head," a tall, thin, swiveling mast of cameras and cables. Shakey's vision sensor was a TV camera that generated a steam of images, each containing just a few hundred pixels.

Shakey wowed the world of machine-vision research by responding to a command typed into his system to "go find a red block" and then, gazing around with his TV camera, slowly rolling around in search of a red block. When his vision system concluded that he indeed "saw" his desired object, Shakey would signal that his mission was complete.

To find his way around, Shakey used a type of artificial-intelligence called *edge detection*, part of a larger family of visual recognition techniques known as *template-based* perception. Shakey could identify objects of a particular shape or color by analyzing images from his TV camera and then simplifying those images into simple line drawings. Once an image was thus broken down, Shakey would identify what the object was by comparing it against a database of line drawings of pyramids, blocks, and cylinders.

Edge detection required relatively little computing power or memory and enabled efficient data storage. Edge detection was a speedy way to extract meaningful information from raw visual data, particularly given the crudeness of the hardware of Shakey's day. Analyzing an entire digital image took several minutes. Breaking apart images into simple line drawings enabled Shakey to respond to commands in a time frame with which humans felt comfortable.

The limitations of template matching using edge detection are obvious. Shakey could function only in carefully arranged environments where he would encounter only objects he was already familiar with against a clean background. If Shakey were to "see" an object that did not match those in his personal collection of line drawings, his software would just have to make its best guess. If a new obstacle were thrown into the mix—a cylinder, or a cat, or a flying plastic bag, or a colleague inadvertently moseying into the lab after a late morning, Shakey's sensors would capture this unfamiliar object, but its mid-level control would not be able to recognize it.

The researchers who followed after Shakey developed several different types of rule-based AI software programs that processed data from a number of different formats, including digital image files, 3-D point clouds, and videos. Some machine-vision programs calculated depth measurements from lidar range data. Other software specialized in recognizing different textures in digital photographs. Some programs recognized the presence of a distinct visual feature in an image and compared that feature against a database of visual features.

Many of these techniques worked well. In fact, many are still used by modern industrial robots to carry out concrete tasks, such as inspecting complex circuit boards or sorting machine parts into bins. A critical limitation of rule-based machine-vision software, however, is that it works best in structured environments where the robot's machine vision will encounter only a selected set of objects. Show a banana to an industrial robot that's programmed to sort only nuts and bolts and it will be dumbfounded, baffled by this novel yellow object that doesn't match anything in its image library.

Rule-based AI fares especially poorly when used to provide artificial scene understanding to a driverless car. While watching several autonomous vehicles race in the DARPA Challenge of 2007, I witnessed an excellent (and unintentional) demonstration of a rule-based AI program's failure to understand a traffic scene, a lapse that caused two autonomous vehicles to crash. (For more detail on the DARPA Challenges, see chapter 8).

In 2007, computer-vision software was still largely rule-based. As the race progressed, my university's car, a vehicle called Skynet (from Cornell University) inched cautiously down the road, followed closely by Talos, a car from MIT. For no apparent reason, Cornell's car suddenly stopped, backed up, then lurched forward and stopped again. The MIT car attempted to pass the faltering Cornell car. As the MIT car slowly moved into passing position,

Cornell's car unexpectedly started moving again and the MIT car crashed into its side.

Fortunately, no one was harmed, and both teams (later) enjoyed the distinction of participating in what was perhaps the first "driverless vs. driverless" accident in history. Analysis of the car's driving logs revealed that the cars crashed because their rule-based machine vision software failed to do its job. In its post-mortem analysis, the Cornell team concluded that the reason its car came to a sudden halt was that "a measurement assignment mistake caused a phantom obstacle to appear, momentarily blocking Skynet's path." The MIT team concluded that "Talos perceived Skynet as a cluster of static objects."[3]

If the software guiding Cornell's car had correctly identified MIT's car as a moving vehicle and vice versa, the crash would not have occurred. This example demonstrates how essential it is that a driverless car's mid-level control software have the capacity to recognize the objects it sees on and near the road. Subtle but critical differences between two similar objects—a parked motorcycle vs. one being actively steered into traffic—can make the difference between life and death.

MID-LEVEL CONTROLS

We will explain how mid-level control software works by considering it in four modules. The first module is a software tool called an *occupancy grid*. The second is a software program that recognizes and labels the raw data that flows into the occupancy grid. The third module uses predictive AI software to generate *cones of uncertainty*. Finally, the fourth module consists of a *short-term trajectory planner* that guides the car past perceived obstacles, while obeying rules of the road. Let's begin with the first module, the occupancy grid.

An occupancy grid is a software tool that provides a real-time, continuously updated 3-D digital model of the environment outside the car. Similar to a back-end database that contains digital records, the occupancy grid is a digital repository that stores

Figure 5.2

An occupancy grid of an intersection with recognized objects; the grid overlays sensor data onto stored data from a high-definition map.
Source: Google, Inc.

information about the physical objects around the car. The grid works in tandem with other modules in the mid-level control software and also serves as a visual model for programmers.

Data flows into the occupancy grid from several sources. Some data is static and originates in stored, high-definition maps. Other data flows in from the car's visual sensors in real time. Most programmers set up their occupancy grid using a system of color coding and easily recognizable icons to represent objects that commonly appear on the road.

Twenty years ago, a typical occupancy grid was blocky and crude with the same level of visual appeal as an old PacMan arcade game. During the 1980s, when driverless cars hauled around hefty minicomputers and TV cameras, their occupancy grids that modeled the data depicted the scene outside the car as a jerky series of static frames. Today's occupancy grids operate in real time, building a dynamic model of the world by making a running list of all the objects near the car.

At this point, an astute reader would pause and point out that for most of its history, software has not proven to be very capable at correctly identifying objects. Since this is indeed the case, we now introduce a new and critical piece of information: an occupancy grid is indeed just a spatial model for planning. To interpret the scene, it relies on a second software module to label the raw data flowing in from the car's sensors. This second module uses deep-learning software to classify the objects moving past the car so the occupancy grid can store this information and make it available to the rest of the car's operating system.

This second module is the force behind the revolution in driverless cars. By simply recognizing objects depicted in images, deep-learning software is finally unlocking the puzzle of artificial perception and enabling the development of robust mid-level control software. We'll explain the inner workings of deep learning software in-depth in chapter 10 Here we will summarize it as a type of machine-learning software that uses artificial neural networks to recognize objects in streams of raw visual data.

In the past, without an accurately labeled data feed, an occupancy grid was fairly toothless, a mere crude approximation of a few large physical objects in the nearby environment. Without knowing what objects lurked outside the car, the rest of the car's software programs could not figure out how best to react to them, or to predict what these unidentified objects would do next. Until very recently, driverless vehicles operated reliably only in static environments that contained almost no moving objects, for example in factories, mines, on agricultural fields, and in deserts. In these static environments, the control software guiding the car worked pretty well by simply avoiding every obstacle it encountered, regardless of whether it could classify it or not.

Deep learning has made possible the use of another technique that has also greatly improved the performance of driverless-car software in dynamic environments. The third module in mid-level control software uses a tool called a *cone of uncertainty* to predict where and how fast objects near the car are moving. Once the deep-learning module has labeled an object and the occupancy grid made note of its presence, a cone of uncertainty predicts where the object is headed next.

A cone of uncertainty provides a driverless car with artificial scene understanding. When a human driver sees a pedestrian standing too close to traffic, she makes a mental note to veer away to avoid him. A driverless car makes the same "mental note" using a cone of uncertainty. A stationary object, like a fire hydrant, will have a tiny, narrow cone of uncertainty since it's not likely to move much. In contrast, a rapidly moving object would have a large and broad cone since the number of potential places it could wind up is larger, and therefore its future position is uncertain.

Human drivers don't explicitly draw out mental elliptical cones around every nearby object. Yet, we do something that's roughly equivalent. We keep a running tally in our minds of who and what is around us. Based on our assessment of their appearance combined with our past experience, we guess at the intentions of nearby pedestrians and we predict what they're going to do next.

Roboticists borrowed the concept of the cone from weather forecasters. If you've ever watched a weather report on TV where the meteorologist shows the trajectory of a tornado across the Midwest plains, you've seen a cone of uncertainty. The apex of the cone begins with the current and known position of the tornado. The broad end of the cone is the tornado's potential path, where it might wreak havoc over the course of the next few days. The broader the open edge of the cone, the more uncertain the tornado's ultimate destination.

Mid-level control software creates cones as follows. Imagine an object depicted on a piece of paper. First, draw a tight circle around that object. Let's call that the *current circle*. Next, imagine that the object is moving through space and draw another larger circle around all the potential future locations that the object might occupy in the next 10 seconds. Let's call that the *future circle*. Finally, connect the small circle and the larger circle with two lines. Voilà: a cone of uncertainty.

Cones of uncertainty provide a digital substitute for human eye contact. From the vantage point of a driverless car, a pedestrian standing near the curb looking onto the street would have a cone with a slightly forward skew, indicating she might move forward any moment. If she was staring at her phone instead of staring forward, her cone might have a different shape, perhaps slightly narrower, since she would not appear to be ready to move forward. If she were to glance at the driverless car, her cone would shrink even further since the car's software would recognize that she saw the car and was unlikely to move into the car's path.

The more unpredictable the pedestrian, the larger the cone of uncertainty. A wobbling bicycle rider would have a larger cone of uncertainty than a stationary pedestrian. A bewildered dog or a child chasing a ball would have an even larger cone.

Sometimes, even a static object can be surrounded by a large cone of uncertainty. Occluding objects, or things blocking something behind them—while they themselves are unlikely to move— might be hiding something else that could be moving. A car's mid-level software would likely draw a large cone of uncertainty near a blind alley, a blind turn, or next to the open door of a parked car that might unexpectedly let out a passenger. A standing school bus would likely generate a large cone of uncertainty. Although the bus itself may not be moving, at any moment a child could pop up behind it.

In the car's mid-level controls, when the first three modules have completed their work, the fourth one, the *short-term trajectory planner*, can kick in. When objects near the car have all been labeled and their cones of uncertainty calculated, a driverless car's trajectory planner can lay out the car's best path forward. The trajectory planner uses well-established planning algorithms to calculate the most efficient path forward while still obeying the rules of the road and minimizing travel time and the risk of a collision.

Computers excel at this type of nonlinear trajectory estimation. In the past few years, software programs have improved to the point where a computer can make better predictions about an object's trajectory than can a person. The more potential outcomes in a certain situation, the better the computer is at calculating all the various possibilities. Add in more potential variables, such as a broader range of possible pedestrian behaviors, and the trajectory planner's performance would improve even more.

As mid-level control software continues to improve at its current rate, it won't be long before the operating system for a driverless car will exhibit perfect mastery of the holy trinity of qualities needed for mainstream application—real-time response, reliability, and intelligence. Does this mean that driverless cars should be permitted to take the road? Probably. But first, human passengers need to demand concrete proof and a clear definition of how reliable, exactly, these new robotic drivers will be.

SUPER-RELIABLE AND SECURE

We've discussed the technological challenges that make it difficult for an operating system to be perfectly reliable. What also needs to be defined and then quantified is a legal standard for reliability. Many people would insist that driverless cars not be legal until they achieve perfect 100 percent reliability, meaning no crashes, mishaps, or blunders—ever. The sad truth is that if perfect reliability is required, driverless cars will never attain legal status. No operating system is perfectly reliable all of the time.

A great deal can go wrong with an operating system, and even the best-designed ones fail periodically. On a personal computer, a user might install a new application that's buggy and hence disrupts the system's core processes. A system can be infected by a malevolent computer virus. A new hardware peripheral can unexpectedly bring down the entire system.

Computer operating systems have two characteristics that make them unreliable and insecure: One, they contain millions of lines of code, too much for a skilled coder to wade through in search of potential bugs. Two, operating systems suffer from what's called *poor fault isolation.*

Windows, IOS, and Linux, for example, are built in such a way that there's little or no isolation between their subparts or procedures. The architecture of Windows XP contains about five million lines of code that runs thousands of procedures in a single, monolithic digital "workspace," or *kernel*. These thousands of procedures are linked together into a single binary program; like mountain climbers attached to a single line, if one falls, they all fall.

Hardware problems are frequently the root cause of a computer operating system failure. A robotic operating system would manage an even larger workforce of hardware components. If simple peripherals such as mice, keyboards, and headphones can cause a computer operating system to crash, imagine the unreliability introduced by a car's "hardware": its tires, brakes, and a steering wheel, not to mention all the sensors needed to drive the car.

Each attached bit of hardware has a special software program called a *driver* that enables that bit of hardware to speak with the rest of the operating system it is installed onto. Driver problems are another major cause of system failure. They can wreak havoc. Driver-induced crashes cause an estimated 70 percent of operating system failures, an error rate that's three to seven times higher than the problems introduced by bugs lurking in software code.[4]

The more complex the operating system, the harder it is to predict how it's going to fail. The number of lines of code is in the tens of millions, and even well-written code can crash. There is also the threat of data security, resulting from malevolent hackers installing rogue hardware onto a driverless car or tinkering with the operating system.

The stakes are higher, too. When a personal computer suffers a catastrophic system failure, the result is frustration. No user ever died from the dreaded Microsoft Windows "blue screen of death." In a driverless car, however, the equivalent of the blue screen of death could be, literally, death. Other less disastrous but still dangerous failure scenarios would be if a specific piece of hardware stopped responding, or if the entire operating system got bogged down in some sort of systemic problem and began to run very, very slowly.

The reality is that driverless cars will certainly suffer from software failure. The open question, however, is how much failure is acceptable. In the established world of server operating systems, system administrators have made a science of counting and documenting their system's *downtime*, the number of hours each year that a server is taken offline because of system failure. Downtime can be planned, as in when an upgrade is required, or unplanned, when there's catastrophic system failure. Downtime, planned or otherwise, costs businesses money.

Mature computer operating systems benefit from the fact that system administrators have figured out several techniques to improve reliability. As a result, the number of hours of server downtime per year has dropped dramatically in the past few years. The typical well-configured Windows or Linux server now suffers just a few minutes of downtime a year, if that. One question that will need to be addressed is: if a few minutes a year of downtime is acceptable for a server farm that supports several businesses, should that level of downtime also be okay for a driverless car?

Some people, tired of the carnage caused by distracted, drunk, or emotional human drivers might be comfortable accepting less than perfect reliability for a driverless car. This pragmatic group of people might agree that driverless cars should become legal once the operating system can drive better than a human driver. Rationally, such a reliability benchmark makes a lot of sense. The challenge, however, would be one of convincing naysayers to give robots a chance. We're used to tragedies caused by human drivers. However, the first tragedy caused by a robotic driver will be cause for outrage, perhaps turning the public against driverless cars for a long time.

Let's propose a bolder baseline: in order to be considered legal, driverless cars must be twice as safe as the average human driver. Let's assign some numbers to this baseline. According to car insurance industry data, on average, a human driver in the United States has an accident every seventeen years. Another way to look at this is that the average human driver will file an insurance claim once every 190,000 miles.

While car accidents are common, very few of these collisions involve fatalities—only 0.3 percent.[5] In other words, a human driver is likely to have some sort of accident, ranging from a minor fender-bender to full-on fatality, once every 190,000 miles driven. Let's take this metric and round it up a bit—one accident per 200,000 miles.

One widely used metric to quantify a robot's reliability is how long it can operate alone, without human intervention. This metric is known as *mean time between failures*, or MTBF. Like humans, all robots sometimes need help. For example, at home, our Roomba needs to be rescued, on average, once every ten hours when it snarls itself in a jungle of chair legs or gets its wheels stuck in a nasty tangle of electric cords. High-end industrial robots have a much longer MTBF, especially if they're operating in remote conditions where their human overseer stops by only once a month or so.

If the average driverless car must be twice as safe as the average human driver, that means an acceptable failure metric for the car would be to average one accident every 400,000 miles driven. That's approximately more than twice the number of miles that an average person will drive accident-free. Let's call this metric *mean distance between failures*, or MDBF. Ideally, a car's MDBF should be measured across a typical suite of road conditions, traffic conditions, and weather conditions.

Let's calculate how long it would take for a driverless car to rack up an MDBF of 400,000 miles. If an autonomous car can drive 1,000 miles per day, then its MDBF could be verified in 400 days, or just over one year. Alternatively, a fleet of 1,000 cars could verify an MDBF of 400,000 miles in twenty-four hours. To add statistical significance, the people testing the cars would probably need to repeat this test a few times.

One of the great advantages of teaching robots how to think is that they have a hive mind. If one robot learns something, that software can be copied to dozens of other robots, who will use that knowledge to continue to learn. As many different robotic systems learn in parallel, their individual learnings can be pooled into a central knowledge base and then poured back into the individual robotic minds, which in turn continue to learn at an even faster rate.

Some call this sort of collective learning *fleet learning*. One of the great advantages of driverless-car technology is that fleets of cars can learn at an exponential rate. Fleets of cars absorb one another's combined digital streams of driving data from past miles driven, an approach used by Google, Volvo, and Tesla to hone their driverless-car technology.

Fleet learning involves repetition, lots and lots of repetition. This was demonstrated in a video posted in April 2014, when a test driver for Google Self Driving Car Project explained that "A big part of our job is to go out into the world and uncover all the potential scenarios that a car might encounter. Then we help the engineers teach the car how to best navigate each one."[6] The blog article posted to accompany the video added, "As we've encountered thousands of different situations, we've built software models of what to expect from the likely (a car stopping at a red light) to the unlikely (blowing through it). We still have lots of problems to solve, including teaching the car to drive more streets in Mountain View before we tackle another town."

TWICE AS SAFE AS A HUMAN

As the stored knowledge base of driving situations continues to grow exponentially, driverless cars will become more and more capable. Yet, in order to gain full social and legal acceptance, driverless cars will need a transparent set of reliability standards, a clearly defined and public standard for what constitutes safe and acceptable mean distance between failures. Ideally, the companies that manufacture driverless cars would work with the federal government to publicly define acceptable MDBF standards for driverless cars.

In the new driverless era, MDBF levels will become as essential a piece of consumer-facing information about a new set of wheels as its horsepower. When consumers decide what car to buy, the driverless car's MDBF level will be one of the car's defining characteristics reported. An MDBF, however, is a bit of a clumsy term. We propose a term that's easier to say.

The MDBF of driverless cars should be measured as a driverless car's *humansafe* level. After all, 100 years ago early carmakers quantified the power of their engines in a metric that people of the time understood, the strength of a horse, or horsepower. Driverless cars should similarly showcase their ability to drive safely in terms of a safety level we're already familiar with, that of a human.

Here's how it would work. A car that can drive twice as many accident-free miles as the average human could be advertised as having a humansafe rating of 2.0. A car that's three and a half times as safe as an average human driver would have a humansafe rating of 3.5, and so on. The humansafe level would depend on the software and computing power, as well as the number and types of hardware sensors.

A federally regulated system of humansafe levels would be a boon for nearly everyone involved in the driverless-car industry. A driverless car's humansafe rating would be a core part of its market appeal. Car companies could build special "super safe" cars with high humansafe ratings and charge a premium for the extra safety. Perhaps a driverless car that ferries unaccompanied children would be required, by laws, to have a safety level of 10.0, but cargo-only vehicles could be permitted to travel with lower rating. Consumers would speak knowledgeably about the trade-off in humansafes vs. horsepower in various models of sleekly designed sports cars.

Some of this work has already been done. A good example of a successful robotic system that has successfully tackled many of these issues are the operating systems that fly commercial aircraft. Commercial airplanes have one of the highest MTBF ratings of all transportation systems. On average, an airplane has one fatal system failure once every two million flights[7] (not counting pilot error, sabotage, terrorism, and other external factors that are responsible for over 80 percent of the fatalities).

One failure every two million flights is a vastly improved level of reliability than what airplanes had in the past, roughly 100 times better than the accident rate in the 1950s. Such an impeccable safety record is even more impressive, considering that modern airplanes fly for longer durations and greater distances than did planes in the 1950s. Modern airplanes also fly faster. Yet, despite these demands, in the past 50 years, the number of avionic system failures has dropped by two orders of magnitude.

What can driverless cars learn from commercial airplanes? One is that federal oversight is key. Modern airplanes are subject to more scrutiny, with tighter federal oversight of maintenance and pilot training. Driverless cars need federal oversight that's robot-savvy and guided by safety data. It's crucial that safety regulations for driverless cars are defined using a rational and transparent process for weighing and quantifying the merits of robotic drivers.

Federal oversight of standards is just one piece of the puzzle, however. Better operating-system design is also essential. You will recall that one of the fatal weaknesses of computer operating systems is that their software architecture was designed so that all of the system processes ran inside one, monolithic workspace. Dumping everything into one software bucket results in computer operating systems being unreliable and insecure, or *leaky*. As one paper on operating system security explained it, "Current operating systems are like ships before compartmentalization was invented: every leak can sink the ship."[8]

Driverless cars need an operating system that's highly modular and redundant, similar to those that guide airplanes. Airplanes are famous for their redundant architectural design, much of it strictly regulated by the Federal Aviation Administration. All critical physical subsystems have double or triple redundancy. For example, fuel lines of commercial aircraft are required to be double-sheathed so that a leak in the inner tubing will be captured and detected in the outer tubing.

A plane's critical software subsystems are also highly modular and redundant. The avionic operating system is composed of several linked but independent electronic subsystems. Separation is key. For example, the software that runs the engines is separated from the software that runs the landing gears, and both are separated from the infotainment system software with which passengers interact.

Redundancy and fault-proofing are also important. Each avionic subsystem is designed so that it can test faults in other systems and if such a fault occurs, it can tolerate it. If several subsystems "disagree," the gridlock is resolved by a digital majority vote.

Driverless cars will need a redundant real-time operating system that contains built-in independent, self-testing systems that are required by law. Perhaps a driverless car could be required to have three separate visual perception subsystems, each using its own visual sensors and its own unique technique for analyzing the data gathered by those sensors. To ensure its safety, a car's operating system would need periodic tune-ups to ensure that it is running the latest software trained by the latest datasets, and that the mechanical systems are speaking flawlessly to the software systems.

Similar to those on airplanes, the car's wiring and on-board computers should be physically walled off, safe from the tinkering hands of innocent passengers or malevolent hijackers. The car's self-driving software should be modular and should be subject to periodic mandatory inspections from an independent third party that's not the manufacturer of the software. If one subsystem disagrees with the conclusion drawn by another, the oversight software should either "tune" the system's performance or drive the car immediately to seek maintenance.

The operating system of a modern driverless car is the fruit of decades of artificial intelligence and controls engineering research. The operating system of a driverless car must not only be reliable and smart, but it must "handle the world" in real time, and never crash. Given these challenges, some people ponder whether driverless cars are possible. They ask, "Will there ever be an operating system that can handle a car as well as a person can?" A more interesting question is to ask is, "Why weren't driverless cars invented years ago?"

6

FIRST THERE WERE ELECTRONIC HIGHWAYS

In 1939, General Motors Corporation, then a young company with an appetite for bold innovation and creative marketing, introduced the world's first driverless concept car at the World's Fair in Queens, New York. The general public was thrilled. Yet, it would take more than sixty years for GM's vision to become Google's highly functional driverless prototype.

Driverless-car development languished for decades because of a phenomenon we call the *Da Vinci problem*, which haunts inventors to this day. The Da Vinci problem arises when an inventor dreams up a technology that doesn't work, not because of a problem with its concept, but because the other technologies that support the invention have not yet come into existence. While an inventor's vision may be right on track, the invention will fail until the eventual maturation of key supporting technologies.

Here's a classic example. In 1493, Leonardo Da Vinci invented the helicopter but alas, Leonardo's vertical flying machine (which he called an *airscrew*) could not fly. Its shortcoming wasn't its fundamental concept. Nor did the problem lie in Leonardo's designs.

The fatal flaw was that in order to fly, Leonardo's airscrew needed a lightweight but strong aluminum body and a powerful power source, neither of which were yet available. The modern helicopter would not lift off the ground until the twentieth century. Several hundred years after it was initially conceived,

Leonardo's design for a vertical flying machine finally took flight when it could be constructed out of lightweight aluminum and powered by a modern internal combustion engine.

The development of driverless cars has followed a similar trajectory. The first driverless cars were a fantasy created by GM's marketing department for the 1939 World's Fair. The fair was a thrilling, massive 1,200-acre tribute to cutting-edge technologies such as television, electric street lamps, fluorescent lighting, and a new must-have device for emerging middle-class families, the automatic washing machine. GM's bold exhibit, the "Futurama," showcased an Automated Highway that by the year 1960 would make "hands-free, feet-free" driving the norm.

GM's Futurama exhibit consisted of a small-scale model of a typical American landscape of the near future. Fairgoers absorbed the scene from the vantage point of moving chairs that carried them through this mesmerizing miniature world.[1] Fairgoers sat and glided past tiny cities, farms, stretches of countryside, even an airport in miniature, all seamlessly connected by ribbons of smooth, high-speed automated highways. Over the course of the eighteen-minute ride, visitors were treated to a recorded narrative that described the delights of this Lilliputian landscape.

During the ride, the Futurama's narrator explained that by the year 1960, regular people would enjoy trouble-free personal mobility on automated highways in cars guided by a system of radio controls (the exact technological details of how, exactly, these radio-controlled cars would work were left purposefully vague). According to the narrative, just twenty-one short years into the future, human drivers would become relaxed passengers, thanks to GM's marvelously engineered automobiles. Radio-controlled cars would steer themselves on and off automated highways, comfortably, safely, and economically, ferrying people from their home to their office to the airport, or wherever else their heart desired.

Today, it's difficult to imagine that a model landscape whose chief selling point was high-speed roads and tiny cities would fascinate millions of people. In 1939, however, the American public

Figure 6.1
As fairgoers listened, the Futurama's narrative read, "The world we are now seeing is a vision, an artistic conception, which may undergo many changes as it develops into the great realities of tomorrow." New York World's Fair, "Futurama: Highways & Horizons," 1939
Source: General Motors

was fascinated by GM's utopian depiction of automated highways. GM's Futurama, one of the most successful exhibits of the fair, attracted an estimated total of ten million riders. On some days, 28,000 people waited for hours in lines that sometimes stretched two miles long.[2]

GM's artificial miniature world was great theater, as seductive and magical as the Technicolor Land of Oz in the film *The Wizard of Oz* (which was released earlier the same year). Unlike the other emerging technological marvels showcased at the World's Fair that eventually became commercial products, however, the Futurama's automated highway—while brilliant showmanship—proved to be as authentic as the flying monkeys in the *The Wizard of Oz*. GM glossed over the technical details of how, exactly, these "hands-free" cars would work, attributing their ability to guide themselves to some clever blend of radio and electronics.

Perhaps it's not surprising that GM's Futurama was conceived not by engineers, but by legendary industrial designer Norman Bel Geddes. Bel Geddes was famous for creating fantastic movie sets and futuristic reinterpretations of everyday household objects such as cocktail shakers, desk lamps, and radios. After the fair, Bel Geddes wrote a book, *Magic Motorways*, about the liberating possibilities of well-designed high-speed motorways.[3] He attributed the popularity of the 1939 Futurama to the fact that people craved the privacy and personal mobility offered by the automobile, yet abhorred its high cost:

> All of these thousands of people who stood in line ride in motor cars and therefore are harassed by the daily task of getting from one place to another, by the nuisances of intersectional jams, narrow, congested bottlenecks, dangerous night driving, annoying policemen's whistles, honking horns, blinking traffic lights, confusing highway signs and irritating traffic regulations they are appalled by the daily toll of highway accidents and deaths; and they are eager to find a sensible way out of this planless, suicidal mess.[4]

Many modern observers might find this negative description of early roadways surprising, given that, at the time, cars were still costly luxury items owned by a relatively small number of well-to-do people. Yet, it seems that even in 1939, trouble loomed in paradise. Years before the interstate highway system was built and before the green-yellow clouds of smog descended into cities like Los Angeles and Beijing, cars were already proving to be an unsafe and costly mode of personal transportation, a "planless, suicidal mess."

Bel Geddes viewed well-designed highways as the foundation for economic prosperity, a better military, and improved public health. Aside from the practical benefits, Bel Geddes believed that an efficient highway system played a vital role in shaping a nation's political climate. As World War II loomed and fascist dictators rose to power in several European nations, for Bel Geddes, convenient personal mobility was the very foundation of democracy.

Bel Geddes concluded *Magic Motorways* with a passionate call to action about the importance of well-designed highways, saying that good roads were the foundation of a free, yet unified, society:

> An America in which people are free ... to move out on good roads to decent abodes of life—free to travel over routes whose very sight and feel give a lift to the heart—that is an America whose inner changes may far transcend the alterations on the surface. If city dweller can know the land, Easterner know Westerner, the man who has lived among mountain know harbors and the sea, then horizons will be broadened, individual lives will grow ... out of that very interchange of diversity will come another thing ... we call it unity. It is not a unity imposed from above, such as exists under a dictatorship, but a unity based on freedom and understanding.[5]

Just a year after Bel Geddes wrote these stirring words, the United States officially entered World War II. GM shifted its attention away from building automated highways and toward manufacturing tanks, aircraft, and armaments for the Allied war effort. The development of automated highways ceased for most of the 1940s, yet World War II would prove to be a technological goldmine in the decades to come.

The war was a battle of technology. As it waged on, massive government investment in research accelerated the development of several important military technologies that today guide the modern driverless car, including computers, lasers, and radar. After World War II ended, these wartime technologies would play a key role in the development of electronic highways in the 1950s and 1960s, and eventually help steer the first fully autonomous robotic vehicles in the 1980s.

THE GOLDEN AGE

The 1950s and 1960s were a Golden Age, both for the automobile and for the development of the automated highway. In the boom of economic prosperity that followed World War II, thousands of people bought their first car. According to U.S. census data, by the end of the 1950s, most U.S. households owned at least one automobile.

To encourage the development of automotive transportation, in 1956 the federal government passed the Federal Highway Act, kicking off several decades of frenzied highway building that would ultimately rearrange the face of American cities, suburbs, and countryside. As the number of new car owners skyrocketed, millions of drivers eagerly put the nation's sprouting network of new roads and highways to use. With tens of thousands of miles of paved roads and a national interstate highway system that sprawled from coast to coast, a U.S. "car culture" was born.

People embraced the low-cost and convenient personal mobility their cars provided them, bringing Bel Geddes's poetic (and prophetic) description of the unifying power of well-designed highways to life. Efficient motorways and cars indeed enabled city dwellers to explore the countryside, and allowed people who lived

ELECTRICITY MAY BE THE DRIVER. One day your car may speed along an electric super-highway, its speed and steering automatically controlled by electronic devices embedded in the road. Travel will be more enjoyable. Highways will be made safe—by electricity. No traffic jams...and collisions...no driver fatigue.

Figure 6.2

"Electricity may be the driver." Driverless Car of the Future, advertisement for "America's Electric Light and Power Companies," *Saturday Evening Post*, 1950s. Source: The Everett Collection

in the mountains to experience the wonders of harbors and the sea, first-hand. Less poetically, a nation on wheels bought meals at new fast-food restaurants like the In-N-Out drive-through burger stand, where customers enjoyed the convenience of eating hamburgers inside their cars. Cars became a new sort of living room. By the end of the 1950s, 4,000 drive-in movie theaters represented a whopping 25 percent of the nation's movie screens.[6]

As people learned the pleasures of eating and relaxing inside their vehicles, the automobile industry created big, powerful, cars whose bodies were beautifully shaped and curved, and whose interiors offered the spaciousness of a living room sofa. Today's cars might be technologically superior, but for many people, they lack the soul of automobiles designed in mid-century. Cars of the 1950s and 1960s embody an optimism, their lush, curvy, aerodynamic bodies inspired by the shape of jet planes and cartoon drawings of rocket ships.

We recently accidentally stumbled upon a collection of old cars during a routine journey to visit relatives. Lured by signs announcing a vintage car show, we parked our modest little black leased Honda—a practical, fuel-efficient but generic little car—and walked over to a parking lot to ogle rows of automobiles from the 1950s and 1960s, all lovingly restored to their former glory. Antique Buicks, Chevrolets, and Cadillacs sat majestically in rows, chrome-laden relics from an era before oil embargos, massive product safety recalls, and competition from overseas automakers. Clusters of mostly older men peered underneath open hoods at gigantic old-fashioned metal carburetors and shiny coils of steel pipe. Like the plumage of exotic birds, the gleaming bodies of these proud painted ladies glowed bright red, tangerine, and aqua blue against the drab gray of the parking lot.

While many Americans during the 1950s embraced the newfound convenience and privacy of traveling around by automobile, they did not necessarily embrace the task of driving. The notion of an automated highway remained popular in the public imagination. In 1957, a coalition of power companies featured a driverless car in an advertising campaign celebrating the nation's rapidly rising rates of electricity consumption, something that in those days was considered a robust sign of economic and social progress. The advertisement depicted an electric car in which members of a family were seated in the back, facing each other around a table playing dominos. The caption under the picture reads:

> One day your car may speed along an electric super-highway, its speed and steering automatically controlled by electronic devices embedded in the road. Highways will be

made safe—by electricity! No traffic jams ... no collisions ... no driver fatigue.[7]

In 1958, Disney ran an episode on its popular television show *Disneyland* entitled "Magic Highway, U.S.A." In the episode's final few minutes, an animated clip shows the family car being automatically washed and electrically charged up in the garage. The family climbs in, dad pulls a few sliding levers to program the car's destination, and the car takes the wheel and drives itself. Dad conducts a business meeting during the drive while his wife and child relax in the back.

Not to be outdone, nearly two decades after its hugely successful Futurama exhibit mesmerized people at the World's Fair, GM continued its efforts to create an automated highway. The notion that the highway, not the car, would guide the vehicle makes sense when you consider the state of information technologies in those early years. A computer was the size of a small room, much too large and heavy to fit inside any car. Vacuum tubes (the precursor to silicon transistors) were too fragile to endure the bumps and sudden turns of the road. Artificial-intelligence software was in its infancy. Cutting-edge research of the day consisted of teaching an IBM 701 mainframe to play games of checkers or blackjack.[8]

The hardware devices of the day were also primitive or nonexistent. Cameras were large, analog, and fragile. Lasers and radar were bulky machines, still confined to military application. GPS had yet to be invented.

To make things even more challenging, most of the world's information and data were still in analog form. At that time, text and numerical data was created manually or laboriously captured via measurement or observation. The data was recorded in tables on paper or, in a few advanced cases, kept in crude database tables stored inside a mainframe computer. In an era that lacked abundant data, detailed digital maps, fast computers, and accurate, mobile sensors, inserting even primitive "intelligence" into a two-ton steel machine was a formidable challenge. Since computing technology was too immature to oversee the task of driving,

GM engineers came up with another solution: color television technology.

GM'S ELECTRONIC HIGHWAY

GM teamed up with the Radio Corporation of America (RCA), at that time a hotbed of electronics innovation. RCA employed the famous inventor Vladimir Zworykin, a pioneer of cathode-ray tubes and automated solutions, to head up the company's research into automated traffic lights and other intelligent highway technologies. Zworykin, already concerned about the negative effects of rapidly increasing traffic density and higher-speed automobiles on the safety of the nation's highways, was convinced that new methods were needed to relieve the driver of some of the mechanical tasks of driving.[9]

Working with GM's automotive engineers, Zworykin's team of electronics experts broke the challenge of designing an automated highway into three problem areas. As he described it, "Any vehicle control system [must] know the position of every car on the highway. This implies some means of vehicle detection. The second requirement is to make known the presence of every vehicle to the other vehicles most immediately concerned. Usually the vehicle following behind. This implies a means of communication between vehicles or between highway and vehicle. The third step is the application of automated controls to a vehicle in response to the information received."[10]

After several years of research, RCA and GM engineers kludged together an ingenious—although by today's standards, crude—solution they named the *electronic highway*. They used a combination of radio technologies, electronic circuits, and logic gates combined with ages-old theories of electromagnetism. A high-profile demonstration of the electronic highway took place in 1958 on a specially equipped 400-foot-long section of highway outside Lincoln, Nebraska. GM and RCA enlisted the enthusiastic support of the state of Nebraska's Department of Roads to weave together a primitive detection and guidance system that remotely controlled the cars' movements along two critical axes: laterally, to steer correctly within the confines of its lane, and longitudinally, to keep the cars' bumpers a safe distance apart. The test vehicles were two majestic 1958 Chevrolets with splendid tail fins and double front headlamps.[11]

Two years later, using a similar approach, GM and RCA created yet another electronic highway test track in New Jersey upon which specially outfitted GM cars were successfully started, accelerated, steered, and stopped, all without direct human oversight.[12] A press release, written by the city of Princeton, New Jersey, in 1960, described the technologies that enabled this electronic highway masterpiece.

> [The] detection system thus keeps cars automatically at a safe
> distance behind those ahead, and causes cars to stop when

Figure 6.3
The electronic highway in action.
Source: Radio Corporation of America (RCA), courtesy the David Sarnoff Library

there is an obstruction or a parked vehicle in the lane ahead. The guidance system consists of a single, continuous cable buried in the pavement in the center of the traffic lane. A signal current in this cable is picked up by two coils mounted at the front end of the car and equi-distant from the guidance cable. If the car moves in either direction away from the center of the lane, the signal becomes stronger in one coil than in the other, generating a "difference signal" that can be used either to warn the driver by lights or by an audible signal, or to operate the steering gear automatically.[13]

The detection system that prevented the cars from rear-ending one another was essentially a communications infrastructure made up of wired-together transistors, radio transmitters, and lights. To create the detection system, RCA engineers first placed a series of rectangular loops of wire, each slightly less than the length of the car, one after the other along the length of the special test roadway. Each time a car drove over a loop of wire, it set off a signal in a special transistorized detection device buried under the roadway.

As the car passed quickly over this series of rectangular loops, the resulting signals were fed into a network connecting all of the detector units. This moving succession of signals lit up a chain of lamps placed along the edge of the road to form an electronic "flying tail" that served as a warning system to other nearby automobiles. Human drivers, at least in theory, could see a driverless car's position thanks to the illumination of the roadside lamps. Or, if no humans were present, the signals could be sensed by a following car so it could automatically correct its position by either hitting its brakes or pressing the gas pedal.

The lateral guidance system that steered the car inside its lane involved slightly more convoluted and imaginative engineering. To mimic the eyes and reflexes of an attentive human behind the steering wheel, GM and RCA engineers harnessed the power of a combination of electronic gadgets and electromagnetic forces. To feed critical information about the car's lateral position inside its lane, GM and RCA engineers used modern electronics technologies and an ancient relationship that exists between electrical current and magnetic force fields.

For more than a century, scientists have known that an electrical current has the ability to generate a magnetic field. A changing magnetic field, in turn, can induce current in any conductive material that's standing or moving nearby. The closer that conductive material is to the source of the magnetic field, the greater the current induced.

Scientists and engineers have become quite adept at measuring and using the relationship between the two primal forces of magnetism and electricity. To quantify the shape and magnitude of a magnetic field generated by flowing electrical current through a wire, scientists and engineers use what's known as *Ampere's Law*. In turn, to quantify how much electrical current will be induced by a magnetic field generated by that conductive wire, experts apply *Faraday's Law*—named after eighteenth-century British physicist Michael Faraday.

Not surprisingly, both Ampere's Law and Faraday's Law prove what most people could already intuitively predict. The greater the amount of electrical current running through a conductive wire or cable, the more powerful the magnetic field that will result. Similarly, the stronger the magnetic field that moves around a conductive wire, the stronger the electrical current that will be induced in nearby conductive materials.

One of the better-known modern practical applications that makes use of the marriage between electrical current and magnetic force fields is the invisible dog fence. Like the beloved but peripatetic family dog, a driverless car is happiest when untethered, yet still safely confined inside a specific geographic area. Similarly, a driverless car on GMs and RCA's electronic highway reached optimal performance when driving freely while still safely confined to its lane.

To contain their dog, suburban homeowners pay to have a live electric cable buried along the perimeter of their property line. The buried cable carries an oscillating electrical current that radiates a magnetic force field. This oscillating magnetic force field is picked up by a special dog collar into which is embedded a conductive metal sensor. When this special collar is affixed to the neck of the family dog, the next time the dog roams too close to the property line (and buried cable), the sensor in the dog's collar will be activated and administer an electric shock, which eventually teaches the dog to stay within the confines of its own property.

The steering system for early self-guided cars used similar principles. Instead of a live electrical cable buried along a homeowner's property line, RCA and GM buried a live cable underneath the center of each lane of roadway of their electronic highway test facilities. Next, similar to the sensor in the dog collar, engineers equipped each car with two metal "pick-up coils," one on each side of the car an equal distance apart. Attached to each pick-up coil was a measurement device that could quantify the strength of any electrical current that passed through it.

Imagine the scenario. A car equipped with two pick-up coils and measurement devices slowly rolled down a road. As the moving car passed overhead, its on-board pick up coils received the electrical current induced by the magnetic field enveloping the buried cable. If the car was correctly driving down the middle of the lane, the amount of induced current in each of the two coils would be roughly equal. However, if the car veered off to the side of its lane, one coil would become much more strongly charged and its sensor would record a much higher measurement than the other. The sensor with the stronger signal would send instructions to the car's specially rigged steering wheel to turn the car slightly until the sensor measurements were once again equal.

This process was known as "feedback control," and at the time, was considered advanced technology. Using a steady stream of measurement data from both sensors attached to the car's pick-up coils, this combination of technologies provided a crude but effective automated steering system. Long before the invention of computer vision, GM's and RCA's rigged steering wheel could adjust its lateral position inside a lane of roadway with the accuracy and responsiveness of an alert human driver.

At the time, optimism for GM's and RCA's crude prototype ran high; the Princeton press release enthused that someday, this electronic highway invention would enable "motorists of the future [to] be able to get in a hand of bridge or take a nap on that weekend drive to the cabin."[14] Despite positive public response, GM's electronic highway never went anywhere commercially. The long research partnership between GM and RCA, however, would prove productive in the decades to come.

The core idea of the detection system used in the electronic highway is still widely used today by modern responsive traffic lights. Automated traffic lights manage traffic flow by changing to green when they detect the presence of cars in the intersection or awaiting their chance to turn left. To detect nearby cars, automated traffic lights use a system of buried-wire inductive loops and sensors that, when triggered, send electronic signals that cause the stoplight to change color.

Perhaps encouraged by its earlier successes, GM took one more shot at a driverless car at the 1964 New York World's Fair in Queens, New York, the very same site where the glamorous 1939 Futurama took place a quarter century earlier. As described by its advertising, GM's concept car, the Firebird, "anticipates the day when the family will drive to the super-highway, turn over the car's controls to an automatic, programmed guidance system and travel in comfort and absolute safety at more than twice the speed possible on today's expressways."[15] The Firebird, despite the appeal of its sleek lines and single, vertical rear fin, would be GM's final high-profile foray into driverless cars for decades.

Throughout the 1960s and 1970s, other researchers continued to refine variants of automated highways using GM's and RCA's basic system of electrical cables, metal coils, and magnetic

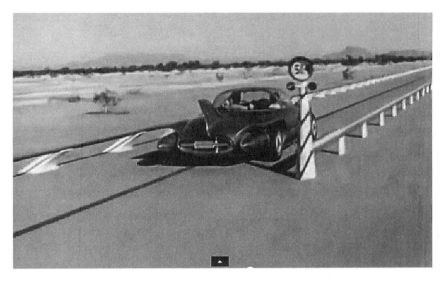

Figure 6.4
The "Turbine-Powered" GM Firebird concept car entering an autopilot lane. This techno-utopian fantasy was set in 1976 but created in 1956 for GM's Motorama Exhibit.
Source: General Motors

sensors. In the United Kingdom, the Transport and Road Research Laboratory tested a driverless Citroen DS that was guided by cables embedded in the surface of a test track.[16] In the United States during the 1960s, Ohio State emerged as a leading research hub for a field of automotive engineering that, by then, was known as automated vehicle guidance and control.

By the dawn of the 1970s, the focus of most academic autonomous vehicle research shifted away from cars. Researchers turned their attention toward another sort of autonomous vehicle, mass transit automated people movers (APMs), that are used today to shuttle passengers at major airports like Heathrow and JFK.[17] The era of the electronic highway was over.

THE SLOW DEATH OF THE AUTOMATED HIGHWAY

One of the primary reasons the dream of the automated highway eventually lost its allure was simple: cost. Rigging up the requisite electronic cables and roadside controls was an expensive and slow process, one that might have been a reasonable expense in a short stretch of test roadway, but was not workable on the massive highway systems that crisscrossed the United States and Europe. Even with the more generous highway construction budgets of the 1960s, equipping and maintaining the tens of thousands of miles of interstate highways with a fragile infrastructure of buried live electronic cables, transistors, and other devices was simply too cost-prohibitive.

In a 1969 paper, Ohio State researchers Robert Fenton and Carl Olson wrote that "the total investment in computers and highway-based sensors would probably average anywhere from $20,000 to $200,000 per lane mile."[18] Not only were automated highways too expensive, the available electronic and computing technologies of the day were too primitive. In the same research paper, Fenton and Olson, both tenacious and well-respected automated highway visionaries, glumly concluded that despite years of intensive research and development, "it is not possible at present to specify completely all of the required system components, because the necessary knowledge is not available."[19]

Cost and technological readiness aside, another reason the Golden Age of automated highway research slowed to a near-halt was that the larger world of automobile manufacturing lost its youthful innocence. The auto industry, once a magnet for the boldest designers and most expert technologists, was forced to grow up and face the consequences of a world where cars were no longer a novelty. Cars and highways had become a practical tool of everyday life.

Consumer advocate Ralph Nadar's instant 1965 classic book *Unsafe at Any Speed* exposed the shoddy engineering practices at the big auto companies, meticulously detailing the safety problems of the Chevy Corvair and the auto industry's overemphasis on styling and profit margins over driver safety. The book was a best seller, and it motivated the passage of the National Traffic and Motor Vehicle Safety Act of 1966 and the passage of seat-belt laws in 49 states (the sole holdout being New Hampshire). The book generated more controversy a few years later, when the U.S. Department of Transportation conducted a series of tests of comparable small cars and concluded that despite Nadar's claims, the safety of the 1960–63 Corvair compared favorably to "contemporary vehicles both foreign and domestic."[20]

Despite the exoneration of the Corvair, it was too late to ease public pressure on GM, Ford, and Chrysler. The consumer-safety movement gained steam as the number of cars on the highway continued to increase. Already both a treasure and a curse, the United States interstate highway system matured into a sprawling transportation infrastructure that faced a new challenge: heavy traffic. Rush-hour traffic jams became part of everyday life as the number of people commuting daily from suburb to city center (and back) more than doubled between 1950 and 1970.[21]

In 1973 the era of cheap gasoline came to a sudden end as several oil-producing nations protested U.S. aid to Israel by raising the posted price of a barrel of oil by 70 percent.[22] The United States auto industry would never be the same. Big car companies gave up their once-bold visions of hands-free, feet-free automated highways and instead focused on practical challenges such as defining safety standards for cars, improving fuel efficiency, and reducing exhaust emissions.

As the 1970s turned into the 1980s, driverless cars remained just a concept, not a reality. As the focus of the automotive industry changed, sleek designs took second place to fuel efficiency, and profit margins triumphed over aesthetics. Despite the efforts of many gifted engineers, for the remainder of the twentieth century, driverless cars continued to suffer from the Da Vinci problem, their development thwarted by the immaturity of the era's information and communication technologies.

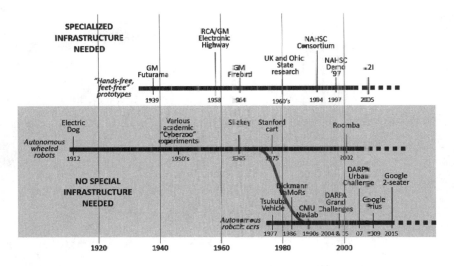

Figure 6.5

The History of Driverless Cars: Key milestones in the evolution of autonomous vehicles.

7

BUILD SMART CARS, NOT SMART HIGHWAYS

Nearly thirty years after the end of the golden age of electronic highways, a conference on intelligent vehicles is taking place in a large, windowless hotel meeting room near Washington, D.C. This gathering of experts was organized by the U.S. Department of Transportation, the federal agency that oversees policy for our nation's airports, trains, and, of course, highways and cars. I'm one of 250 attendees spending the day listening to a steady stream of presentations given by men dressed in conservative dark suits.

I came to this conference seeking insight into driverless cars. Instead, speaker after speaker shows cryptic slides littered with unexplained acronyms: RSU, FCC TMC, and V2I. The day drags on. Finally, in desperation, during a morning networking break, I sidle up to a cluster of people sitting at a table near the obligatory coffee and cookies. These people seem to know what they're doing.

I introduce myself and learn that one of them is a consultant on issues of automation to the automotive industry, the second a postdoc studying automotive engineering, and the third a professor of transportation technologies. I innocently ask them why in a conference about intelligent vehicles, none of the talks have mentioned computer vision or deep learning. In fact, Google's self-driving vehicle experiments have not yet been mentioned— not even once.

Under a glowing light fixture the size of a manhole cover, the small group of sages stares at me as if I had two heads. After a long silence, the automation consultant finally, condescendingly, explains the situation. "Oh, that driverless car stuff. I think there's a separate track for that tomorrow afternoon." My ignorance revealed, the group pointedly returns to its previous discussion and I scuttle away, chastened, exposed as an outsider, but with new clarity.

Thanks to my seat-of-the-pants education at the USDOT conference, I learned that the term *intelligent vehicle* means something different to a federal transportation agency insider than to a university roboticist. When federal policy makers think about intelligent transportation systems, their strategies do not necessarily involve robotics. Instead, for the past few decades, most of the research funded by federal transportation agencies has focused on the development of a *vehicle-to-vehicle* (V2V) and *vehicle-to-infrastructure* (V2I) communication infrastructure (the broader term *V2X* is increasingly used to refer to both V2V and V2I initiatives).

V2X

The goal of the federal V2X initiative is to create a wireless infrastructure to connect cars to one another and to installed roadside transmitters so they can exchange data, thereby saving lives. V2X research uses a set-aside portion of bandwidth on the federal dedicated short range radio (DSRC) network that's regulated by the Federal Communications Commission (FCC). The agency that administers the V2X initiative is a division of the U.S. Department of Transportation called the National Highway Transportation and Safety Administration (NHTSA).

Ordinarily, when I find myself accidentally stumbling into unproductive research conferences, I quickly cut my losses and see whether I can catch an earlier flight home. In this situation, however, I realized that too much was at stake. I had to stay and learn more.

After the lunch break, I marched back into the conference to absorb several more acronym-laden presentations. By day's end, I learned that millions of taxpayer dollars are spent each year on research to enable cars to exchange data with one another. Over the next five years, the USDOT plans to invest an additional $100 million to fund several pilot programs to explore the design and deployment of connected vehicle environments.[1] The problem with this plan is that it's the wrong kind of research.

The fate of driverless cars in the United States lies in the hands of the U.S. Department of Transportation and two key divisions within it: the Federal Highway Administration (FHA) and the NHTSA. As dictated by the legislation that formed the USDOT in 1966, its subagencies have the power to pass federal mandates with which all fifty state governments and automotive corporations have to comply. At least in theory, our friends in the USDOT could dream up mandates that would accelerate the development of driverless cars. After all, this agency had the tenacity to eventually make seat belts a mandatory safety feature in cars despite great public resistance at the time.

As the USDOT conference ended, I found myself asking, "Why not invest less in connectedness and more in robotic technology?" In the year 2014, the USDCT's budget was a mind-boggling $77 billion, of which $41 billion went to the FHA and $0.8 billion went to the NHTSA for projects related to the safety of the nation's cars, streets, bridges, tunnels, and highways. A lot of technological development on driverless cars could be accomplished with just a sliver of a these mammoth budgets

I returned from D.C. wiser and, when I dug into the technology behind V2X, sadder. The underlying goal of federal V2X initiatives is safety. According to the USDOT website, "By exchanging anonymous, vehicle-based data regarding position, speed, and location (at a minimum), vehicle-to-vehicle (V2V) communications enables a vehicle to: sense threats and hazards with a 360 degree awareness of the position of other vehicles and the threat or hazard they present; calculate risk; issue driver advisories or warnings; or take pre-emptive actions to avoid and mitigate crashes."[2]

Here's how the V2X program would work. V2X-enabled cars and infrastructure would be equipped with dedicated short-range communications (DSRC) transceivers to enable the transmission of data over a range of about 300 meters (nearly 1,000 feet). Connected cars and infrastructure would communicate on an allotted 75 megahertz of spectrum, from 5.850 to 5.925 gigahertz. Ten times per second, a V2X-equipped car would transmit data containing a basic safety message to other V2X-equipped cars about their speed, position, size, direction headed, brake status, and so on.

Typical alerts exchanged between cars could include warnings about unsafe weather conditions or the presence of roadside construction up ahead. The road infrastructure (or V2I) would also be specially equipped. Its role would be to capture data from vehicles on traffic volumes, to adjust nearby traffic lights in response, and to alert other drivers so they could take an alternative route. To make this all this communication possible, special traffic lights would have to be installed, short-range radio transmitters built into the roadside, and miles of fiber-optic cables laid in place to connect these roadside devices together.

To be fair, the development of V2X technologies isn't a terrible idea. In fact, the theory behind it is immensely appealing. By modeling a number of possible car-crash scenarios, a study conducted by the NHTSA estimated that if all cars were equipped with V2X capacity, the system could beep warnings to a human driver about blind spots and unseen obstacles, potentially preventing about 4 million (or 79 percent) vehicle crashes a year.[3] That's a lot of money, damage, and potentially human lives spared.

What was disappointing for me was learning that what passed for an "intelligent vehicle" in our nation's capital is so primitive. Why has exchanging data on road conditions via short-range wireless networks—a useful but relatively trivial technological application—become the focal point of the mighty USDOT's strategy to apply information technologies to improve the safety of driving? By focusing on V2X to the exclusion of other intelligent technologies, federal transportation officials remained enamored of a technological paradigm that's conceptually just a few leaps ahead of the primitive radio-controlled electronic highways of the 1950s.

In the past, the USDOT wasn't this conservative. In fact, just a few decades ago, the USDOT was a bold advocate of the development of intelligent vehicles. The problem was that forward-thinking USDOT personnel ran into the same problem as did visionary GM engineers a few decades earlier: their vision for driverless cars preceded the necessary technology to successfully drive them.

THE HISTORY OF INTELLIGENT TRANSPORTATION SYSTEMS

During the 1980s, information technology was reshaping industries. In 1986, to address the state's growing traffic and smog problem, the California Department of Transportation (Caltrans) teamed up with the University of California to explore ways information and communication technologies in vehicles and on highways could help humans drive more effectively. Eventually, this collaboration grew into a new statewide program called Program on Advanced Technology and Highways (PATH). Caltrans and PATH, however, quickly realized that without federal support or widespread buy-in from the big automakers, their efforts would bear little fruit.

Undeterred, PATH stakeholders hosted several more workshops and outreach efforts. Galvanized by the nation's ever-worsening traffic jams and urban air quality, in 1988, a critical mass of interested parties from various federal and state government agencies, industry, and universities formed a taskforce called Mobility 2000. Mobility 2000 lobbied the USDOT to create a formal federal program office whose charter would be to apply advanced technology to improve the safety and efficiency of the nation's highways and roadways. In the early 1990s, the USDOT established a formal program office whose charter was to promote the development of intelligent vehicle and highway systems, or IVHS.

As fitting for its new status as a federal program, the USDOT's IVHS program (now renamed intelligent transportation system, or ITS) had an ambitious mandate. As a full-fledged federal program, ITS was responsible for the research and development of all modes of automated surface transportation, including automated traffic-management systems, driver-information systems, commercial vehicles, and public transportation. That same year, to add fuel to the fire, Congress passed a major new transportation bill, the Intermodal Surface Transportation Efficiency Act (ISTEA).

The act decreed that the secretary of transportation "shall develop an automated highway and vehicle prototype from which future fully automated vehicle-highway systems can be developed. ... The goal of this program is to have the first fully automated roadway or an automated test track in operation by 1997."[4] The USDOT placed responsibility for executing this lofty goal inside the Federal Highway Administration. The FHA named the project the Automated Highway System Program, or AHS, and divided the effort into three phases: analysis, systems definition, and finally, operational evaluation.

Even better, to build this automated highway prototype, Congress authorized nearly $660 million of funding for research, development, and operational tests over the next six years.[5] Given the new wealth of resources and expertise now available to aid the development of an automated car and highway system, it seemed inevitable that the result would be a breathtakingly innovative blend of vehicle, road, and computer. Unfortunately, somehow the combination of money and mandate failed to further the development of autonomous vehicles.

The creation of a formal program inside the USDOT was both a blessing and a curse. On the one hand, an official home in the vast billion-dollar USDOT empire of 55,000 employees could, at least in theory, accelerate the development of driverless-car technology by providing access to policymakers and, of course, research dollars. On the other hand, placing a fast-moving technology-intensive initiative inside a gigantic federal agency responsible for every form of transportation, including airplanes, highways, public transit, and automobiles, introduced the risk that driverless-car technology would die a slow death at the hands of well-intended bureaucrats.

In the beginning of the Automated Highway System Program, optimism reigned. In a document from 1993 that in light of today's cautious federal V2X programs seems like a relic from a lost civilization, at least a few employees in the USDOT passionately believed in the benefits of automating driving. One wrote, "This high-performance highway system, seen as the next major evolutionary stage of surface transportation, is expected to be the focus of major U.S. implementation efforts early in the next century, much like the Interstate Highway System program was the focus of the last half of this century."[6]

In 1994, now that the funding had fallen into place, all the FHA needed was a team of expert stakeholders to actually design and build an operational prototype of an automated highway. By the end of the year, the USDOT created a 120-member consortium called the National Automated Highway System Consortium (NAHSC) whose charter was to come up with a workable prototype of an automated highway system.[7] At this point, the complex organizational tangle of federal initiatives and various agencies and working groups and acronyms began to resemble the complicated genealogical lineages of European royal families.

The NAHSC was made up of members that hailed from several leading organizations, including different federal agencies, big auto companies, electronic and trucking companies, universities, state and local governments, transportation agencies, and consulting firms. From 1994 to 1997, the consortium used a consensus process to try to reconcile its members' diverse views and unique organizational agendas into a single, unified strategy for the gradual deployment of an automated highway system.[8] Alas, rather than coalescing into a well-focused and effective team, the

NAHSC would eventually sink underneath the weight of a welter of agendas and interests.

Once the organizational pieces were in place, the consortium began to move laboriously forward. To fund work in each of the three project phases—analysis, systems definition, and operational evaluation—the USDOT issued federal contracts to various NAHSC members. A tantalizing stream of federal monies started to flow. The queue of well-heeled consortium members eager to scoop up yet another plump pouch of federal research dollars read like a Who's Who of automotive technology experts: Honeywell, General Motors, Ford Motor Company, PATH, Delco Electronics, Carnegie Mellon University, and more.

After three years of hard work and the best efforts of well-established automotive and transportation engineers, ultimately the ambitious federal project to define and create a working prototype of a "fully automated vehicle-highway system" managed to absorb tens of millions of dollars of research money. Yet, as would later be revealed, the consortium's efforts actually yielded very little in the way of usable insight or technologies.

To showcase its research of the past three years, the NAHSC created an event called Demo 97 that would take place just north of San Diego, California. The consortium invited members of Congress, local politicians, and corporate executives to ride in the demonstration vehicles. Despite its high profile attendees, the best efforts of brilliant automotive engineers, and an enthusiastic public reception, Demo 97 would inadvertently pound the final nail into the coffin of an automated highway system.

Before Demo 97, enthusiasm ran high. A promotional article gushed that "highways of the future may feature relaxed drivers talking on the phone, faxing documents, or reading a novel while an automated highway system controls the vehicle's steering, braking, and throttling and allows for 'hands-off, feet-off' driving. … The National Automated Highway System Consortium (NAHSC) will illustrate that the vision of an automated highway system (AHS) that improves traffic safety and highway efficiency can be made a reality."[9]

Demo 97 took place under a flawless blue San Diego sky on a stretch of Interstate 15. For seven days in a row, spectators watched a steady stream of demonstrations. Each demonstration depicted different ways in which an automated driving system could manage a car's lateral control (lane keeping) and longitudinal control (keeping the right distance from cars in front and behind). The goal was to show that despite the absence of a human hand on the steering wheel and stick shift and a foot on the brake and gas pedals, an automated vehicle could handle its own steering, accelerating, and braking.

Spectators were wowed. Using a system of in-road magnets reminiscent of GM's and RCA's experiments of previous decades, the University of California PATH program showed a specially equipped fleet of eight autonomous 1997 Buick LeSabres that saved fuel by driving in a tight, single-file formation known as *platooning*. Honda showed two prototypes called AHS Accords that transitioned control back and forth between the human driver and vehicle using sensors to automatically change lanes and respond to road obstacles. Toyota demonstrated how a laser vision system could warn a human driver of obstacles and blind spots and control lane changes.

Everything worked as planned. The cars performed flawlessly. Various dignitaries such as U.S. senators and corporate executives fearlessly took test drives inside the demonstration vehicles. The media coverage was broad and positive. Yet, Demo 97 was the U.S. Department of Transportation's final investment in research to develop aggressively revolutionary highway technology. The consortium's automated highway failed for the same reasons GM's did: the information technology of the day wasn't mature enough to safely pilot a car without a driver, and the demonstrated system still needed a costly custom infrastructure.

After Demo 97, the notion of automated driving was deemed impractical. The USDOT cut off funding for research on automated highways and, in a mindset that still prevails today, shifted its focus to funding incremental technological enhancements that assist, rather than replace, human drivers. The disappointing result is that today all that remains of the once-bold plans of federal transportation officials is ... V2X research.

RETHINKING CONNECTED CARS

Federal transportation officials have the resources and legislative muscle to throw their support behind driverless cars and save tens of thousands of lives each year. In 2013, the NHTSA took its first wobbly steps toward thinking about full autonomy, releasing a cautious memorandum that outlined several theoretical stages of automated driving. While a good start, more is needed.

The NHTSA continues to doggedly pursue the development of backward-looking V2X technologies despite the fact that in the past decade, rapid improvements in artificial-intelligence software and hardware sensors have made driverless cars an increasingly mature and viable solution. In fact, as recently as 2014, the NHTSA seriously considered using a precious political silver bullet on mandating that all new cars and trucks come equipped with V2X capability.[10] Such a mandate, while well intended, would do little to improve the safety of the roads.

Let us explain both the value and the shortcomings of V2X in the context of driverless cars. The benefit of a networked vehicle (at least in theory) is safety. Crash prevention is one goal; another is better traffic flow and, therefore, fewer polluting carbon dioxide emissions.

Here's how, ideally, V2X could work. A V2X-enabled vehicle would broadcast that it is about to enter an intersection on a specific lane at a specific time and speed. As the car beeps a warning, nearby human drivers in other vehicles could factor the knowledge of the approach of the other car into their driving and brake or slow down accordingly.

At least in theory, wireless communications between cars and infrastructure could be useful. If a traffic light were hooked up to a data network, it could broadcast to the human drivers in approaching vehicles which lanes have the right of way. Human drivers (if they opted to obey the warning) could plan their acceleration or lane-changing strategy accordingly. In bad weather a V2I roadside unit could broadcast information on surface conditions to warn human drivers of slippery spots. Bridges, fences, barriers, and curbs could be marked with data tags to warn human drivers of their presence should the car drift too close.

Those are the potential benefits. Now for the drawbacks. A roboticist would argue that the $100 million that has been earmarked for V2X pilots is money that should have been creatively and intelligently spent on addressing challenges in autonomous vehicle research. Not only is the notion of a "connected car" technologically inadequate and out of date, there are several significant practical barriers that ensure that V2X technologies will probably never gain real world traction.

The biggest flaw in the U.S. Department of Transportation's V2X strategy is that connected cars would improve safety and traffic flow only when two conditions are met: cars are fully autonomous (meaning no human is driving) and the majority of the vehicles on the road and all the roadsides are V2X equipped. Right now, we're not close to either of these conditions. In fact, by presenting V2X technology as a stepping-stone in a gradual progression toward increasing automation, the USDOT is not only wasting money, but may actually hinder the development of fully autonomous vehicles.

First let's talk about the money. A GAO report on V2X estimates that the cost of a single installation of a V2I site is a whopping $51,650, of which a significant portion is made up of the cost of installing new fiber-optic cables to connect roadside units to traffic management centers.[11] Given the sorry state of public roads, tunnels, and bridges in the United States, states are unlikely to be willing or able to make this sort of investment. Since state departments of transportation would have to bear the cost of a V2X system, another significant barrier is the fact that states lack the skilled personnel needed to install, maintain, and operate V2X technologies.

Then there's the conundrum of V2X penetration. Alain Kornhauser, a veteran of automated driving research and a robotics professor at Princeton University, is not a fan of the USDOT fixation on V2X. Kornhauser writes a regular email update on autonomous driving where he demonstrates his keen insights and occasionally biting wit, punctuating particularly foolish news stories with his trademark comments "C'mon man," or, "They didn't get the memo."

Kornhauser provides a devastating critique of the inefficiency of installing V2X only onto new vehicles while the rest of the cars on the road remain unconnected. He points out that if the USDOT were to go ahead and mandate that all new vehicles be installed with V2V technology, not much would improve. V2X relies on critical mass. In other words, a V2X sensor works only if it can speak to another car equipped with a compatible V2X transmitter. Until more than half of the cars on the road are equipped with the right software, mandating the installation of V2X technology onto new vehicles won't offer many benefits.

For any data transmission infrastructure to be effective, penetration is key. As Kornhauser points out, if, for example, only 10 percent of the cars on the road were equipped with V2V technology, then only 1 percent (=10 percent of 10 percent) of pairs of cars will be able to communicate with one another. This means that even if eventually 10 percent of the 250 million cars currently circulating on roads in the United States were to be V2V-equipped, then only 1 percent of the car accidents would take place between two connected cars. Assuming that the car's human drivers were paying attention and reacting appropriately to their beeping in-car warning system, a mere 1 percent reduction in traffic accidents would be an insignificant improvement.

The challenges continue. Right now there are no accepted federal standards for the data that would be transmitted via V2X technologies. Without a widely accepted national-level set of data standards, the risk would be that cities and states would create their own data standards and V2X-equipped cars could communicate only with the roadside transmitters in their city or state of origin. Given the fact that most driving involves going through towns and crossing state lines, tiny regional patchworks of different V2X data standards would render the national infrastructure nearly useless.

Then there are the pesky human-factor issues. Typical of the anachronistic character of V2X research efforts, the human driver continues to play a crucial role. Unlike a fully autonomous vehicle that will someday drive better than a human, a car with V2X technology merely beeps warnings. If the human doesn't react appropriately, the safety benefit is nil. Even worse, at some point, a beeping signal could become an irritant that human drivers tune out, fail to understand, or, worst of all, get so distracted by that they lose focus on the immediate task at hand: keeping the car safely on the road.

Finally, like all peer-to-peer wireless networks, V2X systems are vulnerable to hacks, attacks, intruders, and imposters. If there is any hard lesson that the software industry has learned time and time again, it's that any decentralized communication scheme is vulnerable to hacking and breaking, and that any manufacturing system has its leaks and compromises. No matter how many PhDs and teams of engineers work on designing a fool-proof communication system, invariably someone will break it.

A V2X infrastructure would need to reliably conduct thousands of transactions a day with millions of individual cars. In contrast, a hacker need break the system just once. A V2X signal could be easily jammed using any common communication jammer. A skilled hacker could emulate a trusted source and, from there, wreak havoc. If one car sent a false signal saying "I'm driving into the intersection at 100 MPH," other nearby V2X-equipped cars would respond with a cacophony of frantic warning beeps, throwing their human drivers into a confused panic.

Given all these shortcomings, why would intelligent people continue to promote the notion of V2X technologies? The answer is that V2X networks could offer tremendous value, but only in a world of fully autonomous vehicles, where connected cars could exchange data with the roadside infrastructure to optimize traffic flow in real-time, prioritize the passage of emergency vehicles, and warn other cars of hazardous road conditions. The great irony of federal plans to develop V2X networks is that the benefits of connected cars emerge only when *every single car on the road is fully autonomous.*

Perhaps in the future, a new generation of hardware devices could reduce the cost of creating intelligent highways. As the number of connected devices has exploded in the past few years, the Internet of Things has become a popular phrase in technology circles. A report by Gartner predicts that in 2016, smart cities will use 1.6 billion connected devices, a 39 percent increase from the year before. In 2018, Gartner predicts that the number of connected devices in smart cities will number 3.3 billion.[12] Most of these connected devices will be used for security (e.g., cameras) or to control the indoor climate in commercial buildings and public spaces such as shopping malls, offices parks, and airports. In homes, connected devices will be smart entertainment devices and security and climate controls.

Imagine if most of the cars on the highway were 100 percent autonomous and every intersection and highway on-ramp were equipped with a wireless transmitter. Add intelligent school zones and construction sites to the network. Then imagine that all vehicles were equipped with a foolproof, hackproof wireless transmitter and receiver so they could exchange information with transmitters about traffic patterns or the presence of some kind of on-road hazard.

This is already a lot of "ifs," but for the purpose of this thought exercise, let's continue. Imagine that traffic-control software in each autonomous vehicle had the intelligence to automatically adjust the vehicle's speed and trajectory in response to the information it collected from the surrounding infrastructure. Voilà. No more idling.

Each autonomous vehicle could plan its route based on information gained from this discussion with the roadside

Internet of Things. No more traffic jams. The safety benefits would be tremendous, since a third of all fatal accidents occur at intersections.[13]

Networked, intelligent cars could keep one another informed, adding to a central, collective body of knowledge. When BMW bought the digital mapping company HERE, it described the benefits of such a model.

> The social benefits of swarm intelligence are enormous: They facilitate warnings of hazards in real time, of icy roads for example, based on calculations of individual data such as ABS activations and outside temperature. Upcoming traffic jams will be identified more precisely in the future, significantly reducing the risk of accidents. ... Anticipation of green phases of stoplights could navigate vehicles through an urban area on a "green wave" with the appropriate engine performance and minimized fuel consumption.[14]

Perhaps someday, autonomous vehicles will communicate with one another over some kind of network. Even if this day arrives, however, it's unlikely V2X-equipped cars of the future will use the same costly infrastructure of short-wave radio technology that figures in current USDOT strategy. Once the majority of cars on the road are fully self-driving, by then, it's highly likely that connectedness will be achieved for a lower price. Fully autonomous cars will be able to communicate with one another and with roadside traffic-management servers using cheaper forms of networks such as the existing cellphone infrastructure.

THE VALUE OF DUMB HIGHWAYS

Perhaps because of decades of federal and private sector investment in intelligent highway systems, a common myth that lingers about driverless cars is that they require extensive investment in the highway infrastructure. As recently as 2014, Volvo proposed embedding magnets in the road to help driverless cars see in the fog.[15] It is tempting to suggest improvements to highway infrastructure. Even advanced programmers wistfully daydream about how much easier it would be to program a driverless car if only there were barcodes embedded into the road or radio-frequency identification (RFID) tags placed at every intersection.

Investing in intelligent highway infrastructure is a poor strategy for many reasons. One is practical: there is no ready money to pay for non-essential highway infrastructure and asking for it would doom any proposed initiative to develop the technology. In the United States, the question of who will pay for highway infrastructure continues to be a political hot potato in an era of crumbling public roads and a nearly bankrupt federal highway trust fund. Even if funding for intelligent highway infrastructure were to become available, the more money spent on highway infrastructure, the less money left over to invest in more valuable research on robotic technologies that will someday drive better than a human can.

Another argument against investment in intelligent highway systems is that as cars gain their own ability to safely navigate the roads, the need for signs, traffic lights, and guard rails will diminish. When driverless cars take the road, the most important road infrastructure will be the low-tech painted-on lane markers that provide critical visual information for the car's deep-learning software. Even today, the visual crispness of lane markers varies dramatically from place to place. Driverless-car advocates should save their political capital to lobby for a federal quality standard for painted lane markers, a complicated battle that will take place across a crazy quilt of municipalities, counties, and states.

Third, investment in intelligent infrastructure is risky since hardware technologies rapidly and inevitably become obsolete. Software is usually updated at a much faster rate than the hardware that supports it. The best place to invest precious research dollars would be in developing intelligent robotic operating systems for driverless cars whose abilities will improve continuously, maybe even exponentially.

The best infrastructure is "dumb infrastructure." Autonomous driving expert Brad Templeton from Singularity University believes that the internet is a good example of the value of dumb infrastructure. Internet infrastructure contains little built-in intelligence, a characteristic that, counterintuitively, has enabled it to adapt and evolve. Routers and cables transmit data packets without understanding a thing about the content of those packets—be they e-mail, video, or web pages. Because the internet was structured to be as dumb as possible, it has enjoyed rapid, unencumbered technological growth.

Imagine if internet infrastructure were "smart" and made routing and processing decisions based on understanding the content of each data packet. Each time the network's software applications changed, the underlying infrastructure would also need to be upgraded. To see the cost of internet intelligence in action, recall the politics around a simple quality of service (QOS) routing update in which routers were required to prioritize streaming content over nonstreaming content. More recently, in battles over net neutrality, consumers fought telecommunication companies to prevent telecommunications companies (telcos) from charging more for prioritized routing. The very simplicity of internet infrastructure reduces its potential management headaches and minimizes potential political controversy.

Similarly, in the case of driverless cars, the simpler the transportation infrastructure, the more bureaucracy-free, flexible, and adaptive it will be. Brad Templeton draws another useful analogy between intelligent cars and rail transportation. The infrastructure that supports trains is significantly more specialized than the paved roads that support cars. Paved roads are versatile, capable of accommodating a broad range of vehicles, from bicycles, pedestrians, and donkeys, to private cars and semitrailers. Paved roads also permit more complex traffic patterns. Drivers can weave between multiple lanes, while a rigid and expensive train track permits only one train to pass at a time.

UPDATING TRANSPORTATION POLICY

Since the doomed Demo 97 a few decades ago, the U.S. Department of Transportation and its organizational offspring, the NHTSA, and the FHA have been content with taking a largely passive

approach toward driverless cars, sitting back to see where industry and individual states take them. Once upon a time, a cautious
approach—given the absence of critical enabling information
and communication technologies—was a sensible decision on the
part of federal officials. As driverless-car technology continues to
advance at a breakneck pace, however, there's no excuse for the
agency's continuing focus on incremental initiatives such as V2X
research pilots.

There are some positive indications, however, that the situation may be improving. In December 2015, Congress passed a
long-awaited bill to improve the infrastructure of the federal
highway system and transit systems called the Fixing America's
Surface Transportation (FAST) Act. The FAST Act provides
roughly $300 billion for roads and transit systems for over five
years. The act establishes grant money for advanced transportation management technologies and requires the GAO to submit a
regular report to Congress on the status of autonomous transportation technology policy.

In 2016, U.S. transportation secretary Anthony Foxx
announced that over the next ten years, the federal government
will invest nearly $4 billion to accelerate the development and
adoption of transformational, automotive technology through pilot
projects.[16] (At the time of this writing, it wasn't clear exactly what
these pilot projects would focus on; we hope not just V2X). Taking
a more proactive approach than in the past, the USDOT said it
will aim to provide guidance to industry on establishing definitions for safe operation of autonomous vehicles. The agency has
also stated it will work with states to craft model policy guidance
on the testing and deployment of autonomous vehicles.

If we could worm our way into the upper echelons of the
federal government, here's what we would do to accelerate the
development of driverless-car technology. First, we would create
an agency devoted to the topic of fully autonomous driving. Let's
call this new agency the Federal Autonomous Vehicles Agency, or
AVA, similar to the Federal Aviation Administration (FAA) that

governs air traffic. The AVA would be responsible for setting aggressive and visionary strategy to make driverless cars a reality across all fifty states.

The FAA rigorously defines standards for redundancy and self-testing for aircraft; driverless cars need the same level of oversight. Federal transportation officials need to take a leadership role on defining key questions such as at what point is a driverless car "safe enough." For example, is a self-driving car that averages one collision in 500,000 miles sufficiently safe to be allowed on public roads? (That's a higher bar than we demand of taxi drivers.) Once defined, safety standards will need to be enforced.

One aspect of discussions of safety that's difficult for many people to deal with is the uncomfortable fact that the introduction of driverless cars involves risk, uncertainty, and probably even some accidents. The problem is that the alternative solution, human drivers, has already proven itself to be even worse. We human drivers are a well-documented menace. Regulators must resist the temptation to wait until driverless cars are perfect drivers, since that day may never come. Instead, federal regulators need to set a practical new goal line for safety: as we discussed earlier, driverless-car technology should be considered viable when a driverless car drives twice as safely as a human.

Another way this hypothetical new agency, the AVA, could help would be to generate public and corporate excitement about driverless cars. To ensure that more minds than just those employed by Google, Apple, and car companies are thinking about driverless cars, the AVA should earmark funding for regular competitions where teams from industry and universities compete to create better solutions to the hard technical problems. If an annual driverless-car competition sounds familiar, that's because it is. The DARPA Grand Challenges of 2004, 2005, and 2007 showcased the best autonomous vehicle technology of the day, catalyzing the careers of dozens of bright minds who have since helped spark today's renaissance in driverless technologies.

States and cities need federal guidance. The AVA should mandate that all states offer a standard driver's license for autonomous vehicles provided the technology passes a certain minimal safety record. In 2015, only four states had a driver's license for autonomous vehicles: California, Nevada, Michigan, and Florida. In addition, states with long empty stretches of highway should be encouraged to create designated lanes for testing and validation of fully autonomous vehicles and trucks.

None of these goals will be easy to accomplish and writing good technology policy is notoriously difficult. When the technology involves cars and safety, striking the right balance between encouragement and prudence becomes even more challenging. Recent, updated regulations for driverless cars passed by the state of California are a good example of the regulatory landmines that lie ahead, highlighting the need for strong and well-defined federal oversight.

On December 16, 2015, the California DMV released its first draft of proposed new regulations governing driverless cars for public feedback. The most controversial new regulation proposed by California's DMV was that all driverless cars possess a steering wheel and brakes and have a human on-board at all times. One drawback of such an approach is that it's risky. Forcing humans to maintain oversight of a driverless car invokes serious safety issues (as we discussed in chapter 3). Humans don't drive well when they believe a capable computer is handling things for them.

Another drawback of requiring a human driver to be present at all times is that such a law maintains the "human in the loop" paradigm. Such an approach flies in the face of Google's bid to build a car that leaps directly into full autonomy. As California's drafted regulations stand now, Google's autonomous prototype (which features a simple black button to make it go and a red button to make it stop) would be illegal.

One problem with a poorly thought out state regulation is that once passed, it's difficult to retract. In a blog article, Brad Templeton summed up the challenge:

The state proposes banning Google style vehicles for now, and drafting regulations on them in the future. Unfortunately, once something is banned, it is remarkably difficult to un-ban it. That's because nobody wants to be the regulator or politician who un-bans something that later causes harm that can be blamed on them. And these vehicles will cause harm, just less harm than the people currently driving are doing.[17]

One of the new regulations proposed by the California DMV, however, sets a good precedent. The state is considering requiring that driverless-car manufacturers be subject to safety tests from an independent third party. Given that at the time of this writing such testing entities did not exist, the rule will be difficult to apply. However, it's a sensible regulation that will not only spark the development of a new industry (driverless-car testing) but will also serve to protect consumers against shoddy or malfunctioning software and inflated claims. This proposed regulation, in fact, should go further and define the process for state inspection for individual autonomous vehicles. Similar to the periodic inspections of car brakes and emissions, driverless-car technology will also need to be periodically inspected by city governments to make sure the car's software and hardware are functioning properly.

The AVA should lead states to define and clarify another core challenge related to safety, that of liability. Who is at fault in a driverless-car accident needs to be clarified. While accidents involving driverless cars are likely to be relatively rare and the question may wind up being irrelevant, the issue stills requires examination. In the United States, insurance law is defined and enforced at the state level. If the federal government can clarify standard performance metrics for each major system in a driverless car (i.e., the software, hardware sensors, and the automotive body), insurance companies will have a clear framework for quantifying risk, and manufacturers will be protected from frivolous lawsuits.

Another issue where federal regulation will be needed at the state and city level is that of privacy. Driverless cars will be a goldmine of data on passenger comings and goings and a treasure trove of visual data of roads and roadsides. So far, there have been some promising first steps being taken to deal with privacy issues. In 2015, a bill to protect consumer privacy in autonomous vehicles was introduced by New York state representative Grace Meng, a step in the right direction.[18]

We hope that soon the USDOT will broaden its definition of what constitutes an intelligent vehicle. Its best path forward would be to focus on improving public safety by making intelligent policy that smooths the path for robotic vehicles and helps cities and states make it possible for autonomous vehicles to flourish. The regions and nations with the most forward-thinking policy will reap future economic benefits associated with being the epicenter of driverless-car technology.

If the development of driverless cars had stopped dead after Demo 97, this book wouldn't exist. Our brief tour through history has revealed that for most of the twentieth century, inventor after inventor tried and failed to deliver a viable driverless car, held back by the lack of critical enabling technologies, such as deep-learning software, data, fast computers, and modern sensors. The good news is that there's more to the story.

The modern driverless car appeared at the dawn of the twenty-first century in the middle of an empty desert, far from the electronic highways and cinderblock corridors of federal transportation think tanks. Freed from the shackles of highway infrastructure, this new generation of driverless cars broke tradition by tapping into breakthroughs in mobile robotics and carrying their intelligence around on their own back. This new species of driverless car was a robot.

8

RISE OF THE ROBOTS

Modern driverless cars began to emerge from the labs of robotics researchers in the final decades of the twentieth century. Throughout the 1980s and 1990s, German autonomous-vehicle pioneer Ernst Dickmanns built several prototypes that used sensors and intelligent software to steer themselves. In Italy, Professor Alberto Broggi created a car that used machine vision software to follow painted lane markers. As primitive as these early driverless cars were by today's standards, they had a major advantage over the radio-guided Buicks of the past: their intelligence was carried on-board the car rather than buried in the road.

Two catalysts helped make modern robotic cars a reality: The first was that microprocessors shrank and grew more powerful. The second catalyst was a 2001 U.S. Congressional mandate that dictated that by the year 2015, one-third of the vehicles used in military war zones should be fully autonomous. Like cell phones, GPS, and the internet, driverless cars are yet another consumer device whose origins are in military technology.

As part of the mandate, Congress tasked DARPA with driving the development of the necessary technologies and authorized the agency to give out cash prizes to anyone who could demonstrate they could build an autonomous vehicle. Equipped with an alluring pot of prize money, DARPA officials laid out a plan. The agency would sponsor a series of road races where researchers could compete for cash prizes by pitting their robotic vehicle against those of their colleagues from other universities and companies (readers will recall that DARPA later used a similar technique to motivate the development of disaster recovery robots like CHIMP).

Between 2001 and 2007, DARPA sponsored three road races, the DARPA Challenges of 2004, 2005, and 2007. The first DARPA Challenge of 2004 offered a cash prize of $1 million to the team whose autonomous vehicle could win a 150-mile long race through an uninhabited section of the Mohave Desert in the southwestern United States. The desert was a natural choice for the first challenge. Given the primitive state of autonomous vehicle technology in those early days, it was crucial that the roboticists test their work far from busy places such as shopping malls and streets crowded with pedestrians, baby carriages, and other potentially disastrous obstacles.

It turns out the desert was the right choice of venue. The robotics software and hardware with which the fifteen competing teams equipped their cars was too crude to handle the task at hand. Hardware sensors and GPS devices were slow and unreliable. The competing vehicles' machine-vision software performed even more poorly, stranding vehicles in embankments and on rocks. Other vehicles were felled by mechanical problems. After a few hours of race time, none of the fifteen competing vehicles made it further than eight miles into the course. The $1 million cash prize remained unclaimed.

It would have been easy for everyone involved to give up after such a crushingly disappointing outcome. In an interview to CNN following the 2004 race, Tom Strat, deputy program manager of the DARPA Grand Challenge, remained firmly optimistic, saying "Even though nobody got more than about 5 percent of the way through the course, this has made these engineers even more determined."[1]

Undeterred, DARPA ponied up funding to repeat the race again the next year. The 2004 race involved a fascinating but motley crew of all kinds of diverse autonomous vehicles, ranging from a small, two-ton truck to a sprightly dune buggy with oversized wheels. The second time around, for the 2005 race, DARPA tightened up its selection process for competitors, holding site visits and a National Qualifying Event to winnow down the field. The purse for the winning team was increased to $2 million.

Based on performance in the qualifying event, DARPA selected twenty-three teams to compete in the 2005 DARPA Challenge. The 2005 race also took place in an uninhabited desert. The rules were roughly the same as for the previous year: competing vehicles had to drive themselves through a 132-mile-long off-road course without relying on support from roadside infrastructure or human assistance.

By the end of race day, it was clear that DARPA 2005 represented a critical tipping point in the development of modern robotics. If only the engineers who built GM's and RCA's electronic highway half a century ago could have been witness to the miracle that took place on the unpaved desert roads. For the first time ever, five autonomous vehicles safely steered themselves through a treacherous sandy race course using only their own artificial perception to find their way.

The winner of the 2005 challenge was the Stanford Racing team that came in first place in just under seven hours. Close on their heels were two cars from Carnegie Mellon University that took second and third places. Fourth place went to a car from the Gray Insurance Company, and fifth to an entry built by the Oshkosh Truck Corporation.

Equally exciting was the software that Stanford's victorious vehicle used to win the race. While the other competing teams planned their vehicle's course in advance with topographic maps and aerial imagery, Stanford's champion car, a souped-up VW Touareg named Stanley, used another approach. During the months leading up to the 2005 challenge, Stanley's mid-level controls learned to drive.

Figure 8.1
An infamous stretch of road in the DARPA Grand Challenge of 2005 called Beer Bottle Pass, approximately seven miles from the finish line, featured over twenty twists and turns.
Source: U.S. Federal Government (DARPA); Wikipedia

MACHINE LEARNING AND DRIVING

Sebastian Thrun, the Stanford professor who led the team of students that developed Stanley, did a few key things differently. First, he realized that software, not hardware, would determine who won the race. Second, to create the mid-level control software, the "perceiving" and "reacting" portions of the car's guiding software, Thrun and his team opted to not use rule-based software, the prevailing AI paradigm at the time. In the early days of their project, Thrun and his team decided that attempting to write a logical set of rules to deal with the vast array of topographical details and random objects the car would encounter during the race was simply not going to work.

Instead, Thrun and his team used machine learning. Thrun explained:

> Many of the people who participated in the race had a strong hardware focus, so a lot of teams ended up building their own

robots. Our calculus was that this was not about the strength of the robot or the design of the chassis. Humans could drive those trails perfectly; it was not complicated off-road terrain. It was really just desert trails. So we decided it was purely a matter of artificial intelligence. All we had to do was put a computer inside the car, give it the appropriate eyes and ears, and make it smart.

In trying to make it smart, we found that driving is really governed not by two or three rules but by tens of thousands of rules. There are so many different contingencies. We had a day when birds were sitting on the road and flew up as our vehicle approached. And we learned that to a robot eye, a bird looks exactly the same as a rock. So we had to make the machine smart enough to distinguish birds from rocks.

In the end, we started relying on what we call machine learning, or big data. That is, instead of trying to program all these rules by hand, we taught our robot the same way we would teach a human driver. We would go into the desert, and I would drive, and the robot would watch me and try to emulate the behaviors involved. Or we would let the robot drive, and it would make a mistake, and we would go back to the data and explain to the robot why this was a mistake and give the robot a chance to adjust.[2]

To understand why Thrun's decision to use machine learning was a radical approach at the time, let's revisit the two prevailing paradigms of artificial-intelligence software we covered in previous chapters: rule-based AI and data-driven AI (increasingly known as machine learning). As we discussed earlier, rule-based AI demands that its programmer first devise a theoretical model of the world, then write a set of rules called if-then statements to logically interact with that model. In contrast, machine learning involves applying an algorithm to large amounts of data and using statistical techniques to process that data, eventually exposing the software to enough data that it "learns" to recognize patterns without human oversight

In chapter 5, we conducted an exercise in writing mid-level control software to guide a car through a busy intersection. We learned that rule-based code falters when asked to handle the wide variety of obstacles a car might encounter in the real world. Software that uses logical if-then statements to oversee a car's perception and response will quickly be derailed by corner cases and exceptions to the rules.

Now imagine that we are undertaking a similar exercise, but this time our goal is to write mid-level control software that can guide a car through a desert. Our software must be capable of identifying which portions of ground in front of the car are safe to drive upon ("driveable"), and which portions are not ("undrivable"). One solution could be to use aerial images and GPS data of the desert landscape to manually chart a path for our car. After some thought, however, it would become apparent that such a solution would not anticipate all the obstacles that our car will face on the ground level as it navigates around uncharted potholes, debris, big rocks, and ditches.

For the purpose of this exercise, let's assume that we all arrive at the same conclusion: the best way to keep the car on ground that's safe to drive upon is to build mid-level control software that, similar to a human driver, identifies "driveable" ground in real time, but without using rules or logic. I witnessed one memorable demonstration of the futility of applying rules to driving in the 2005 challenge. One of my colleagues led a team that spent months writing a set of logical rules and applying them to the stream of data flowing in from their vehicle's visual sensors. When sensor data indicated a substantial rise in the ground in front of the car, the control software would respond by turning the wheel and steering the car around the obstacle.

After months of hard work, this team's code base was voluminous and detailed. Unfortunately, their quest for the million-dollar purse came (literally) to a screeching halt when during the race, their vehicle slammed on its brakes right before it entered a tunnel. The team later figured out that their mid-level control software lacked a specific rule that dealt with tunnels since none of the programmers had anticipated that one would appear on the course. Without clear guidance, the car took its best guess. Based on the height of the tunnel ceiling and the fact that it loomed large over the road in front of it, the car's software classified the tunnel as a gigantic and steep wall. Unexpectedly presented with what it thought was a wall, its software did the right thing: it slammed on its brakes and refused to move until its human programmer came and coaxed the car back onto safer ground.

Rule-based software can be a valuable part of a driverless car's toolkit for high-level control applications like route planning, and to manage low-level activities, such as checking the status of the gas tank. However, rule-based artificial intelligence has a tendency to break down in unstructured environments, leading some roboticists to refer to top-down AI software as "brittle." In the 2004

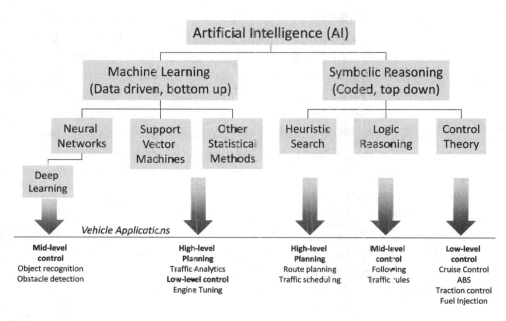

Figure 8.2

AI techniques used in driverless cars. Most robotic systems use a combination of techniques. Object recognition for real-time obstacle detection and traffic negotiation is the most challenging for AI (far left).

and 2005 challenges, the software used by most of the contestants proved to be too brittle to do its job, one reason why so many of the competing vehicles failed to complete the course.

The third and final DARPA Urban Challenge took place in on an unused U.S. Air Force base seventy-five miles northeast of Los Angeles. To keep competing teams on their toes, it was decided that the sixty-mile race course would be an unstructured and dynamic environment, similar to what an autonomous vehicle would encounter in a chaotic war zone (or busy freeway). To win the first place prize of $2 million, teams would have to build mid-level control software that could guide their vehicle safely around other moving cars on an unfamiliar course without being explicitly programmed to do so. At that time, such an assignment was as formidable a challenge for an autonomous vehicle as climbing Mt. Everest during a blinding snowstorm without a map would be for a human.

The rules of the 2007 Urban Challenge were straightforward: without a human driver on board, each vehicle had to complete a list of simple driving tasks, or "missions," in an urban environment. Missions included turning left into an intersection, going through a traffic circle, parking, and maintaining proper position in a two-lane road without colliding into on-coming traffic. To ensure that the vehicles were truly autonomous (rather than pre-programmed for this particular environment), just an hour before the race began each team was given a crude digital map of the local geography.

As race day for the 2007 challenge dawned, hundreds of egos were on the line. Eleven robotic cars from elite universities and companies lined up at the starting gates. The starter, a man in a baseball cap, dropped a green flag and the race began. One by one, the driverless cars cautiously rolled out of the gates, their trunks and back seats stuffed with computers and their steering wheels spinning back and forth as if guided by an invisible set of hands. Inside a nearby tent large enough to stage a circus, thousands of fans and spectators watched the action unfold on gigantic movie screens.

The race proceeded with mixed results. Judges in reflective orange safety vests scurried around holding stopwatches as competing teams tackled their assigned missions under the relentless sun of the Southern California desert. Like a squadron of visually impaired octogenarians, vehicle after vehicle chugged cautiously along while DARPA program managers monitored the race from behind giant concrete barricades.

Even in this face-off of the world's elite roboticists, the best driverless-car technology of the day was still unpredictable. To ensure the safety of traffic judges and competing teams, each autonomous vehicle was trailed by a human "babysitter" vehicle, a professional driver in a specially reinforced Ford Taurus. Should a car's on-board artificial intelligence fail, each robotic vehicle was equipped with a mandatory emergency remote E-stop button to be used if it posed a danger to nearby humans or other vehicles.

The sandy desert terrain, once the training ground for fighter pilots, began to resemble a movie set for a comedy about slow-motion fender benders. Talos, the entry from MIT, drove slowly into the side of Skynet, Cornell's autonomous vehicle (an accident we described in chapter 5).[3] Another competing vehicle quickly got itself eliminated from the race after it rebelliously steered itself off course and dove headfirst into the wall of a nearby building; the collision was noted in race logs as a "vehicle vs. building incident," which is exactly what it sounds like. Two other vehicles, like adolescents paralyzed by stage fright at their first high-school dance, froze in place while pondering which way to turn, one at an intersection and the other at a traffic circle.[4]

Despite the vehicular high jinks, the race ended well, as six of the eleven competing teams completed their missions and finished the course. The winning vehicle was a vehicle named Boss, built by Carnegie Mellon University and its industry partner for the race, automotive giant GM. Boss completed the course in four hours and ten minutes, maintaining an average speed of fourteen miles per hour. Stanford University's entry, a robot named Junior, came in a close second, while Odin, the vehicle from Virginia Tech University, was third.

The real winner of the day, however, was the robotics community. The results of the 2007 challenge proved that autonomous vehicles could someday be a viable technology, capable of successfully navigating bustling urban environments, negotiating four-way intersections, and detecting the presence of other cars on the road. Finally, perhaps the Da Vinci problem that had plagued the development of driverless cars for decades was coming to an end.

PLAYING CHECKERS

There is no exact birth date for the modern autonomous vehicle. In reality, the modern driverless car emerged in stages. In DARPA's previous sponsored races in 2004 and 2005, the cars' performance improved from one competition to the next. By the time the third challenge rolled around in the year 2007, competing teams benefitted not only from hard-won experience, but also from rapid advances in hardware technologies and breakthroughs in artificial intelligence software, in particular, in machine learning.

A useful explanation of machine learning comes from a lively website called Stack Overflow, where a global community of several million programmers answer one another's technical questions and then vote on the quality of the responses. On the site, the top-voted response to the question "What is machine learning" states:

> Essentially, it is a method of teaching computers to make and improve predictions or behaviors based on some data. What is this "data"? Well, that depends entirely on the problem. It could be readings from a robot's sensors as it learns to walk, or the correct output of a program for certain input. The ability to react to inputs that have never been seen before is one of the core tenets of many machine learning algorithms. Imagine

trying to teach a computer driver to navigate highways in traffic. Using your "database" metaphor, you would have to teach the computer exactly what to do in millions of possible situations. An effective machine learning algorithm would (we hope!) be able to learn similarities between different states and react to them similarly.

The similarities between states can be anything—even things we might think of as "mundane" can really trip up a computer! For example, let's say that the computer driver learned that when a car in front of it slowed down, it had to slow down too. For a human, replacing the car with a motorcycle doesn't change anything—we recognize that the motorcycle is also a vehicle. For a machine learning algorithm, this can actually be surprisingly difficult! A database would have to store information separately about the case where a car is in front and where a motorcycle is in front. A machine learning algorithm, on the other hand, would "learn" from the car example and be able to generalize to the motorcycle example automatically. Another way to think about machine learning is that it is "pattern recognition"—the act of teaching a program to react to or recognize patterns.[5]

While machine-learning techniques sound organic—the software learns to recognize patterns or to solve certain problems— what's actually happening is that an algorithm parses vast amounts of data to look for statistical patterns. Using the statistical patterns found, the algorithm then builds a mathematical model that ranks the probability of various possible outcomes to make predictions or reach a decision. The algorithm then validates whether its predictions are accurate (or its decisions appropriate ones) by testing them on new, unseen data. If they're wrong, it goes back to update the model. In this way, a machine-learning program is fed data to "learn" from "experience" under the supervision of its human programmer, whose job consists of selecting the algorithm and providing the data and the initial right or wrong feedback.

Board games have long been a favorite of AI researchers to demonstrate new paradigms, and machine learning was no exception. When machine-learning techniques were first developed during the 1950s, limited computing power greatly restricted what board games they could be applied to. Since the computers of that era could not handle the number of calculations that a game of chess would require, researchers used the game of checkers instead.

In 1949, Arthur Samuel, an early artificial intelligence researcher and at that time a brand-new IBM employee, wanted to prove that a computer could perform complicated intellectual tasks. The year Samuel joined IBM, the company was still primarily known for making calculating machines. Samuel had an idea for how to increase the company's visibility. He figured that if he could come up with some sort of application that a computer could do but an adding machine couldn't, he could showcase the analytical power of IBM's first commercial computer, the IBM 701.

Samuels decided that the best application for demonstrating the cognitive ability of a computer was a good game of checkers. Even better, Samuel's goal was to teach a computer how to play checkers at a world-class level. If he had opted to solve the problem using the prevailing AI paradigm of his day, Samuel would have written copious amounts of if-then statements in an attempt to anticipate and guide the computer through any possible board configuration it might encounter.

Such a rule-based approach would have been a laborious undertaking. Every possible board configuration would need to be addressed in advance by a rule that dealt with that particular situation. Using a rule-based approach would go something like this: one rule might say "Give priority to moves that eliminate an opponent's piece"; another rule might say "Give priority to moving pieces that are closer to reaching the opponent's back line."

The problem with this sort of AI, as Samuel quickly discovered, is that the number of rules needed to play a single game of checkers ballooned into a unmanageably long list of instructions. A more troubling problem, however, was that even if somebody created an exhaustive list of rules to address every possible board position, the computer following those rules would still be a mediocre checkers player. Similar to a novice human player who is guided by rigid protocol rather an intuitive sense of strategy, the computer would lack an appreciation for nuances and seemingly illogical moves, qualities that define a great checkers player.

Many AI experts would have gotten pretty good results by writing more elaborate sets of rules, perhaps tossing in some exceptions and pseudorandom moves to create the illusion that a strategy was being employed. Samuel, however, chose a different path. He decided to use machine learning, so the computer could learn to play checkers, not from a set of formal rules, but from its own experience.

A human player becomes an expert not by calculating all possible outcomes, but by observing typical board situations, memorizing them, and remembering what their outcomes were. Human players remember the moves that led to defeat; a similarly valuable lesson is offered by remembering the moves that led to victory. Samuel decided to program his computer to emulate a skilled human, to play by learning to recognize the patterns of particular board positions, particularly those that led to a winning game.

Samuel programmed the computer to begin learning by making random legal moves by playing against a software copy of itself. Sometimes the original copy of the checkers program would win, sometimes it would lose. After every game the computer would take a moment to record, in a large database, all the moves that led to a win and all the moves that led to a loss. This was how the computer gained experience.

The next time it played, armed with its ever-growing database of experiences, before making a move the software would look up the board configuration in its database. This way, it could see whether it had already encountered that particular configuration and, if so, what moves had led to a win. If it happened to be a configuration of pieces that the software had never before encountered, the software would make another random but legal move, and then store the result of that move.

Initially, Samuel's machine-learning software played randomly, like a child stumbling through his first game. But after a few thousand games, its database of good and bad moves grew. After a few thousand games more, the software began to play with what some observers might call "strategy." Since most moves can lead to both a loss and a win, depending on subsequent moves, the database didn't just record a win/lose outcome. Instead, it recorded the *probability* that each move would eventually lead to a win. In other words, the database was essentially a big statistical model.

As the software learned, it spent countless hours in "self-play," amassing more gaming experience than any human could in a lifetime. As the database grew, Samuel had to develop more efficient data-lookup techniques, leading to the invention of *hash tables* that are still used in large databases. Another of Samuel's innovations was to use the database to factor in how the opponent would mostly likely respond to each move, an algorithm known today as *minimax*.

Ultimately, Samuel succeeded. His checker-playing program would later have an impressive impact on the world outside his lab. A few years later, on February 24, 1956, the program was demonstrated to the public on live television. In 1962, the computer beat checkers master player Robert Nealey, and IBM's stocks rose 15 percent overnight.

It was impressive that the software could win against a master checkers player. But even more impressive was that the program became skilled enough to play checkers better than its creator, Samuel himself. A rule-based artificial-intelligence program's expertise is bounded by that of its human creators. Samuel taught his machine-learning program something limitless: how to learn.

Figure 8.3
Arthur Samuel playing checkers on the IBM 7090 (February 24, 1956).
Source: Courtesy of IBM Archives

Many people reject the idea that a machine, a computer, can learn. We frequently hear misguided statements such as "a computer can't be more intelligent than the human who programmed it." That idea is rooted in the old way of thinking of a computer as an automated machine that simply carries out a prescribed set of instructions. The power of machine learning enabled Samuel's computer to acquire skill the same way a human does, by learning from its own successes and failures. Just a child can eventually know more than its parents, a student can surpass her teacher, and an athlete can beat his coach, a computer can ultimately outperform its programmer.

Some expert chess players who have played against a software opponent have reported that they feel as if the computer program plays with intention, strategy, even passion. In 1996, Garry Kasparov lost his first match against IBM's Deep Blue, the greatgrandchild of Samuel's checkers-playing algorithm. In an interview with *TIME* magazine, Kasparov said "I could feel—I could smell—a new kind of intelligence across the table." He later concluded, "Although I think I did see some signs of intelligence, it's a weird kind, an inefficient, inflexible kind that makes me think I have a few years left."[6] Kasparov was wrong. The next year Deep Blue won the tournament.

Deep Blue's "weird, inefficient new kind of intelligence," was at its heart just an application of statistics. One of the fascinating and frustrating characteristics of machine learning is its opacity. Some engineers feel uncomfortable with machine learning since they never completely understand exactly how AI reaches its conclusion.

One of the defining characteristics of machine learning, for better or for worse, is that the internal mathematical model that the machine-learning algorithm develops to make its predictions is usually incomprehensible to a human. As a result, a human supervisor can't take a look at the software code to see whether it's sound. The only way a human supervisor can validate a machine-learning model's prediction is by feeding it new test cases.

INFINITE STATE SPACE

Although robotics researchers have used machine-learning techniques for decades, these robots worked in highly structured environments. Machine learning worked well for a checkers game, since a checkerboard is a simple state space that offers its players a finite number of possible moves. Samuel's checkers program recognized board positions by looking them up in its database. Each board configuration was distinct and well defined, therefore easy to store.

Playing chess is more difficult than checkers because each board configuration has many more possible future moves, or what AI scientists call a *higher branching factor*. More complex still is a city street or a busy freeway that presents a state space that contains an infinite number of possible "moves" and "board positions." In artificial-intelligence research, an environment that serves its robot an endless supply of novel situations is called an *infinite state space*.

Driverless cars must deal with an infinite state space. A robotic vehicle constantly encounters new situations, which makes it impossible to create a lookup table to store these experiences. Not only is each new experience difficult to boil down into a finite storable unit (such as a board position), storing an infinite number of experiences would result in a look-up database so large it would quickly outgrow even a powerful modern computer.

For years, the barrier of infinite state space has prevented roboticists from using machine learning for robots operating in unstructured and dynamic environments. It became possible to apply machine learning to infinite state spaces only recently, when new algorithms were developed, computing power improved, and sufficient amounts of training data became available. One of the reasons Stanford's victory in the 2005 DARPA Challenge was significant was that their autonomous vehicle, Stanley, was the first successful application of machine learning to driving.

Stanley's team cracked the problem of infinite state space by simplifying the real world outside the car into just two categories: drivable and not drivable. They trained their machine-learning software to sort the raw, real-time visual data from the lidar and cameras mounted on their car into one of these two finite categories. To teach the machine learning-software how to recognize drivable ground, every weekend the Stanford team returned to the desert to collect more visual data of the desert landscape. They adjusted the program when it made a mistake and continued the training.

To build a visual model of the processed data for their mid-level controller's occupancy grid, the team color-coded the data streams. The portions of the ground in front of the car's front bumper that the machine-learning software deemed drivable were assigned one color, and the portions deemed not drivable were assigned another color. Videos of Stanley's dynamic occupancy grid show hypnotic brightly colored swirls drifting around the screen as the car moves forward, the machine-learning software simplifying the infinite state space of the desert into just these two categories.

Stanley's victory in the 2005 DARPA Challenge proved that computer-vision applications can use machine learning to navigate complex and unpredictable real-world environments. One of the key enabling factors in the development of machine-learning software has been a new abundance of training data, previously a scarce resource. In the case of driverless cars, training data originates from several on-board hardware devices whose performance has improved dramatically over the past several years.

THE MODERN TOOLBOX

Driverless cars are a prime example of a force called *recombinant innovation*, the process of combining several existing technologies in new ways. Despite the popular stereotype of the lone, genius inventor, in reality many emerging technologies—particularly complex ones—are actually fresh combinations of old technologies put together again in a novel way.[7] Recombinant innovation is an indirect by-product of Moore's Law, the now-famous principle that over time, the performance of semiconductors improves at an exponential rate while their cost shrinks at a corresponding rate.

Moore's Law has held true for semiconductor technologies for a few decades now. Its effect has carried over to other types of hardware that use computer chips such as digital cameras, televisions, and electronic toys. The effect of Moore's Law has led some experts to describe any technology whose performance improves at an exponential rate as an *exponential technology*.

The gradual improvement of autonomous vehicle prototypes since the 1970s demonstrates the power of recombinant innovation, and also the beneficial effects of Moore's Law.[8] In the 1980s, Carnegie Mellon's Navlab built an autonomous-vehicle prototype named Codger that was the size of a UPS delivery truck. Codger had to be hefty since it carried an expensive assortment of high-end technology, including a bulky color TV camera, a GPS receiver, a laser range finder, and several general purpose Sun-3 computers. Codger's top speed was about 20 mph on empty roads. The vehicle was unsafe for city streets since it took about ten seconds for the software to work through each navigation "task" on a clear stretch of road and up to twenty seconds or more in "cluttered" environments.[9]

Fast forward to another state-of-the-art autonomous vehicle in the year 2007 and the situation looked more promising. To equip their SUV for the 2007 DARPA Challenge, the Cornell team spent $195,850 to buy lidar and radar sensors, a GPS, and a camera, and $46,550 to purchase several desktop computers, laptops, and peripherals.[10] Although it cost less to outfit an autonomous vehicle in 2007 than it did in 1980, computers and sensors were still too slow to support autonomous driving. In a postmortem analysis of the 2007 DARPA Challenge, the leader of the CMU team, Chris Urmson (who later helped lead Google's self-driving car initiative), ruefully noted that "available off-the-shelf sensors are insufficient for urban driving."[11]

Fast forward again to the present day and the situation looks much more promising. Today the cost of providing the data needed to feed a car's mid-level control software is significantly less than in 2007. At the time this book was written, the cost of rigging up the hardware needed for an autonomous vehicle was roughly $5,000 per car, and in five to seven years will be even less.[12]

Modern hardware devices are not only cheaper but also smaller, so they can be discreetly tucked inside the car's body and interior. A radar detector is the size of a hockey puck. A GPS receiver fits easily into a car's dashboard. One slim laptop computer has more processing power than a 1960s mainframe that was the size of a minivan. A few lidar devices can be inserted next to a car's headlights.

Today's enabling hardware technologies also work better. In 2007, driverless cars were an intriguing "someday soon" technology. Just seven years after describing the inadequacy of off-the-shelf sensors, in 2014, Urmson noted that as Google's cars reached their 700,000 mile mark, "thousands of situations on city streets that would have stumped us two years ago can now be navigated autonomously."[13] As the momentum continues, another few short years later, Google's advanced prototypes have successfully driven more than 1,500,000 combined miles on city streets.

When Google's driverless Prius captured the public's attention in 2011, it appeared that the team of people on Google's Chauffeur Project designed and built a functioning driverless car in just a few short years. While it's tempting to see Google's success as just another example of the company's seemingly magical ability to stay a few steps ahead of the rest of the industry, Google enjoyed several other advantages. One obvious advantage was funding. Google has a generous, multiyear R&D budget to throw at thorny engineering problems.

As a point of comparison, in 2007, Google's annual expenditures for research and development were a hefty $2.1 billion, or an estimated 12 percent of the company's annual revenue.[14] While it's not clear how much of that was allotted to driverless-car research, in contrast, that same year, DARPA gave each competing team roughly $1 million apiece to outfit their vehicle with the pricey technological gear it required (and to buy free pizza for the students contributing their time to the team).

Another advantage Google enjoyed was lots of top-notch personnel. DARPA's investment in the series of challenges created a pool of talent and brainpower that was mined by recruiters for Google's Chauffeur Project, which was launched in 2007. In fact, Sebastian Thrun was hired by Google shortly after the final DARPA Challenge.

Later in an interview, Thrun described how Google built its team of experts by "cherry-pick[ing] the top talent from the Grand Challenges. ... Then they branched out to prodigies of other sorts."[15] Once the rich vein of talent drawn to the DARPA Challenge was mined out, Google lured away more of the world's best and brightest (and highly paid) experts from a number of different fields, such as machine learning, robotics, interface design, and laser technology.

Some of the Grand Challenge alumni that Google hired designed the company's first-generation autonomous Prius. DARPA Challenge veteran Anthony Levandowski, famous for creating the world's first "driverless motorcycle" while a student at Berkeley, cofounded a company after graduation called 510 Systems. Shortly afterward, 510 Systems was hired by the Discovery Channel in 2008 to transform a Prius into an autonomous pizza-delivery robot.

The "Pribot" delivery succeeded and Google took notice. Bryon Majusiak, an employee of 510 recalls: "From then on, we started doing a lot of work with Google. ... We did almost all of their hardware integration. They were just doing software. We'd get the cars and develop the [low-level] controllers, and they'd take it from there." Several autonomous Priuses later, in 2011, Google bought 510 Systems, lock, stock, and barrel.[16]

Money and the right staff are certainly critical success factors in large and ambitious engineering projects. But there's a third reason that Google's cars were able to outperform earlier attempts: time to prepare. Machine-learning software, like teenagers, needs time to learn to drive. The cars that competed in the different DARPA Challenges were the fruit of a mere 12–18 months of hard intellectual labor by students, professors, and professional engineering teams.

Because of the way the rules of the DARPA Challenges were structured, none of the participating teams had the luxury of years of development time, nor the opportunity to privately test their software on the actual race course. To ensure that no participant gained an unfair advantage, DARPA intentionally prevented competing teams from rehearsing their robotic cars on the streets and roads of the shuttered air force bases (or deserts) where the competitions took place. Instead, teams refined their machine vision software without knowing the exact details of the obstacles and situations their car would encounter in the actual race.

On race day, participants put their reputations on the line and publicly demonstrated their cars. In contrast, determined to uphold its public image of a software company known for providing rapid and eerily accurate insights into data, Google conducted its initial driverless engineering experiments in private. Its early technological failures—whatever they might have been—will never see the light of day or be painfully documented in the media. By the time Google's fleet of Priuses were finally publicly unveiled in 2011, they were honed to near perfection and could perform flawlessly.

Several advantages, including a big research budget, talented developers, and the time to prepare in private have enabled Google to create a fleet of driverless cars that seemed to work on their first try. Important as these factors have been, we wonder whether there's actually another more mundane reason for Google's success: timing, the fact that between 2007 and 2011, the invisible, but powerful forces of Moore's Law and recombinant innovation were in full swing. Today, driverless cars are finally hitting their stride, guided by intelligent software that's fed by data from high-speed digital cameras, high-definition digital maps, radar, lidar, and GPS devices.

9

ANATOMY OF A DRIVERLESS CAR

Driverless cars "see" and "hear" by taking in real-time data that flows in from several different types of on-board sensors. Cars recognize their current location using a GPS device and a high-definition stored digital map. Lets take an in-depth look at the suite of hardware devices that provide data to the car's operating system.

HIGH-DEFINITION DIGITAL MAPS

Humans learn their way around a new neighborhood by recognizing distinctive landmarks. Driverless cars find their way around with a GPS, with visual sensors, and by following a high-definition (HD) digital map, a detailed and precise model of a region's most important surface features. Driverless cars use machine-learning software to deal with real-time traffic situations, and rich, detailed, and constantly updated high-definition digital maps to handle longer term navigation.

A driverless car knows its ballpark location by looking up its GPS coordinates on a high-definition digital map. GPS coordinates, however, tend to be a few feet off the mark, making them insufficient for autonomous driving. Driverless-car designers have come up with different techniques to compensate for the inability of GPS data to pinpoint the car's exact location. The operating system of early driverless cars placed more weight on stored data from digital maps and less on real-time GPS and sensed data. As the performance of machine-learning software and visual sensors—particularly digital cameras—improves, it's increasingly common for a car's operating system to calculate its current location by relying on visual cues in the flow of real-time sensor data that depicts the nearby environment.

HD maps differ from standard digital maps in their degree of detail. An HD map depicts both big geographical features, such as mountains and lakes, and minor topographic details, such as the presence of trees and sidewalks. An HD map for a driverless car focuses on the static surface details of a road or intersection, for example, its lane markings, intersections, construction zones, and road signs.

Traditional maps created for human eyes were two-dimensional pictorial depictions of a particular place where notable landmarks were indicated by static labels. In contrast, HD digital maps have a concealed powerful back-end. While an HD map usually offers its user a pictorial depiction of the region, behind the scenes, it's actually a database that contain millions of

Figure 9.1
High-definition map of an intersection, overlaid with sensor data.
Source: HERE

stored entries of topographical details, each logged along with other relevant details such as its geographical location, size, and orientation.

The brain of the average human houses a high-quality local map. In fact, our brains enjoy an "auto-update" and "auto-correct" capacity that any software engineer or digital cartographer would envy. Updating a high-definition digital map is a laborious process that involves exhaustively driving around with several cameras and *lidar* (laser radar) sensors, a process we will discuss in detail later in this chapter.

DIGITAL CAMERAS

Digital maps are stored, static data that help identify a car's location. In contrast, digital cameras are the equivalent of human eyes, capturing the visual environment outside the car in a stream of real-time data. As digital camera technology continues to get faster and more precise, roboticists have eagerly harnessed these rapid advancements to improve the performance of mid-level control software.

Just two decades ago, Apple's Quicktake 100 was considered a cutting-edge digital camera. The QuickTake, manufactured by Kodak, was famed for its portability and the fact that it could store eight 640 × 480 color images at a time (while weighing in at a dainty 16 ounces). Today an average consumer camera can take thirty high-resolution images a second.

It's important to understand how digital cameras work, since the structure of a digital image feeds directly into the deep-learning software. A digital camera gathers light through a lens in the form of photons. Each photon carries a certain amount of energy. As the photons stream through the camera's lens, they land on a silicon wafer that's made up of a grid of tiny individual photoreceptor cells.

Each photoreceptor absorbs its share of photons and translates the photons into electrons, which are stored as electrical charges. The brighter the stream of light, the higher the number of photons and the stronger the electrical charge. The amount of light hitting the grid of photoreceptors is then transformed into a format a computer can understand: a collection of numbers on a grid that represent the location of each individual "picture element," or *pixel*. JPEGS, GIFs, and all other image files are just different ways of storing this array of light intensities.

Digital cameras borrow some concepts from mammalian eyes. The silicon sensor is somewhat analogous to the retina: in both, visual data is broken up into several smaller units in order to be processed. On the retina, millions of specialized biological photoreceptor cells called *rods* and *cones* absorb photons and convert the energy into neural signals that are sent to the brain to be processed into visual information.

In the human eye rods and cones are arranged in a random fashion, densely packed in the center of the retina and less densely packed around the edges. In contrast, in a silicon sensor inside a digital camera, individual pixels are arranged in a rectangular pattern with regular spacing. A one megapixel camera contains a silicon sensor that has an array of 1000×1000 individual photoreceptors that correspond to a total of 1,000,000 pixels.

Some specialized digital cameras used for autonomous driving do more than just record pixel values. Rather than outputting an array of raw numbers direct from the silicon sensor's grid of pixels, advanced automotive cameras also analyze the image data in real time, inside the camera's hardware. This way, image processing is faster and the camera can eliminate irrelevant information before sending it upstream to the mid-level control software.

More sophisticated automotive cameras take it one step further and begin the process of making sense of what's contained in the images by making a list of objects being detected and tabulating the result. For example, an automotive camera will describe a scene, "1. There's a pedestrian in the upper left corner, moving left at a speed of 1.23 meters per second. 2. Far right, fire hydrant. Static. 3. Left lane, truck approaching at a speed of 5 meters per second 4. Southeast, unidentified object. Static."

Figure 9.2

What your eye sees (left) versus what the cameras sees (right). Can you tell the difference between the human and the background just by looking at the numbers?
Source: Photo of Manhattan 14th Street, looking west from Fifth Avenue; Wikipedia.

Biological life forms have two (or more) eyes placed side by side, an adaptation that enables depth perception, or what biologists call *stereo vision*. Digital cameras, however, do not have stereo vision, a limitation that has been one of the biggest problems in their application to autonomous driving. Digital cameras capture information on the intensity of light into a grid of pixels, an elegant way to digitally capture a three-dimensional world into a two-dimensional format. What gets omitted during this capture process, unfortunately, is a piece of information critical in enabling depth perception: how far away objects are from the camera.

Several different techniques are being explored to overcome this inherent limitation. One solution is to place multiple digital cameras on the same car. On a driverless car, many cameras are strategically placed to capture the same scene from slightly different viewing angles, a placement that enables the car's on-board computer to reconstruct a 3-D model of the scene, enabling better understanding of the surrounding space.

Another potential solution is structured-light cameras that use a camera-projector combo that augments image data with depth information. To emulate depth perception, structured-light cameras project a pattern onto a scene and measure its distortion. By the degree of distortion, a structured-light camera can calculate depth. While structured-light cameras like the XBOX Kinect are great for indoor applications such as interactive video games, it's not clear yet whether they'll find a home in driverless cars.

One of the biggest weaknesses of structured light cameras is that while they offer rapid depth perception, they don't work so well during daylight hours, since the reflected light pattern can get muddled by natural light. Nor do they work well beyond about ten meters, a potentially fatal shortcoming when placed on speeding vehicles. Because of these limitations, the best application for structured-light cameras is in indoor settings, perhaps guiding driverless cars through parking garages, or inside the car's cabin, sensing the physical whereabouts and movements of the car's passengers.

Digital cameras continue to improve by leaps and bounds, yet ironically they have a low-tech Achilles heel: dirt. Even the best automotive digital camera will be rendered blind by a splash of muddy water. Roadside dust, sand, bird droppings, bugs, and other indignities of outdoor driving can render useless the most sophisticated digital cameras and machine-vision software. Perhaps the solution will be similarly low-tech—equipping on-board cameras with their own cleaning mechanism similar to the windshield wiper that human drivers rely on, or tears and eyelids that their human counterparts use.

Many of the solutions to the limitations of digital cameras will eventually lie in the car's operating system. To ensure its on-board cameras are clean and dry, each driverless car should be equipped with a software tool that executes a periodic self-test on the quality of the data from the digital cameras. As the artificial-intelligence software that guides the car's mid-level control software continues to improve, someday it will have the ability to autocorrect faulty visual data, helping a car see in conditions that would blind a human driver, such as fog, heavy rain, and blinding sun.

LIGHT DETECTION AND RANGING (LIDAR)

Another primary image sensor is the *lidar*, an acronym of "light detection and ranging," also called *laser radar*. A digital camera works by breaking down the three-dimensional visual world into a two-dimensional matrix of pixels. In contrast, a lidar device "spray paints" its surroundings with intense beams of pulsed light, measures how long it takes for each of those beams to bounce back, and then calculates a three-dimensional digital model of its nearby physical environment.

Like digital cameras, lidar sensors have also followed the Moore's Law trajectory, morphing from gigantic and expensive stationary devices in the 1960s to today's robust and portable devices. Unlike digital cameras, however, lidar sensors are still more expensive than the average person can afford. While their cost is dropping each year, in 2016 a sixteen-channel lidar sensor made by a company called Velodyne, weighing 600 grams and accurate to within a few centimeters, cost $8,000.

Lidar sensors have been used for decades by surveyors to capture the topographic details of parcels of land. The notion of mounting a device onto a moving vehicle to shoot laser beams into the environment is a more recent innovation. During the early years of robotic autonomous vehicles before the advent of modern digital cameras, lidar was the gold-standard sensor for visual data in autonomous vehicles. In all three DARPA Challenges, lidar played a critical role in capturing the visual scene in front of the car. The iconic cones on top of Google's first-generation fleet of self-driving Priuses were lidar sensors.

Lidar sensors have been a crucial tool in driverless cars since the 3-D digital model they generate is highly detailed and contains accurate depth perception. They work by sending one or more laser beams into the surrounding environment and recording the time it takes for the laser signal to reflect off of the object. Since light travels at a speed of about one foot per billionth of a second, a lidar sensor with gigahertz speed microprocessors can measure depth at single-centimeter resolution.

A laser beam is an ideal measurement tool. Unlike a candle or an incandescent lamp, which radiates light in all directions, a laser beam shines in a straight line for a great distance. The laser beam does not spread out like light from a flashlight; it remains collimated—that is, parallel—no matter whether it's striking an object just a few feet or dozens or yards away.

To create a full 3-D digital image of the surrounding environment, a lidar sensor spins its laser beams around and around at high speeds. A set of rotating mirrors deflects the laser beam in a rotational scanning motion. A lidar sensor, like a digital camera, can vary in resolution. Multiple beams can work together continuously to scan and measure the surrounding environment in parallel. The more laser beams there are in play, the higher the resolution of the resulting digital model of the scene.

Imagine a room full of ornately shaped but invisible objects. Then imagine taking a can of red spray paint and coating all the invisible objects with paint until they are fully visible. If you were armed only with a single can of paint, it would take you a long time to "see" the shape of the invisible objects. However, if several people had cans of red spray paint, the invisible objects would quickly be coated with paint, and therefore visible. Lidar sensors work much the same way.

In a driverless car, the data generated by a lidar is fed to software that arranges the information in a digital model called a *point cloud*. If the laser beams had been pointed straight up into the distant sky, the digital model would be blank, void of solid objects that would reflect the beam's light. If the laser beams were directed onto a city street during rush hour, however, the resulting point cloud would be full of interesting details.

Watching a digital point cloud emerge is somewhat akin to watching a hologram emerge in thin slices. The lidar's laser beams are aimed outward in a specific pattern. The spinning mirrors train the lasers into a series of rapid, horizontal passes over the road in front of the car. The digital point cloud that's built from lidar data is made up of lots of finely textured scan lines, each row in the digital model corresponding to one scan line of the spinning mirrors.

Figure 9.3 shows a point cloud generated by lidar. If you look closely, you can see the scan lines from the horizontal sweeps of the spinning mirrors. A casual observer might conclude that a lidar point cloud is pretty much the same thing as a digital image. In reality, a lidar point cloud and a digital photograph differ from one another in many ways.

One critical difference is that lidar sensors do not capture color information. The image shown above has a ghostly, romantic feel as if it were generated during a moonlight drive right after a snowstorm. In reality, the software that interpreted the point cloud adds the color, artificially, coding closer objects in blue tones and more distant objects in red ones. The black sky indicates

Figure 9.3
View of 3-D point cloud data captured from a lidar mounted on a car driving through a bustling intersection.
Source: Alex Kushleyev and Dan Lee, University of Pennsylvania

the absence of any physical object, or that the laser beam was not reflected back.

A second difference between lidar point clouds and a digital photograph is the point in time that's depicted. A spinning lidar sensor continually refreshes the digital model it generates. On the one hand, this is advantageous since the point cloud is constantly updated; on the other hand, however, the entire process is nowhere near the instantaneous "snap" of a digital camera. Lidar sensors are slow, and while highly effective for depicting the contours of a static landscape or a slow-moving traffic jam, they cannot feed visual data to a computer fast enough to provide the split-second reflexes needed in some emergency driving situations.

Today's driverless cars use both digital cameras and lidar. In the AI-poor world of decades past, lidar was the more essential visual sensor. Today, lidar sensors are expensive and slow compared to digital cameras, but the point clouds they generate can guide a moving car through the majority of routine driving environments.

In the past few years, digital cameras have finally come into their own as a tool for mobile robotics. The long-standing bottleneck that delayed the use of digital cameras as a machine-vision sensor was their poor 3-D perception. Unpacking arrays of pixels in order to process them requires vast amounts of computing power, which results in very poor real-time performance, a serious shortcoming in a mobile robot. As microprocessor speeds continue to improve the performance of both the digital camera and the software that processes the digital images, it's quite likely that digital cameras could replace lidar as the queen of the visual sensors.

Some experts agree. In a press conference in October 2015, Tesla CEO Elon Musk commented on technologies for Tesla's future driverless cars. "I don't think you need lidar. I think you can do this all with passive optical and then with maybe one forward RADAR," he said. "I think that completely solves it without the use of lidar. I'm not a big fan of lidar, I don't think it makes sense in this context."[1]

Chapter 9

RADIO DETECTION AND RANGING (RADAR)

In addition to cameras and lidar, driverless cars use radar sensors to "look" at the nearby environment. If digital cameras capture a scene in a pixelated grid and lidar sensors are the equivalent of a can of digital spray paint, a radar sensor is similar to the surface of a pond. The way a radar sensor works is reminiscent of the process of throwing stones into a body of water and keeping track of where the ensuing ripples go as they ricochet back and forth.

Radar has its roots in military applications. During World War II, radar towers were placed on beaches and fields to detect the approach of enemy aircraft, ships, and incoming missiles. After the war, air-traffic controllers used radar to track and confirm flight trajectories of commercial airliners. Many people have felt the direct effects of radar technology if they've ever received a speeding ticket from the highway patrol.

In another demonstration of Moore's Law, radar sensors have become small and robust enough to be mounted on a moving car. Radar sensors are used in modern human-driven cars in adaptive cruise control technology. A built-in radar device senses the speed and location of cars in front of and behind a car, so the cruise control can adjust the brake and gas pedal accordingly. Another

Figure 9.4

Raw target density plot of a forward-looking radar (left), and corresponding front view from the car (right). Large static objects are captured (parking cars, building barriers, street lamps). Gric based operation at 24Ghz.
Source: SmartMicro 3DHD

common driver-assist application for radar sensors is to warn a driver if another car is in his blind spot.

A radar sensor detects the presence of physical objects in the nearby environment using electromagnetic wave echo. A radar device sends out a series of electromagnetic waves that radiate outward. A radar sensor consists of a transmitter, the unit that sends out the electromagnetic waves, and a receiver, the device that awaits their return.

If the waves do not encounter an object in their path, the waves continue their circular expansion outward until they are lost in the distance. If they do encounter an object in their path, the wave ricochets off of it and changes direction. Since electromagnetic waves, also known as radio waves, travel at the speed of light, this entire process works very rapidly.

Radar sensors are increasingly sensitive and intelligent. Since the returning waves are significantly weaker than when they departed, the receiver uses amplification techniques to detect the whisper-quiet echo. To prevent the sensor from accidentally picking up the waves emitted by another nearby radar transmitter, the electromagnetic wave is sent out accompanied by a unique signature "chirp."

Waves convey a surprising amount of information. Shape and timing of the reflected waves provide insight into the reflecting object's shape and what material it is made of. Some radar sensors can calculate which direction a reflecting object is moving by analyzing changes in the frequency of the reflecting wave.

The wavelength of an electromagnetic wave is the distance from the crest of one wave to the crest of the one behind it. Different radar sensors employ different wavelengths. Waves spaced further apart—long wavelengths—travel farther. Yet since they are more likely to overlook small objects in the environment, they tend to offer a less precise reading of what's in the nearby environment. Short-range radar sensors that send microwaves into the distance can detect objects as small as a cat or as thin as a bicycle.

Electromagnetic waves reflect best off surfaces that have high electric conductivity—think smooth, glossy surfaces such as those of a shiny metal bicycle or a wet road surface. Nonconductive objects, things made of porous plastic or wood, appear relatively "transparent" to the radar and are more difficult to detect. Fortunately, most cars, even those made up of a lot of plastic parts, have plenty of metal in them, and hence are easily detectable to a radar sensor.

A radar sensor can "look" only in a particular, narrow direction, so most radar sensors are mounted in arrays that overlap slightly. On a driverless car, a typical configuration will be that three radars will be mounted side by side in a way that gives them good 180-degree coverage of the field of view. For autonomous driving, the great advantage of radar sensors is that, unlike cameras, they can "see" through fog, rain, dust, sand, and even blinding headlights.

Another advantage is that electromagnetic waves travel easily through nonconductive and thin materials, so they're not going to be distracted by a plastic bag blowing across the highway or a tumbleweed. Electromagnetic waves prefer larger objects, therefore they "notice" bulky obstacles that drivers care about. Conversely, the biggest drawback of a radar sensor is its relatively low resolution.

Another advantage of a radar sensor is that it can detect not just the position of an object, but (much to the chagrin of speeding drivers) also its speed, using the *Doppler effect*, named after the nineteenth-century Austrian physicist Christian Doppler. One of the most commonly observed manifestations of the Doppler effect is when a person standing near the side of a highway hears the "ZZZZOOOOooom" of a fast-approaching car that suddenly drops in pitch as the car speeds past. The sudden drop in pitch happens because the sound waves emitted by a speeding engine get compressed (sounding higher pitched) as the car speeds closer. After the car roars past, the sound waves expand, resulting in a lower pitch.

Radar sensors use the Doppler effect to track the speed of moving objects. By recording the change in frequency between outgoing and incoming electromagnetic waves, a radar sensor can determine if the sensed object is approaching or moving away. The sensor can also calculate the object's speed. This velocity information is helpful for classifying exactly what a sensed object is. Something moving along the roadside at thirty miles an hour is probably not a human pedestrian.

On a driverless car, radar detectors complement the visual sensors in figuring out the surrounding environment. By sensing the size, density, speed, and direction of nearby objects, the radar sensor passes along useful information that can be compared against the images from the digital camera and the 3-D point cloud from the lidar sensor. Is that small object sitting by the side of the road a cat or an empty cardboard box? Watch out! A big metal box-like object is tailgating us!

Today's radar detectors are much smarter than their ancestors. The radar of WWII displayed the raw analog echo signal on a greenish screen, with a rotating line representing the current scanning direction. Similar to the process used by advanced cameras, a modern radar sensor processes raw information into a *target list* consisting of objects, along with their size, location, and speed. That information is much more compact, requires less bandwidth to communicate, and is easier for the driverless "brain" to digest.

In order not to over-report, radars try to omit the presence of the road pavement itself from the list of sensed objects, even though the tarmac reflects waves. For this reason, some radar sensors automatically eliminate any nonmoving object from the report. While eliminating static objects from the target list is more efficient, it has its risks. The radar could overlook something large and deadly such as a stalled car parked under a bridge by assuming that the static car is merely part of the bridge's infrastructure.

ULTRASONIC SENSORS (SONARS)

If lidar and cameras are the equivalent of human eyes, sonar is like a human ear. Sonar is the close-range cousin of radar. Like radar, a device emits waves and detects their echoes, but sonar uses sound waves instead of radar's electromagnetic waves. The term *sonar* combines "sound navigation" and "radar."

A sonar sensor detects the position and speed of objects based on the time, frequency, and shape of sound waves reflecting off their surfaces. A sonar device is composed of two subunits: an emitter and a receiving sensor. The emitter generates sound waves that have a frequency above 20 kHz, a sound beyond the range of human hearing. The receiver listens for the echoes from the emitted sound waves and processes them.

Sonar sensor share many of the benefits and drawbacks of lidar and radar. Like radar sensors, they can see through fog and dust, and they are not blinded by sun. Since sound waves travel much more slowly than electromagnetic waves, they can see much smaller objects at much higher resolution. But because their energy decays rapidly with distance and wind, sonar can detect objects only at a much closer range. Sonar therefore often complements radar for applications that require close-range precision detection, such as parking.

GLOBAL POSITIONING SYSTEMS (GPS)

So far, we've covered digital maps and sensors. One of the more critical technologies of mobile robotics is neither map nor sensor, although it plays an essential role in guiding a driverless car. A *global positioning system* (GPS) device supplies coordinates to pin down a car's exact location on its HD digital map.

GPS is another decades-old technology with roots in the military that, following Moore's Law, has blossomed into a reliable, low-cost consumer appliance. Just a few decades ago, the typical GPS receiver was the size of a refrigerator; today they are small chips that can be embedded into cell phones, cameras, laptops, and cars.

GPS devices are miracles of advanced engineering that listen to signals from satellites rotating in the heavens. A GPS receiver in your car or cell phone determines your latitude and longitude by listening to beeps that arrive from a family of satellites spinning high above the earth. Each satellite follows an exactly prescribed orbit, all the while emitting a steady stream of electric pulses precisely once a second.

Twenty-four satellites provide GPS signals, but the GPS receiver needs only four to calculate its own location on Earth. Each satellite emits its own unique signature beep, which enables the GPS receiver to attribute a particular beep to its satellite of origin. As beeps stream into the GPS receiver, the receiver listens carefully. By calculating the time lapse between beeps, a GPS receiver is able to calculate its own exact location using a mathematical process known as *triangulation*. If beeps from two satellites arrive at exactly the same time, then the GPS receiver knows that it must be somewhere on the bisector plane that is half way between them. A total of four satellites are needed to pinpoint exactly where the receiver is; additional satellite signals refine the position even further.

In a normal driving environment, a typical GPS receiver is accurate to a distance of about four meters, or roughly thirteen feet.[2] If the location information GPS receivers provide were perfect and up-to-date, the job of building a driverless car would be much easier. Unfortunately, satellite signals can be blocked or delayed as a result of atmospheric turbulence, clouds, or rain, which can result in an inaccurate calculation.

Another serious problem in urban driving is that of reflected pulses. If you have ever used a GPS receiver in Manhattan, you've experienced what happens when satellite pulses bounce off tall skyscrapers. The confused GPS begins to go berserk, informing you of a new location position every few minutes in a seemly random fashion. What's happening is that pulses arriving from satellites ricochet off tall skyscrapers, giving the GPS receiver an illusion that the pulses are arriving at a slightly different time. This *urban canyon effect* can mislead even the best GPS receivers.

THE INNER EAR (IMU)

GPS failure can be catastrophic. The solution to the potentially deadly problem of losing satellite reception is another descendent of military technology, a device that serves two critical functions: it compensates for GPS inaccuracies, and it serves as a driverless car's "inner ear," sensing, literally, which way is up.

An *inertial measurement unit* (IMU) is a multipurpose device that serves several functions. An IMU contains acceleration and orientation sensors that keep track of the car's position, which way it's nose is pointing, whether the tires on the left side are level with those on the right, and so on. A modern IMU is a complex bundle of devices including an odometer, accelerometer, gyroscope, and compass, whose combined data is fused together and parsed with sophisticated estimation algorithms.

An IMU is a unique sensor in that its purview is confined to the car's own body. Humans have a set of roughly equivalent senses called *proprioceptive senses*. Proprioceptive senses, unlike our outer-facing ones such as sight and hearing, keep track of what's going on inside our bodies. The sense of balance is a proprioceptive sense. If you close your eyes in a train leaving the station, the sense of acceleration you feel, knowing you're moving forward without visual confirmation, is another proprioceptive sense.

To keep track of a car's exact location between GPS readings and to compensate for GPS inaccuracies, an IMU uses an ancient navigational technique known as *dead reckoning*. For centuries, mariners navigated the open seas by referencing the location of the stars. Problems arose, however, during stretches of stormy weather, when the stars were hidden behind a layer of clouds. Dead reckoning enabled sailors to calculate their ship's location by measuring how far their ship had traveled since the last time they saw the stars. By measuring relative, rather than absolute, geographical location, sailors could keep their ship mostly on course until the skies cleared and the stars were once again visible to guide them.

Dead reckoning worked as follows. During a stretch of cloudy weather, sailors would drop a rope with regularly spaced knots over the back of the ship as it sailed forward. They would count how quickly the knots on the rope flew overboard, which enabled the sailors to calculate their ship's speed. Even today the rate at which a ship is moving forward is measured in *knots*. Once sailors knew how fast their ship was moving and in which direction (using a compass), even without seeing the stars, they could calculate how far their ship had traveled from their last known location, a navigation point known as a *fix*.

On a driverless car, the IMU uses a similar approach when a car goes into a tunnel or travels through an urban canyon that blocks satellite signals. Rather than counting the rate at which knots on a rope slide overboard, the IMU uses its odometer to count the number of wheel revolutions from its last known location. Although wheel revolutions are a fairly precise mechanical action to count, the tally still accumulates uncertainty. The tires might slip as tire pressure changes or if the car changes lanes several times. On a curving segment of highway, the odometer reading might wind up with a different wheel revolution count depending on whether the car had driven on the inner or outer lane, a difference that, depending on distance traveled, can add up to tens of meters.

Since a simple odometer read from the fix isn't perfectly accurate, an IMU brings in its accelerometer sensor to help address the problem. When a car is traveling at a constant speed, its acceleration—perhaps counterintuitively—is recorded as zero. Its acceleration varies only when the car increases its speed, slows down, or suddenly changes direction.

To calculate how far the car has driven since the GPS signal failed, the IMU combines data from the accelerometer and the odometer. An accelerometer, however, does not provide insight into which direction the car is driving. That's where the compass comes in. An IMU paired with a GPS and a compass is a powerful and foolproof combination. But the IMU is more than just a pinch-hitter when the GPS fails. The IMU also provides a driverless car with a sense of balance.

Roboticists call a robot's orientation in space its *pose*. A car's pose is a measurement of which direction its nose is pointed and to what degree its body is tilted. To measure pose, we need to add another sensor to the bundle that makes up the IMU: a gyroscope. A gyroscope is a spinning wheel—either mechanical or, in some cases, optical—that is used to measure pose.

The IMU needs three pieces of information to measure and track the car's physical orientation in space: which direction it's

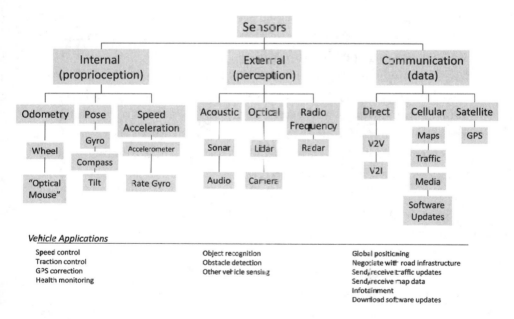

Figure 9.5

Key sensors used in driverless cars. Most autonomous vehicles use multiples and combinations of some of these sensors.

facing, at what angle its nose is tilted up or down, and at what angle it's tilted to the side. Once again, the ancient art of nautical navigation has left its imprint on the modern IMU. Ancient ship-builders and modern aerospace engineers alike call these three different dimensions of a vehicle's (or ship's) orientation *yaw* (the degree to which a vehicle is turned left and right), *pitch* (how high or low the ship or vehicle's noise points), and *roll* (how much it is tilting side to side).

That a car understand its own pose is an important safety feature, even if the GPS device is working just fine. Imagine an icy road where a car starts to skid. Its yaw measurement rapidly spins from zero to 360. As it skids downhill, its pitch shifts forward. If the downhill skid continues and two of its wheels leave the road, the car will begin to roll. Many modern cars have a built-in IMU that measures the car's roll, pitch, and yaw in real time and feeds this data into software that can help the car right itself, unlock its brakes during a skid, or send out a call for distress if it is tipping precariously. Since the IMU tracks the car's motions, it can respond by tightening seatbelts or dynamically stabilizing the shock absorbers on the car's wheels.

The modern IMU is another example of the effect of Moore's Law. IMUs developed during World War II, before the advent of silicon chips, were elaborate mechanical devices that were built to calculate optimal launch trajectories for rockets. In the 1980s, IMU technology was transformed by software and the invention of tiny sensors called *micro electro-mechanical systems* (MEMS) devices. The invention of MEMS technology changed IMUs from expensive and highly specialized devices used in space travel and military operations, into relatively tiny, affordable navigational units.

A high-end IMU that's precise enough for commercial ships and submarines costs about a million dollars, but Moore's Law is relentlessly driving down their cost. Simple IMU's are inside every cell phone. Most smartphones can tell which direction the cell phone is pointing using a built in compass. If you're stuck on a long flight and watching your fellow passengers play with their iPads, when they shake or jiggle to control a bouncy video game avatar, they're using IMU technology.

Regardless of the price, the biggest weakness of the technology is that an IMU can't work without a GPS for long without gradually drifting off course. The calculations from the various sensors contain tiny inaccuracies that become a problem when they accumulate over time. Without the guidance of accurate satellite data, like an ancient ship navigating through weeks of cloud-covered night skies, even high-end IMUs gradually wander off course.

DRIVE BY WIRE

The driverless car's sensors—its digital cameras, lidar, radar, sonar, and IMU devices—supply a steady stream of real-time data. The magic happens when these data streams are merged so the car's operating system can process the data. As we covered in previous chapters, the car's operating system uses several types of artificial-intelligence techniques to make rapid-fire decisions. The final step is converting these decisions into actual physical motions such as turning the steering mechanism or pressing the brake or gas pedal.

In the old days, engineers transformed a regular car into a driverless car by retrofitting it with special custom-built mechanical "drive by wire" contraptions that substituted for human hands and feet. These contraptions, called *actuators*, had to actually swivel the steering wheel or compress the brake pedal. Building accurate and reliable mechanical actuators was an engineering specialty of its own, nearly as complex a process as that of creating workable artificial intelligence to guide the car.

As car subsystems have become progressively more automated over the past two decades, the work of creating artificial driving "muscles" has gotten considerably easier. Computer-guided controls have replaced hydraulic and mechanical controls. Most modern cars have several computer-guided subsystems (that is, low-level controls) that contain embedded microprocessors that run several millions of lines of code. These days, a roboticist rigging up a driverless car, rather than creating a special mechanical "foot" to press a gas pedal, simply tinkers with the car's electrical system.

Software is the ghost in the machine. A driverless car translates instructions from its operating system to its high-, low-, and mid-level controls using an electronic communication system. Today, the average human-driven car contains several subsystems—for example, the *engine control unit* (ECU), the *antilock braking system* (ABS), and the *transmission control unit* (TCU). These subsystems communicate with each other using a *bus*.

In computer lingo, a bus is a communication channel that transfers data from one component inside a computer to another. Fittingly, a city bus and a computer data bus have a similar etymological origin, both deriving from the Latin word *omnibus*, meaning "for all." Like a city bus that delivers people from place to place, in a driverless car a data bus transfers data between different subsystems, similar to the *universal serial bus* (USB) that yokes together your computer's mouse, keyboard, and printer.

Many vehicles today use the *CAN bus* protocol (CAN stands for "controller area network") that ferries data back and forth at a rate of approximately 1 megabit per second (Mbps). The CAN bus protocol is a "point-to-point" protocol governed by the international standards ISO 11898 and 11519. The fact that it's held to a publicly open standard means that any device that can plug into the CAN bus and "understand" the protocol can chime in to the conversation between the car's modules.

Car companies will not normally advertise their specific control protocols publicly. However, they often share that information with other manufacturers that require access to vehicle's controls to install a new built-in device. Or, they may share a detailed description of network protocols with an automotive manufacturer that sells a vehicle chassis to another carmaker that builds RVs, for example.

In an automotive CAN bus, as in any network, key challenges are the network's bandwidth and its reliability. *Bandwidth* is the maximum rate at which data can be transferred through the wires that make up the network, a metric that's usually measured in bits per second (bps). In a wireless network, physical wires are replaced by radio waves, or frequency channels. A network's bandwidth is determined by the speed of the microprocessors that encode and decode the electric pulses sent along the wires or channels, and how many parallel channels are available in the bus.

Bandwidth is important in any network, but the speed of a network inside a moving car is even more critical. Most networks save time by using a set of agreed-upon codes to represent specific actions. For example, imagine that a driverless car's software just issued a command, "BRAKE!" The car's software would have ready a specific two-digit number that means "BRAKE," which it would send through the network to the braking subsystem. Because a two-digit number is a small and efficient unit of meaning, it would take the system only about sixteen microseconds to transmit and receive the message.

Sixteen microseconds is an acceptable response time for a driverless car. It is about a thousand times faster than a blink of an eye, which takes about 100–400 milliseconds.[3] Although a CAN bus can rapidly stream tiny units of data, bandwidth challenges arise in a driverless car when the car's CAN bus is asked to handle data streams that pour from its various sensor systems.

The system slows down when streaming large globs of real-time data from the car's sensors. On a network that passes along data at a rate of one million bits per second, it will take an endless eight seconds to send a one-megabyte image from a camera to the car's mid-level control software module. If you imagine adding to the network load the data flowing in from the car's other sensors it quickly becomes apparent that a million bits per second isn't fast enough for driving. Under the load of real-time visual data, the car's CAN bus would wind up limping along at a response speed unacceptable for real-world driving situations.

At some point in the future, automakers will need to agree on a robust and transparent communications standard for driverless cars that can handle large amounts of streaming sensor data and is resistant to data breaches. In other words, driverless cars need a high-bandwidth bus. On any network there are basically two ways to resolve communication bottlenecks: one, by increasing the number of electrical wires or channels available and streaming data through in parallel streams; and two, by using a compression algorithm to compact large chunks of data into more compact and therefore more efficient units. The point of compression can take place at the sensor level. For example, some automotive cameras contain built-in software that analyzes the images in real time and sends along only the information the camera considers relevant.

In addition to bandwidth, reliability is another critical characteristic of an on-board automotive network. Network reliability takes several forms. One is the ability to withstand hackers. A CAN bus can become a battlefield if a malevolent third party creates a device that interferes with the network's ability to transmit data, somewhat like a belligerent and unruly guest who interferes with the polite conversation at the dinner table. A truly malevolent device could do more than just interfere; it could hijack control of the car once it gained access to its on-board network.

Another facet of reliability is the network's tolerance of errors and its ability to correct ones caused by network noise. The CAN bus on a driverless car needs to use error-correction protocols that are as resilient and efficient as those used by aircraft avionics. Driving should be as smooth a process as downloading a music file, and more secure than the process of making a financial transaction.

Imagine the carnage that would result if a driverless car's software sent along a message along the bus saying "increase throttle by 1 percent" which was misinterpreted by the fuel injector subsystem as "increase throttle by 100 percent." To prevent such errors of miscommunication, an error-correction protocol provides oversight similar to that offered by a calm yet stern proofreader, double-checking the content of every message sent. Subsystems on a driverless CAN bus need to trust one another. A good communication protocol also enables subsystems to verify that the message they received was actually the message sent.

Given how vulnerable we humans are to malevolent attacks when we're speeding along inside a vehicle—whether autonomous or human-driven—one would assume that carmakers would carefully encrypt the communication protocols on the CAN bus. Unfortunately, a security mindset has not yet taken root in the automotive industry.[4] The modern car is not that difficult to hack into, perhaps because, in the past, some car owners delighted in tinkering with their car engine.

Some of a car's vulnerability is intentional. Most cars have a physical connector called the *on-board diagnostics* (OBD) jack that mechanics plug into to diagnose mechanical problems. The OBD jack can be used by hobbyists to plug their own devices into the CAN bus. The physical port for the jack is typically hidden somewhere near the steering column. Carmakers consider the jack to be secure because it is inside the car's cabin, and is therefore accessible only to people who have a key to the car.

Several commercial products take advantage of the fact that the OBD jack offers an easy window into a car's operational back panel. One ingenious product called DASH[5] is a phone app that uses Bluetooth to connect to the car's diagnostics, or as the company's advertising proclaims, "give your car a voice." The way DASH works is that it "eavesdrops" on the CAN bus, tracking how many times a driver presses the brake or gas pedal.

DASH is a well-intentioned device that's intended to help car owners drive more efficiently. It also aggregates the data and lets municipalities know statistics such as where on their roads drivers tend to hit the brake or swerve abruptly. The problem with devices such as DASH is privacy. As DASH knows everything about your driving habits, your car becomes as intriguing to bosses and marketers as your web browsing habits.

Are we there yet? From the point of view of the hardware sensors that provide the data, the answer is a resounding "yes." The quality and cost of today's sensor suite is more than adequate for driverless cars. In fact, as Moore's Law continues to prevail, sensors will continue to become faster, cheaper, and better at exponential rates, doubling their sensitivity and halving their costs every so many months. Now let's turn our attention back to software and delve into one missing piece of the puzzle that is finally falling into place: deep-learning technology, the crown jewel of the control software that guides a robot's artificial perception and response.

10

DEEP LEARNING: THE FINAL PIECE OF THE PUZZLE

Deep-learning software is a key catalyst behind recent advances in driverless-car performance and safety. Remember the challenges of object recognition and scene understanding? Deep-learning software is breaking down decades-old barriers in artificial intelligence research, demonstrating human-level capacity to recognize objects in digital images, even when the objects are depicted in unusual contexts or in varying levels of light.

We may be finally seeing the resolution of Moravec's paradox, as roboticists and computer scientists find creative new ways to apply deep learning to automate artificial perception and response. Since 2012, deep learning has given driverless cars the ability to "see," and has improved the language comprehension of speech-recognition software. In a high-profile demonstration of its power and versatility, in 2016, deep-learning software enabled Google's AlphaGo program to trounce the world's best players of go, a board game considered by many to be more challenging than chess. To encourage third-party developers to build intelligent applications using their software tools, Google, Microsoft, and Facebook have each launched their own version of an open source deep-learning development platform.

Despite its usefulness, it has taken decades for deep-learning software to develop. Like other types of machine-learning software, a deep-learning network is data driven, consuming huge amounts of visual data in the form of digital images or videos. Improved performance, enabled by the recent maturation of enabling technologies such as high-speed computers and digital cameras, isn't the only reason deep-learning software has recently gained acceptance, however. The other reason is political. For decades, the development of artificial neural networks—the technology underlying deep-learning software—was slowed to a glacial pace by a series of periodic ideological deep freezes in university computer science departments.

Since its emergence as a formal field of research in the 1950s, the field of artificial-intelligence research has been an ideological war zone. Since no one really understands how the brain works, for centuries, philosophers have waged fierce scholarly battles over the mysteries of the human mind. What is the difference between brain and mind? What is intelligence? What is knowledge? In modern academe, those who toil to build artificial brains find themselves wrestling with the same thorny questions that centuries of philosophers have failed to answer.

In the formal study of human knowledge, researchers tend to align themselves with a particular school of thought that they dedicate much of their career to defending. The study of artificial knowledge follows a similar dynamic, except, of course, the competing schools of thought take a somewhat different form. To someone outside the university, scholarly debates about the superiority of one approach to artificial intelligence versus another seem like battles over abstractions. To someone inside the field, these debates are not abstract at all, but actually cloak a very concrete struggle over scarce resources.

As young AI researchers quickly learn, the particular school of thought they align themselves with will determine the trajectory of their careers. One way professors and researchers define the boundaries of what's considered acceptable research is by deeming some approaches to AI more "rigorous" than others. Not surprisingly, only research on "rigorous" forms of AI is considered worthy of publication. In turn, a graduate student's ability to publish her work determines whether she gets a job at a prestigious university. Once employed, her ongoing publication record determines whether she receives federal funding to continue her AI research, which in turn, enables her to make a strong case for tenure.

Over the past several decades, neural network research has come in and out of ideological favor in university computer science departments. AI researchers who dedicated themselves to its pursuit knew they were perhaps embarking on a risky career path. During the periods in which research on neural networks was not viewed as worthwhile, federal research funding would dry up. During these lean years that came to be known as "AI winters," neural network researchers faced a difficult choice. They could choose to continue their work despite the chilly research climate, or they could shift gears and embrace another more fiscally and professionally rewarding form of artificial-intelligence research.

NEURAL NETWORKS

To understand the politics that have dogged the development of deep learning, it helps to understand the broader history of neural networks. In previous chapters we explored the limitations of artificial-intelligence software that attempts to automate perception by breaking down the world into a series of logical if-then statements. Neural networks research takes a different approach. Unlike logic-driven software, a neural network is modeled on the nervous system of humans and other animals. While we don't know exactly how the brain works we do know that it's composed of billions of cells called *neurons*. Neurons are the building blocks of the nervous system and are also found in the spinal cord and throughout the body.

Neurons regularly send signals to one another using an electrochemical process. A neuron consists of a cell body that receives incoming signals from other neurons via series of tiny branching dendrites. When the neuron's cell body receives a signal from another neuron, it sends the signal along a long appendage that resembles a dandelion root, the cell's *axon*. Axons thus convey signals from the cell body to other cells. The point of connection to other cells is called a *synaptic interface*. When a neuron fires, it release chemicals called *neurotransmitters* into these synapses.

In the brain, neurons "fire," or pass signals to one another, when they're activated by a particular stimulus. If a neuron in the eye's retina is activated by ray of light, it fires, releasing electrical energy that runs along its axon, which, in turn, signals the synapses to release neurotransmitters. Other neurons pick up on the released neurotransmitters and, in turn, activate several other neurons that activate others neurons, and so on.

Eventually, after a long series of activations, somewhere a neuron is activated at the highest executive level of the brain, the prefrontal cortex. Somewhere along that long chain of neurons touching each other, the magic happens and our conscious mind says "Aha! There's my friend!" Or, "Watch out! A bear!"

In a process that no one fully understands, the neurons in our brain somehow learn to fire only in response to an appropriate stimulus and to ignore stimuli that aren't relevant. This notion that connections between neurons either weaken or become stronger over time and experience is called *synaptic plasticity*. Some brain scientists believe that when a brain undergoes a positive experience, endorphins strengthen the connection between active neurons, while negative experiences inhibit or weaken these connections. The concept of synaptic plasticity plays a key role in neural-network research and is at the heart of deep learning.

To a neuron, the key question is "should I fire or not fire?" When a neuron is not sending a signal, it is at rest. When the network of neurons surrounding it sends along a signal, the neuron may or may not fire. Whether or not the neuron will fire depends on whether the strength of the cumulative signal it received from the other neurons was strong enough to reach a critical threshold. If the signal was just under the necessary threshold, then the cell would not fire at all, not even weakly.

This simple picture of how a network of neurons work is a gross oversimplification of how real biological neurons function. For purposes of artificial-intelligence research, however, it provides a foundation. Now let's turn to the role of artificial neural networks in computer vision.

There's no widely agreed upon birthday for artificial neural network research, but a good place to begin is the 1940s. In 1943, two electrical engineers, Warren McCulloch and Walter Pitts, published a paper that laid out a mathematical model for the first artificial neuron, called a *threshold logic unit*.[1] This simple model of what they described as a "nerve net" in the brain would later serve as the foundation for several types of artificial neural networks.

In 1949 psychologist Donald Hebb proposed a biological model of learning based on neural connections. Hebb postulated that brains learn when active connections between neurons are strengthened by positive reinforcement. Brains also learn when active connections between neurons are weakened by negative reinforcement. Hebb laid out this new theory of how the brain operates in his book *The Organization of Behavior.*

In what's commonly referred to as *Hebb's Law*, "neurons that fire together, wire together." Hebb's simple conjecture about synaptic plasticity was later dubbed *Hebbian learning*. Hebbian learning theory was applied to artificial neural networks and the science of training computers how to learn was born.

Today the field of artificial neural network research includes several different approaches that have in common a few core concepts. One is the idea that neurons are connected to one another in a decentralized network. Another is that the larger brain learns as the connections formed between individual neurons strengthen and weaken. A third is that, in order to fire, or pass along a signal to other neurons, a particular threshold must be reached. In artificial neural network research, these key concepts are fine-tuned in many different ways depending on what sort of neural network is being designed.

THE PERCEPTRON

One of the first artificial neural networks was built in 1957 by Frank Rosenblatt, then a professor in the psychology department at Cornell University in Ithaca, New York. Rosenblatt named his hulking creation the Mark I Perceptron. Although it used primitive technologies such as wooden racks, tangles of electrical wires, and lightbulbs, the Perceptron was the great, great grandparent of modern deep-learning neural networks.

What made the Perceptron so brilliant was its simplicity. The Perceptron was arguably the simplest possible realization of a machine capable of learning to recognize patterns. It learned to recognize patterns of simple shapes by fine-tuning the strength of its own connections between eight artificial neurons.

Another feature of Rosenblatt's Perceptron, unusual at the time, was that it would not be hard-coded by a human programmer. Instead, the machinery would "learn" to recognize patterns on its own through a training process akin to how a human would learn: experience. Consider how radical such an approach would have been at a time when dominant artificial-intelligence techniques consisted of template matching and logic rules.

The physical make-up of the Perceptron consisted of six racks of electronic equipment.[2] Each rack corresponded to a theoretical layer in a biological vision system, consisting of a few hundred connections. Altogether, the racks implemented a single layer of eight neurons. Today, modern deep-learning networks contain over 150 layers of artificial neurons, interconnected with almost a billion connections, a feat made possible by fast and powerful computers and sophisticated training algorithms.

In biology, the strength of connections between neurons is governed by the concentration of neurotransmitters. Rosenblatt decided that the appropriate electrical analog of chemical

Figure 10.1

Frank Rosenblatt and the Perceptron, shown here in connection with a television appearance. The 20 × 20 "eye" is shown, alongside wires from the "A" unit. Source: Robert Hecht-Nielsen, "Perceptrons," UCSD Institute for Neural Computation Technical Report #0403, 17 October 2008. Photo courtesy of Veridian Engineering/General Dynamics Corp.

neurotransmitters would be the degree of resistance of the electrical wires connecting the artificial neurons. Low resistance (high conductivity) would correspond to high neurotransmitter levels, and high resistance (low conductivity) would correspond to low neurotransmitter levels.

The Perceptron used wires, variable resistors, and motors to emulate the structure of a biological brain. The Perceptron's first layer emulated a biological retina. It consisted of 400 light sensors arranged in a 20 × 20 array. If this grid of light sensors in the Perceptron reminds you of the grid of sensors on a silicon light sensor in a digital camera, hang on to that thought—it's an important insight that we'll return to later. This first layer would serve as the sensory units, or what Rosenblatt called *S units*.

The second layer emulated the dendrites of neurons in a biological vision system. Rosenblatt dubbed this rack the *association units*, or *A units*. The A units were a rack of 512 connections that were physically wired to the light sensors in the first layer. Each of these connections served as a synapse.

The third rack served as the output layer of the Perceptron. This layer was the equivalent of the response neurons in a biological system, or what Rosenblatt called *R units*. It consisted of eight neurons with light-bulbs, each labeled for a specific shape; for example "triangle" or "square." Neurons fire only when they experience an electrical signal that's above a critical threshold. The R units in the Perceptron followed the same principle. Each R unit had its own individual threshold. Each R unit would fire a light bulb only when its specific threshold of current was reached by the A-unit wires connecting it to the light sensors in the first layer of the Perceptron.

The idea was that if the Perceptron was shown a triangle, then the machine would eventually learn to "recognize" that particular shape and announce its answer by illuminating the light bulb labeled "triangle."

How, exactly, did such a crude mechanical contraption learn to recognize patterns? First, Rosenblatt would project an image from a slide projector onto the 400 light sensors. The projected image would be of a simple shape, say a triangle, circle, or square. The rest of the projected image would remain dark background. Therefore the shape pattern was much brighter than the non-shape parts of the projected image. The array of light sensors would react accordingly.

If a light sensor was hit by bright light, it would react by sending along a jolt of voltage to the middle rack, the A units. Light

Figure 10.2
Sampling of images from ImageNet 2012. Similar images are placed closer to each other.
Source: Andrej Karpathy and Fei-Fei Li, Stanford University

sensors that did not receive light sat quietly. If enough A units were jolted by enough voltage from the light sensors, those jolts would eventually trigger the R unit's particular threshold. As that R unit fired, it lit up the light bulb labeled with the appropriate shape.

Machine-learning algorithms, ancient and modern, need to be trained to learn their trade. In the case of the Perceptron, as light shapes were projected onto the array of light sensors, a human operator sat and graded the machine's responses. The human operator would project a slide, wait for the machine to light one or more bulbs, and then press a "right" or "wrong" switch for each bulb.

This training process consisted of painstakingly adjusting the firing thresholds of the machine's (or software's) artificial neurons, and the strength of connections between the neurons (called *synaptic weights*). If the machine answered incorrectly, the connections between artificial neurons that fired were reduced. If the machine answered correctly, the connections between those artificial neurons that fired were either left alone or, in some types of neural networks, strengthened.

To train the Perceptron, each time the human operator pressed the "wrong" switch, the Perceptron got the equivalent of a bad grade in the form of an increase in the resistance of the wires in the A unit that were responsible for lighting up the wrong light bulb. After several training exercises, wrong answers resulted in certain wires in the A units being taken down a notch. That way, the next time that particular A unit received a jolt of electrical current from a particular light sensor in the first layer, that artificial neuron, the R unit, would be less likely to reach its threshold. If an R unit did not reach its threshold to fire, the next time it was shown the pattern it would be less likely to light up. If the machine got it right, then no adjustments were made. It's as if the teacher said "Good job. Keep doing what you're doing."

When the Perceptron was brand new and untutored, most of its responses would be incorrect. The training process was then iterated, repeating the same series of images over and over again, until the machine eventually got them all right. In the decades that followed the Perceptron, neural-network researchers pursued endless variations on this same theme, trying out the effect of increasing the strength of the connection in the case of a right answer, changing the way the wires were connected, or increasing the number of neurons and rearranging connections.

The secret to human success is to "practice, practice, practice." Regardless of what flavor of artificial neural network is being trained, the secret to machine learning is pretty similar: repetition, repetition, repetition. To learn to recognize the difference between a circle and a square, the Perceptron needed repetition so the machine could crank up the resistance settings of the connections involved in each wrong answer. In modern machine learning the same technique is used, but the manual training process has been replaced by an automated, digital process based on inputting data, data, and more data through the software.

The Perceptron's recognition repertoire was admittedly limited. Like Shakey, the Perceptron could operate only within a narrow set of parameters. Yet, unlike Shakey, the Perceptron's artificial intelligence was not the product of a human programmer. The Perceptron's machinery learned how to distinguish between a circle and a square on the basis of right/wrong feedback from a human "teacher," not by being programmed in an explicit, top-down fashion.

When it was introduced to the press, the Perceptron was a huge success. Rosenblatt stoked the fires of hype, claiming that the Perceptron was a machine that was capable of learning anything. *The New Yorker* admired the Perceptron as a significant technological accomplishment, and in 1958 the *New York Times* went so far as to call it a revolution, publishing an article with the headline "New Navy Device Learns by Doing."

Rosenblatt's Perceptron earned him a place in artificial-intelligence history. In my introductory course on machine learning, the first homework assignment is to build a software reincarnation of Rosenblatt's machine. Yet Rosenblatt's success, and the resulting media frenzy, brought on the wrath of computer scientists from competing schools of thought.

THE FIRST AI WINTER

If more researchers in the brand-new field of artificial intelligence had followed Rosenblatt's approach, we would have succeeded in automating perception decades earlier. Yet shortly after its successful introduction, the Perceptron lost its allure. One reason was that the computing power and sensor data needed to properly train a neural network were still insufficient. The second reason was another sort of people problem, that of political rivalry.

In Ithaca, home of Rosenblatt and the Perceptron, winters are long and dark. Yet, no Ithaca winter could have prepared Rosenblatt for the chill that would descend after his first flush of success. The ringleader against the Perceptron was, ironically, Rosenblatt's former high-school classmate, Marvin Minsky, at the time an accomplished professor of computer science at MIT. As the media celebrated the Perceptron's astonishing ability to learn by itself, Minsky publicly challenged Rosenblatt's claim that a Perceptron could, potentially, "learn almost anything." Minsky insisted that this claim was not true and that the Perceptron was "without scientific value."

The stage was set for a long ideological battle between two major schools of thought in artificial-intelligence research: symbolic AI, characterized by painstakingly human-programmed logical models, and neural networks, characterized by a machine-learning, data-driven approach. The source of most of the funding for artificial-intelligence research, the military, was keeping a close eye on the battle for superiority between the two AI camps. Fearing that only one AI paradigm would be deemed worthy of support, uneasy researchers whose careers were invested in symbolic AI strode into battle: neural-network research had to die.

Minsky issued his final blow to Rosenblatt when he and MIT colleague Seymour Papert published their book *Perceptrons* in 1969. The book included, among other things, a mathematical proof that showed that a Perceptron could never learn to recognize even a simple pattern that in AI research is a core expression: the XOR pattern. In the same way that musicians use a C scale to test and warm up their instrument, AI researchers used the XOR pattern to test their machine-learning algorithms. If an instrument is out of tune, its C scale will reflect that. If a machine-learning algorithm can't even learn the trivial XOR pattern, then it is not effective.

The XOR pattern performs what's called a *logical exclusive operation*. If two bits are different, the XOR operator returns a value of "1." If the two bits are the same, it returns a value of "0."

Minsky and Papert did not actually apply the XOR pattern to Rosenblatt's Perceptron. Instead, they modeled the pattern mathematically. Their simple proof showed that no matter how long Rosenblatt's Perceptron would be trained, it would never learn to recognize that particular pattern. Because of that, Minsky and Papert argued, the machine could clearly not "learn anything," not even a basic pattern.

Both sides were correct. Indeed, a single Perceptron can learn little by itself, as Minsky pointed out. But Rosenblatt did not claim that his Perceptron could learn anything. Although Minsky took Rosenblatt's boast literally, what Rosenblatt was referring to was the theoretical, potential learning ability of a machine made up of multiple layers of Perceptrons stacked one on top of one other.

Ironically, Rosenblatt's prophecy would become true almost fifty years later, when computing power became sufficient to enable neural networks made of dozens of multiple digital layers, with millions of connections between each layer. Unfortunately, however, at that time, Rosenblatt lacked the technology he needed to defend himself against Minsky's and Papert's challenge. A modern multilayer network would have proven Rosenblatt correct, but at the time, his "Perceptron training algorithm" worked only for a single Perceptron.

It didn't help Rosenblatt that at the time of this raging ideological battle in the late 1960s, computers were bulky and slow. Minsky's argument was crafted well enough to win the minds of the federal scientific funding agencies, who accepted Minsky's topdown AI paradigm as the best path forward. As a result, federal funding for neural-network research dried up.

The Perceptron program fell by the wayside, and any researcher who chose to work on neural networks did so at his own academic peril. Shortly thereafter, in the summer of 1971,

Rosenblatt died on his birthday in a boating accident on the Chesapeake Bay, a tragic and untimely death at age 43. His victory over his former high school classmate complete, Minsky went on to become a leader in the development of symbolic artificial-intelligence techniques that would dominate artificial-intelligence research for the next several decades.

Interestingly, Minsky later followed Rosenblatt down the path of temptation, famously overstating the potential of an artificial-intelligence technology to the press a few years later. In a 1970 interview published in *Life* magazine, Minsky made a small media splash of his own, notoriously claiming that "in from three to eight years we will have a machine with the general intelligence of an average human being. I mean a machine that will be able to read Shakespeare, grease a car, play office politics, tell a joke, have a fight. At that point the machine will begin to educate itself with fantastic speed. In a few months it will be at genius level and a few months after that its powers will be incalculable." Minsky was proven terribly wrong by the passage of time, yet, his career would continue to thrive for the next several decades.

In the MIT Museum of Robotics in Cambridge, Minsky is presented as a hero and a great visionary. Yet his dogged determination to destroy early attempts to build neural networks actually steered artificial-intelligence research down a long, blind alley for decades. In part as a result of Minsky's influence, the 1970s was the golden age of symbolic AI. The more researchers tried to emulate human intelligence by programming it, however, the more they unwittingly demonstrated how little we understand how the brain really works.

THE NEURAL-NETWORK RENAISSANCE

Meanwhile, the development of neural networks for pattern recognition continued to lurch forward. In 1975, Harvard PhD student Paul Werbos created a new and improved Perceptron. By now, the term *perceptron* had become generic, meaning a layer of artificial neurons in a neural network. By this time, analog hardware contraptions like the original Perceptron had been set aside and artificial-intelligence researchers built neural networks in software.

Werbos offered two key improvements that would accelerate the development of artificial neural networks. First, his artificial neurons could output not just a "1" or a "0," but also fractional values; for example, a resulting value of 0.5 might mean that the neuron was "not sure." Compare this to Rosenblatt's original machine that offered just two crisp outputs: either a 1 or a 0; the light bulb providing the "answer" was either on or off, with nothing in between.

The second improvement that Werbos provided was a new training algorithm called *error backpropagation, or backprop*. Now that the artificial neurons could handle uncertainty in the form of fractional numbers, the backprop algorithm could be used to train a neural network with more than one layer. One major limitation of Rosenblatt's Perceptron had been that its output layer could handle only two answers rather than a range; therefore, the learning curve was too steep to climb.

Werbos's new generation of artificial neural network had multiple layers of artificial neurons greatly increasing its pattern-recognition capacity, and thereby increasing its range of potential applications. This new architecture enabled the network to handle pattern-classification problems of much greater complexity. In fact, one of the first things Werbos did with his new network was to solve the deadly problem of XOR, previously considered unsolvable using neural networks.

Let's walk through Werbos's approach and imagine we're training an artificial neural network to recognize pictures of dogs. First, we would present a pattern to the network, let's say a digital image of a dog in the form of a 20×20 grid of pixels. The sensor layer would propagate its signal to the first layer of 400 artificial neurons, which in turn would pass their signal through weighted connections to the second layer of neurons, which in turn would propagate their signal through weighted connections to the third layer, and so on.

Finally, after passing through all the middle layers, the signal would reach the output layer, which would have just one neuron. This neuron would respond with an answer to the question, "Is this a picture of a dog?" Now that fractional responses were possible, the network could offer an answer on a spectrum between zero and one corresponding to the network's degree of confidence. For example, if the network responded with an answer of 0.9, that meant it was fairly confident that object in the image was a dog, but not 100 percent sure.

The training process looked like this. If the answer the network provided was incorrect, Werbos's algorithm would calculate which specific connections contributed the most to the wrong answer. These unfortunate connections would be schooled. In Rosenblatt's Perceptron, the machine adjusted its A units (the weighted connections) by changing the electrical resistance of the wires. In a software-based neural network, the software adjusts its connections by changing the *weight coefficient* of those particular connections that contributed to the wrong answer. Typically, in an artificial neural network, these connectivity weights are given in the form of a percentage, and exactly how they are adjusted is a key component of any training algorithm.

If the answer were correct, Werbos's training algorithm would calculate which connections contributed most to the correct answer and would reinforce those connections by increasing the connectivity weight of those particular connections. This process would be repeated again and again using different images of dogs and counterexample-images of things that are not dogs. Finally, after much repetition, the neural network would achieve mastery in its ability to recognize dogs in the images presented to it during the training process.

Even with Werbos's improvements, however, neural networks still had a severe limitation. A large-enough network was mathematically guaranteed to eventually master all the images presented to it. However, when presented with new and unfamiliar images of dogs, the network's competence would erode dramatically. The network could usually tell the difference between a dog and an entirely different object, say, a bridge. But when presented with pictures depicting somewhat similar four-legged animals, the network's performance would deteriorate to just above randomness, somewhat like a student circling just any answer to get through a multiple-choice exam.

Nevertheless, hope springs eternal. Better digital-camera technology combined with the timely release of Werbos's backprop algorithm sparked new interest in the field of neural-network research, effectively ending the long AI winter of the 1960s and 1970s. If you dig through research papers from the late 1980s and 1990s, you'll find the relics of this brief period of euphoria. Researchers attempted to apply neural networks to classify everything under the sun: images, text, and sound. Neural-network research, now renamed *connectionism*, showed up in a wide range of applications, from estimating an applicant's credit card worthiness to medical diagnosis.

The neural-network renaissance of the 1990s did not last long, however. While research papers demonstrated numerous successes of neural networks in carefully structured settings, in practice, neural networks did not perform well. The problem was, strangely, that they learned too well. Neural networks tended to overspecialize, or overfit, the problem, like a child memorizing the answers to mathematical questions without understanding the general principles behind them.

The problem with overfitting is that neural networks could learn to classify images that they were trained on, but they didn't have the capacity to generalize much beyond what they had seen. The problem of invariant representation remained unresolved. If trained to classify 100 pictures of dogs and cats, the network would typically be able to reclassify those specific images with 100 percent correctness. But the same neural network would then fail miserably on unseen, "out-of-sample" images that were not used for training. It took the connectionist community another decade to figure out how to stop the training before the network began to overfit, using a method called *early stopping*. But that was too late.

The next blow to neural networks came not from the logic-AI camp, but from competing machine-learning camps. New machine-learning methods, and especially *support vector machines* (SVMs), became popular. Their demonstrated performance improvement over neural networks was slight, but seductive. For visual-recognition tasks, such as those that would become essential for driverless cars, the performance boost amounted to fractions of a percent. But like a fraction of a second in an Olympic race, when competition is fierce, any margin is enough to turn the tide. It was winner-takes-all.

Most of the improvement shown by support vector machines, in retrospect, could probably have been attributed to the development of clever ways to avoid overfitting, a technique known as *regularization*. When the same overfitting mitigation approaches were applied to neural networks, they improved performance, but it was too late. Neural networks fell out of favor again by the mid-1990s, and the problem of invariant representation remained unsolved.

THE NEOCOGNITRON

In another ironic twist to the saga of neural-network development, long before the brief but doomed AI renaissance of the 1990s, a neural network designed in 1980 actually solved the seemingly unsolvable problem of invariant representation. But after the scientific paper detailing the architecture of this neural network was published, no one besides a few other neural-network die-hards paid much attention.

In 1980, Japanese researcher Kunihiko Fukushima proposed a new kind of neural-network architecture: the Neocognitron.[3] This new neural network used many of the same techniques used by modern deep-learning networks that today are hitting the ball out of the park in their image-recognition capability. However, in a theme that's no doubt becoming familiar, Fukushima's ingenious invention lacked critical enabling technology to make the world pay attention.

Fukushima's goal was to create a multilayered neural network capable of robust visual pattern recognition. His more specific goal was to create machine-learning software that could recognize handwritten digits for automatic sorting of mail.

Fukushima's network offered three major and much-needed improvements. First, when "feeding" an image to the network, the image was segmented into subgroups of pixels rather than feeding the entire image into the input layer, all at once. This way, rather than connecting each neuron in the second layer to all the photo-receptors in the input layer, each neuron was connected to just a patch of pixels. These patches slightly overlapped each other. This "sliding window" idea was used in all layers.

The second improvement was neuron cloning. Instead of using lots of neurons, each with their separately tuned connections, all the neurons in each layer of the Neocognitron were identical clones

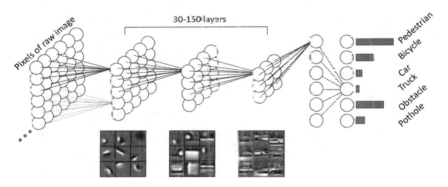

Figure 10.3

Schematic structure of a deep neural network. Spheres represent individual neurons. All neurons in a single layer are identical clones. Insets show actual visual features that some individual neurons respond to when trained on images of cars. Leftmost features represent edges; center features represent car segments such as doors and wheels; rightmost features represent nearly complete vehicles.
Source: Feature insets from Honglak Lee, Roger Grosse, Rajesh Ranganath, and Andrew Y. Ng, "Convolutional Deep Belief Networks for Scalable Unsupervised Learning of Hierarchical Representations," in *Proceedings of the 26th Annual International Conference on Machine Learning*, pp. 609–616 (ACM, 2009)

of each other, with exactly the same synaptic connection strengths. That way, even though a layer might have hundreds or thousands of synaptic connections, only a handful of parameters were needed to set the strength of those connections. This idea was rooted in the observation that identifying a digit in the upper left corner of an image should require the same neuron as identifying a digit in the bottom left corner. In other words, invariance in the image implied invariance in the network architecture as well. This idea made training faster and more robust.

The final improvement was that the network's artificial neurons consisted of two types of neurons, *S-cells* to extract features, and *C-cells* to tolerate these features' deformation. These neurons were arranged in alternating layers.

Fukushima's Neocognitron used Werbos's backprop training algorithm. A *stimulus pattern* was presented to the sensor layer. This pattern would be broken into several smaller *patches*. A typical patch might consist of connecting a window of nine sensors in a 3×3 array to each neuron in the next layer.

Throughout the network, S-cells and C-cells, the artificial neurons, were arranged in overlapping patches. The partial overlaps ensured that if a certain feature of the image did not fall squarely within the receptive field of one neuron, it would likely be captured by the neuron right next to it. Alternating layers of S-cells and C-cells worked together to gradually aggregate information from the patches of the image to process an entire visual field.

Each layer of cells was arranged hierarchically so that the next layer would see a patch of neurons in the previous layer. That way, the deepest neurons would be sensing, indirectly, the entire visual field, by aggregating information from multiple cells that each saw a finer and finer patch of the image. Until the development of the Neocognitron, all neural networks, including Rosenblatt's Perceptron, fed the entire sensory scene into the entire first layer, and that was too big a bite for it to swallow.

The Neocognitron was a wonder. Its unique architecture was robust enough that it could classify individual characters in a dataset of handwritten letters, recognizing shifts in the position of characters with ease. The Neocognitron's architecture would become the direct ancestor of modern deep-learning networks. It performed better than other image-recognition networks of the time. Fukushima's ideas were later generalized by Yann LeCun, Yoshua Bengio, and colleagues to create what we now call *convolutional neural networks* (CNNs).[4] The term *convolution* refers to the process of cloning a mathematical function and applying it repeatedly in an overlapping regular array.

In a fate similar to that which befell the Perceptron, the Neocognitron couldn't perform at a reasonable speed using the computing power available in the 1980s. It seemed that Werbos's backprop training algorithm was not powerful enough to train networks more than three or four layers deep. The reinforcement signal would fizzle out and network learning would cease because it couldn't tell which connections were responsible for wrong answers. We know today that the backprop algorithm was correct in concept, but in execution it lacked the underlying technology and data that it needed to work as its inventor intended.

During the 1990s and 2000s, some researchers tried to make up for the lack of computer power and data by using "shallower" networks, with just two layers of artificial neurons. It didn't help matters that a mathematical theory of artificial networks, the *universal approximation theorem*, gained traction. The universal approximation theorem stated that, at least in theory, a neural network needs only one "hidden" layer of artificial neurons to approximate any measurable function to any desired degree of accuracy. In other words, according to the theorem, mathematically speaking, there should be no theoretical constraints for the success of a shallow neural network.

One the one hand, the universal approximation theorem was a boon for neural networks. After all, it's good news that the overall core concept of neural networks is (at least mathematically) theoretically sound, and therefore worth investing in. On the other hand, yet again, a mathematical proof sent researchers scurrying in the wrong direction, trying to improve the performance of their single-hidden-layer neural networks not by adding more layers, but by improving their training algorithms.

Given the technological constraints of the 1980s and 1990s, unfortunately, most practitioners interpreted the universal approximation theorem to mean that there's no point in trying to build a neural network with more than two layers. The notion that one would spend precious time and resources on building multilayer neural networks seemed risky at best and, at worst, a waste of time.

The passage of time would later prove that what artificial neural networks needed wasn't better training algorithms or gigantic arrays of a single layer of artificial neurons. What neural networks needed were layers—lots and lots of layers and specialized neurons, arranged in a cascading, overlapping fashion. The other critical missing ingredient emerged at the dawn of the new century, thanks to social media: data—lots and lots of random digital images to train these deep networks.

THE BIRTH OF DEEP LEARNING

Like a newborn baby, machines learn through exposure to large amounts of information, a data-intensive activity. The amount of data needed to train an algorithm is generally proportional to the difficulty of the problem. Teaching a machine to distinguish between images of triangles and rectangles is a relatively easy problem; teaching a machine to distinguish between images of men and women is relatively hard.

Rosenblatt's Perceptron algorithm needed to tune the weights of only 512 connections, so it needed relatively few training images. A large neural network—deep or not—can contain millions of connections so it needs millions of images.

If algorithms are like an engine, then the fuel that feeds the algorithm is data. A combustion engine without gasoline can't run. A machine-learning algorithm without data to feed it is a toothless set of instructions.

During the twentieth century, most machine vision researchers recognized the need for training data. The reality was that
for most of computing history, digital images have been hard to
come by. As a result, image-recognition algorithms were developed using relatively data-sparse approaches. Because of the
scarcity of data, machine-learning research, similar to biological
life forms adapting to food-scarce environments, focused on developing algorithms that could run efficiently without requiring
much data.

For decades, the quest for efficient machine-learning algorithms sent researchers down rabbit holes of inquiry, tweaking
algorithms in order to squeeze out fractions of a percent better
performance out of a small dataset. The same kind of thinking
also valued hand-designed provably correct algorithms over
approaches inspired by biology. Human cognition is marked by
plentiful data, and very rapid, massively parallel computation.

Biology, however, does not place a premium on computational
efficiency alone. It also values adaptability and robustness. The
fate of a living thing rests on whether its neural algorithms can
quickly adapt to a new situation. If there were really a set of learning algorithms running in our brain, it's quite likely that they
would be simple in structure and possibly quite inefficient, at least
in a traditional computer science sense.

The transition from data-poor "clever" algorithms to data-rich
"simple" ones happened in the 2010s. A convergence of forces made
this possible: computers became cheap and fast, digital cameras
appeared in cell phones, and the internet offered people plenty of
places to post their digital images. Every minute, some 208,300
new images appear on Facebook.[5] Goodbye data scarcity, hello
Google image search.

In the world of computer vision research, the dam started to
burst in 2003 when a graduate student named Fei-Fei Li created
the Caltech-101, a dataset of 9,146 images broken down into 101
different categories. Li's goal was to build a collection of images
that depicted the breadth and variety of random everyday scenes

in human life and then feed those images to machine-vision algorithms in order to train them to see.

By 2006, Li's image dataset had grown into the Caltech-256, a repository of 30,607 images in 256 categories. In 2009, after spending some time at the University of Illinois at Urbana–Champaign and Princeton, Li joined Stanford's Computer Science faculty. Despite advice from concerned but well-intentioned colleagues to "do something more useful," Li persisted in creating and sharing an even larger image dataset, ImageNet. ImageNet was to become the world's first "mega dataset," containing over one million labeled images. Stanford's ImageNet is still a growing resource. As of the time of this writing, ImageNet contained over 14 million images spanning over 20,000 categories.

ImageNet photos were raw and uncurated. Objects appeared in cluttered, if realistic, contexts. A photo of a beer bottle, for example, was not a glamor photo from an advertisement, but an action shot of a discarded beer bottle lying on the sidewalk.

ImageNet contained a rich variety of images in different categories. Of course the requisite cat and dog photos were well represented. The collection also included pictures of lizards, snails, snakes, snowmobiles, and socks. There were strange and amateurish snaps of toads, toasters, and tomatoes.

Li's goal was not merely to stockpile a random collection of digital images. These images were also categorized. The internet was bursting with images, and somebody had to peruse and then correctly categorize the content of these images so they could be used to train neural networks to see. A human had to manually examine millions of images and create appropriate categories for them. Someone, somewhere, had to do the time-consuming and tedious task of flipping through a stack of dog pictures and deciding that image X is of a Yorkshire terrier, whereas image Y is of its distant cousin, the Staffordshire bull terrier.

Right on cue, another emerging cultural trend came to the rescue: crowdsourcing. The Herculean task of classifying ImageNet's millions of images was accomplished using thousands of

Mechanical-Turk workers on Amazon, who, for pennies per image, labeled each one. At one point, Fei-Fei Li recalls, ImageNet was the largest employer of freelancers on Amazon, employing thousands of people twenty-four hours a day across the globe.[6]

GPUS

We've already discussed faster computers, more data, digital cameras, and adding more layers to artificial neural networks. One more critical technology had to slide into place: fast graphics cards. Why? Because neural networks have a massive appetite for computing power.

The best source for good graphics cards is the gaming community. Though the gaming community is sometimes subject to negative stereotypes of idle youngsters wasting their productive years slavishly playing in their parents' basement, in reality it is also a major source of innovation, particularly in image processing.

Gaming tests the limits of computing power. Gaming computers render three-dimensional graphic scenes at high definition and rapid frame rates. A gaming computer must respond in real time to user inputs, compensate for network latency between multiple gamers, and accurately simulate the physics of splashing water and shattering chairs. Everyday gaming applications demand a far more sophisticated computing environment than applications generally considered more sophisticated, such as modeling numbers in a spreadsheet or searching a database.

Even Moore's law could not keep pace with gaming industry's appetite for low-cost and high-performance computing. The gaming industry solved its processing bottleneck in another way: by running several processes in parallel. Instead of making faster processors, hardware manufacturers catering to gaming companies created special graphics cards containing thousands of processors running in parallel.

Graphics cards contain massively parallel graphics processors called *graphics processing units,* or GPUs (to distinguish them from the more traditional general-purpose central processing units, CPUs). For years, GPUs were confined to niche applications in graphic design and gaming. Performance improvement curves for CPUs are exponential. GPU performance curves have even steeper exponentials, a trend that did not go unnoticed. In 2006, Nvidia, one of the largest graphics card manufacturers, introduced the GeForce 8 series, the first GPU architecture that was specifically designed to be used for more than just graphics.

To market its new chip, Nvidia coined the term *general-purpose GPU* (GPGPU) and launched what was to become a new field of massively parallel desktop computing. Before Nvidia's GeForce 8 series was introduced, general purpose parallel computing was used only by serious graphic artists or hard-core scientists. Now, GPUs found their way into a range of other computing-intensive applications where high intensity parallel computing power was needed, including stock trading, engineering analysis, and, of course, neural networks.

Neural networks lend themselves to parallelization. A neural network involves many neurons, each processing its inputs locally and then deciding whether or not to fire an output. This is particularly true for multilayer convolutional networks that have an array organization that closely aligns with the graphics application for which GPUs were originally designed.

In most computing applications, speed is of the essence; in a neural network, speed is critical. The speed in which the neural network calculates its answer to an image-classification problem is fractions of a second faster on a GPU that it is on a CPU. But the training of a neural network can be hundreds of times faster, because training requires millions of backprop iterations.

Researchers who used GPUs to run their convolutional neural networks began seeing an improvement factor of almost ten compared to their colleagues who were using ordinary desktops. In principle, the speed of the training process is not that critical for most applications; after all, training needs to be done just once. But in practice, an algorithm that takes a month to train cannot be developed and debugged by anyone on a realistic development schedule. A network that can be trained in three days—now that's a different story.

MODERN DEEP LEARNING

Modern deep learning burst forth in 2012 at a machine-vision competition. The stage was set two years earlier, when Fei-Fei Li and her colleagues realized they needed a public venue where researchers could showcase their machine vision software programs. They established the annual Large Scale Visual Recognition Competition, the world's first image-recognition competition, open to anyone who wished to compete. The raw material for competing machine vision software programs was the massive trove of classified images stored in ImageNet.

The rules were as follows. Competitors would submit their image-recognition software to a server managed by the competition's administrators. The software would be prompted to classify the contents of 100,000 new images. Since these images were likely to be cluttered and full of many random objects, the software should be programmed to name the top five objects it recognized in each image.

The competition has three tracks: classification, classification with localization, and detection. The classification track measures an algorithm's ability to correctly label an image. The classification with localization track assesses how well an algorithm is able to model the labels of an image, as well as the location of underlying objects in the image. Finally, the detection challenge borrows elements of the other tracks, but uses stricter evaluation criteria and includes lots of images depicting several tiny objects. New tracks, like recognition in video streams, are being added so that the competition can keep up with the technology.

The first competition in 2010 was won by a team from NEC and the University of Illinois at Urbana–Champaign. Of the 100,000 test images, the winning neural network was incorrect 28 percent of the time.[7] The two runners-up had error rates of 33.6 percent and 44.6 percent. To provide some perspective into this outcome, an ordinary untrained human is pretty good at categorizing images with an average error rate of roughly 5 percent.

In 2011, the second competition showed that machine-vision algorithms were getting better, although almost none of them used neural networks. A team from a tech company called XRCE was wrong only 25 percent of the time, a 2.4 percent improvement from the previous year's winners.[8] The runners-up had error rates of 31 percent and 36 percent.

The field of machine vision changed forever when the third competition concluded at midnight on September 30, 2012. There was no media frenzy or lavish half-time ceremony. But if the rack-mount servers administering the competition could have responded, they would have probably given one another celebratory hugs.

A neural network named SuperVision, created by a team of researchers from the University of Toronto, correctly identified objects 85 percent of the time, a phenomenal performance in the world of image-recognition software.[9] A drop from a 25 percent to 15 percent error rate might not sound like a lot, but for the computer-vision community, which was used to seeing annual improvements of a fraction of a percent each year, it was like seeing a man run the first four-minute mile.

SuperVision's creators were students Alex Krizhevsky and Ilya Sutskever, and their professor, Geoffrey Hinton. SuperVision was a type of neural network called a *convolutional network*. Many of the convolutional network's features were based on techniques laid out more than thirty years earlier by Dr. Fukushima for the Neocognitron. Additional refinements stemmed from work conducted by the research groups of Yann LeCun at NYU, Andrew Ng at Stanford, and Yoshua Bengio at the University of Montreal. SuperVision was a gargantuan neural network made up of thirty layers of racks of arrays of artificial neurons. In a bold move, the Toronto group proceeded to open-source their code so anyone else could use and modify it, creating a sensation in the computer-vision world.

Deep-learning artificial neural networks have become the new gold standard in image-recognition software. Before SuperVision's massive victory in 2012, almost no one used convolutional neural networks. After 2012, no competitors dared enter without one.

The year following SuperVision's triumph, the winner achieved a 11.2 percent error rate, with runners-up close behind at 12 percent and 13 percent; all used customized variants of deep-learning convolutional neural networks.[10] In 2014, a team from Google achieved 6.66 percent error and a team from the University of Oxford achieved 7.1 percent error.[11] In 2015, a team of researchers at Microsoft's Beijing research lab (led by principal researcher Jian Sun) used a network that was 152-layers deep to win first place in all three categories.[12] Most remarkably, Microsoft's team achieved a 3.57 percent error rate, surpassing for the first time the previously unbeatable 5 percent error rate of human-level perception.[13]

After these triumphs, suddenly alternative research approaches in machine vision became obsolete. The string of watershed breakthroughs in object recognition quickly spilled out of the computer vision field into all other areas of artificial-intelligence research. Derivatives of the algorithm that ran SuperVision oozed into other AI fields, such as speech recognition and text generation. The final remaining barrier to the development of driverless cars—software capable of artificial perception—finally began to melt away.

Soon after this big success, the pieces started coming together. Nvidia launched a deep-learning card that implemented a derivative of Krizhevsky's Supervision network on low-power hardware. Nvidia's target commercial application was driverless cars. The system was aptly named Drive-PX, and it could process up to twelve real-time video channels simultaneously. A year later, a faster, cheaper, and better card was released, and the race to build technologies to enable automotive deep learning was underway.

INSIDE THE NETWORK

There are several different types of deep-learning networks for image recognition, each with its own twist on the basic architecture and unique refinements in the way the training algorithm is applied. Deep learning is a fast-growing field and new architectures and algorithms appear every few weeks. One common characteristic, however, is that deep-learning networks use a cascade of many layers of artificial neurons to "extract" features from digital images that the software then identifies and labels. Cutting-edge deep-learning networks often have more than 100 layers of artificial neurons (contrast this to Rosenblatt's Perception, which had only a single layer of eight neurons).

Some people believe that deep-learning networks recognize objects the way humans do, by first recognizing a particular tiny feature, then abstracting that to a broader, more abstract concept. For example, a human eye sees a pair of pointy ears, whiskers, and a tail and rapidly abstracts that visual information into a classification: "Aha, cat!" How, exactly, biological systems recognize objects still remains a mystery. Yet, classifying objects by conducting a rapid analysis of individual features is an approach that when architected into a neural network, results in artificial perception that approaches that of the average human being.

Let's take a closer look at the deep-learning network called SuperVision to get a sense of how these multilayer analytical engines work. One practical improvement made by Krizhevsky and his team was to use GPUs to speed up the training process, reducing the time between cycles from weeks to days. Given the size of the SuperVision network, a massive analytical thicket involving sixty million tunable parameters and 650,000 neurons, shaving weeks off the training process provided considerable advantage.

Inside the layers, SuperVision (nicknamed "AlexNet" after its creator) used a simpler form of thresholding. This simplified transfer function enabled the neurons to work faster and also enabled Werbos's training algorithm to tune connections deeper through many layers—a common problem with multilayer neural networks of the past. Finally, to avoid the dreaded overfitting problem, the SuperVision team used a technique called *dropout*. The dropout technique involved randomly disabling the connections of some portion of neurons during the training process, to make sure that no single neuron is doing all the work, and all the neurons were taking on their fair share of computation.

To create a deep-learning network, the first step is to feed the network raw visual data. A digital image consists of an array of numerical values that quantify the amount of red, green, and blue light present in each individual pixel. The input layer of a deep-learning network has three similar complementary arrays of inputs that accept each numerical value.

The remaining layers of the deep-learning network are where computation takes place. Different types of deep-learning networks lay out layers in various ways. In a convolutional neural network, each neuron in the second layer is connected to a small rectangle of inputs in the first layer. For example, each neuron in the second layer might compute a weighted sum of the pixels in a 3×3 patch in the first layer, much like Fukushima's Neocognitron.

These set points are where the art of tuning the network comes into play. If the sum is larger than a particular threshold, the neuron will "fire" or output a signal that travels to the next inner layer of neurons. If the sum does not meet the level, the neuron just sits, rests, and waits silently. As the signal propagates, or passes from neuron to neuron, the next neuron in the chain computes the sum of signals from its 3×3 window. This process continues all the way through the network.

Most deep-learning architecture also contain *max-pooling* units, similar to the Neocognitron's C-cells, that take the maximum value from a pool of neurons, ignoring all the rest of the signals. It turns out that this kind of unit is essential for making the network robust. Most deep-learning networks also contain two or more layers of an old-fashioned "fully-connected" two-layer perceptron at the last two layers. At the end of the day the convolutional neural network learns to find the best features so that an ordinary perceptron finally can do its work.

When the signal reaches the end of the line, in the final layer, output neurons tally up the "votes" of the inner layers of neurons. In Rosenblatt's Perceptron, the output took the form of a labeled light bulb lighting up. In a modern deep-learning network in software, if the network is being trained to classify images of dogs and cats, the output value that represents the network's degree of certainty of what it is looking at is a number between 0 and 1. If the output value for "dog" is 1, then the network is absolutely certain it's a dog in the picture. If the output value for "cat" is 0.5, then the network is uncertain about whether the object depicted is a cat.

Clearly, this explanation of how a deep-learning network does its analysis is greatly simplified. As the field has advanced, most networks now include enhancements to the process. Some examples of enhancements include inserting specialized layers of artificial neurons into the middle layers that perform real-time statistical analysis to normalize the signal as it propagates through. Other variations involve experimenting with clever ways to extend training to even more layers, a process the 2015 Microsoft team called *residual learning*.

One of the great strengths of a deep-learning network is that if properly arranged, the network creates its own ability to recognize objects based on repeated exposure to new data. Ironically, the fact that the network, not a human programmer, created the machine's ability to recognize objects can create problems. A deep-learning network is a classic example of what programmers call a *black-box architecture*, meaning it's virtually impossible to reverse-engineer the steps the software program takes as it generates output.

Imagine if a driverless car miscategorized a group of pedestrians crossing the road in front of it as a harmless reflection off of a glass-and-steel skyscraper. If the car's visual recognition software were later examined to figure out what caused it to malfunction, the answer might never emerge. Modern multilayer deep-learning networks have dozens of layers that contain millions and sometime billions of connection points. Like a person who can't trace the exact logic of her own thoughts but comes up with an answer that just "feels right," a deep-learning network comes up with an answer that just "feels right" to its millions of artificial neurons.

A NEW SORT OF EDGE DETECTION

One way to unpack the cognitive activity of a deep-learning network is to individually isolate the artificial neurons and test their response when presented with a particular pattern. Researchers who have examined the process by which deep networks learn to classify visual information have discovered that the deeper an artificial neuron is located in the network, the more abstract the pattern it responds to; conversely, the closer a neuron is to the initial outer layers of the network, the simpler the pattern it responds to.

In an interesting twist, the visual systems of cats (and perhaps other animals as well) break down the world the same way.[14] In 1959, biologists David Hubel and Torsten Wiesel recorded the activity of the visual cortex cells in lightly anesthetized cats. The cat's retinas were stimulated with different types of visual data, spots of light and black and white stripes of different sizes.

When they examined the neurons' response to the visual stimuli, Hubel and Wiesel found that cells on the cats' retinas responded to the pattern of stripes but not the spots. For some reason, the stripes triggered a response in the cats' visual cells. Hubel and Wiesel called these cells *bar detectors* or *edge detectors*.

It turns out that the outer neurons in a deep-learning network also present a strong response to lines and edges. Deep-learning networks first break down complex images into simple lines and edges in order to figure out what, exactly, is in the image. In decades past, human programmers hand-coded robots such as

Shakey to break down visual information into lines and edges in order to make sense of it. Today, deep-learning networks use a similar process—automatically.

In a deep-learning network, the deeper you go, the more complex the patterns the individual artificial neurons respond to. In the third layer, if the network is trained on a dataset of cars, the neurons might respond to a pattern resembling the round edges of wheels. The neurons in the fourth layer might respond to patterns that resemble specific parts of cars like a trunk, or a front grille. Even deeper inside the network, neurons might respond to more abstract concepts such as a pattern that matches a particular 3-D orientation of the world, as seen from the driver's seat, and so on.

Over time, deep-learning researchers have picked up on some learning habits of deep-learning networks. Regardless of the

Figure 10.4
Deep learning recognizing objects on the road, in real time.
Source: Courtesy of NVIDIA

application for which a CNN is being trained, the network's first layer will almost always contain edge detectors. It seems as if edge detection is universally useful for image understanding.

Deeper inside, however, neurons in inner layers begin to "specialize": networks that are trained to classify cars home in on "features" relevant to cars. Neurons specializing in shapes of car bodies might emerge, as well as others specializing in the hue of reflections. Networks trained to classify dogs might give rise to neurons that respond to specific patterns of fur, or shapes of ears.

We call the patterns that the neurons respond to *visual features*. In the lower levels, the image features are simple: lines and patches. As we go higher and higher, these features become more complex and more abstract and the word *feature* no longer does them justice. Individual neurons at higher layers of the network might be responding to subtle combinations of visual cues. For example, one neuron might be responding to the "Chevy-ness" of a front grille.

Philosophers have long struggled to describe the individual sensory experiences that are unique to each person, and hence are impossible to quantify or directly compare against another person's individual sensory experiences. The term *qualia* refers to the sensations a person experiences directly. We all know what we feel, but we'll never know how, exactly, our conscious experience compares to that of somebody else. For example, does everyone see the same redness in tonight's evening sky? Does the taste of chocolate explode on your tongue the same way it does on mine?

Perhaps someday deep-learning networks will experience their own qualia. A few years ago, I experienced first-hand the ghostly sensation of having a deep-learning network discover something on its own. My students and I were preparing a demonstration of one of our deep-learning networks to a live audience. To train our network to classify everyday objects, we spent several hours waving random things we found in the lab in front of the live video camera attached to the network.

Our network was humming along as it should, correctly classifying the content of most of the digital images we were showing it. But then something strange happened. We realized that our network, like a month-old human infant, was tracking our faces. Each time I moved my head closer to the camera, the network reacted. The same thing happened when my students put their faces next to the camera.

We discovered that somewhere on the seventh layer of the network, there was one artificial neuron that lit up every time a human face appeared in the image. Somewhere along the way in its long training process, one of the artificial neurons made the

Figure 10.5

A snapshot of our network as it spontaneously learned to respond to faces in a live video stream. Note that the two blurry white areas in the highlighted circle correspond to the two faces in the image frame.
Source: Jason Yosinski, Cornell University

decision to detect human faces. Why faces? Nowhere did we explicitly train the network to detect faces.

After a few baffled moments, we figured out that the presence of a face was actually a useful bit of information to the neural network for classifying other things. We humans tend to hold certain objects close to our face—for example, cell phones. After observing us for a while, our neural network spontaneously decided on its own that it should identify faces so it could better recognize the objects we were training it to recognize.

It was a spooky moment.

Our network's ability to decide what it needed to learn was significant for a few reasons. One reason is that I know many students who spent several precious years in graduate school developing face-detection software and their results were nowhere near as effective as our network's "self-discovered" solution. Another reason is that our network's unexpected capacity for spontaneous learning raises an interesting question. What else (without our knowledge or input) might our network decide to detect? Perhaps our network has also learned to recognize meaningful visual patterns we humans do not have a vocabulary for, or that our brains may not even be able to imagine.

My experience makes me wonder whether someday deep-learning networks will someday have their own artificial qualia. Imagine feeding multispectral images to a network at the rate of a thousand frames a second. Imagine using ten cameras at a time. Toss in other raw sensory data such as audio in frequencies we humans can't hear. I wonder what would happen after a few weeks of training the network.

In theory, software could develop artificial neurons that respond to qualia that we humans cannot imagine, let alone have the vocabulary to describe. The thought of this alternative machine intelligence is humbling. When humans proclaim that a computer will never understand the finer things in life such as a sunset or the taste of fine, red wine, I think, "True, but they'll have sensory awareness of experiences that we will never know to ask about."

In the shorter term, deep-learning techniques are showing up in several practical applications related to driverless cars. The Israeli company Mobileye uses algorithms similar to deep learning in the visual-recognition software it sells to car companies, including Tesla. When Google's cars prowl the streets of Mountain View, California, they're training their driverless-car fleet's collective ability to recognize objects commonly found near the road. Companies such as Google have purchased startups that specialize in deep learning to quickly gain the human expertise and intellectual capital to apply deep learning to Google products.

Deep learning provides fertile ground for future artificial-intelligence research. Unlike the human brain, artificial neural networks are not limited to the use of only two eyes to acquire their raw visual data. Some researchers are experimenting with vision systems that combine data from lidar, radar, and cameras to produce an artificial eye that could see better than a human one. Other intriguing areas to explore are fleet-learning techniques to combine the data collected from several cars to accelerate the rate at which the network's visual perception improves.

New deep-learning algorithms can analyze multiple frames from streaming video signals and create visual features that involve movement and depth perception. For example, dynamic deep-learning algorithms can learn to recognize a cat not by its distinctive ears and whiskers, but from the way its body moves, how it slinks around. If applied to driving, such a deep-learning network could learn to make sense of what's happening on the road according to the way things move: a car cannot just appear out of thin air, and a pedestrian cannot walk at fifty miles per hour. One could even go so far as to claim that a network that has the capacity to recognize objects by the way they should behave is exhibiting a trait we humans call common sense.

As deep-learning software gains the capacity to see the world in new ways, the result will be that autonomous cars will rely on data as heavily as they rely on fuel. Driverless cars consume vast amounts of data through their artificial senses. Yet, as much data as they consume, they also provide. As cars and roads become increasingly rich sources of data, the result will be safer streets and better traffic flow, but also a new front in the ongoing battle over personal privacy.

11

FUELED BY DATA

Driverless cars both consume and generate data. As driving becomes increasingly datafied, the way we travel will change in several ways. One development will be that driverless cars will be guided by high-definition digital maps, creating a new marketplace for companies with the resources to make and maintain them. Another consequence of self-driving cars will be that cities will gain control over municipal traffic patterns. The datafication of driving will introduce new gains, but also new risks.

Once cars are fully automated, our personal privacy, already eroded by smart phones and the internet will be further compromised. Driverless cars will have the technological capacity to collect a full run-down on both passengers' and pedestrians' identities and habits, including where they travel and with whom. Another ethical challenge will be that we as a society will have to agree on standard quantitative values for human lives so that in an accident, a driverless car's software will be able to (literally) weight the value of human lives at stake and calculate an optimal response in an accident.

Let's begin with the opportunities. HD digital maps represent an emerging industry and a strategic battleground. In 2015, Nokia sold its digital mapping and navigation division to a German consortium of automakers that plans to harvest the data to improve their location-based services The corporate titan that's already leading the pack in the race to build highly accurate and up-to-date digital maps is, of course, Google.

Google has invested decades of human labor and billions of dollars to build its treasure-trove of highly detailed and up-to-date digital maps. Some of the original data in Google's maps was initially collected and organized by government projects developed for the U.S. census and to depict the topographic details of the fifty United States.[1] Since then, the maps have been constantly updated. New data is added manually by teams of Google employees dispatched to drive around streets with video cameras and lidar on their cars, filming buildings and street signs and other critical topographic details, hidden or too fine-grained to show up in an aerial image.

Over the years, the teams working on Google's map-building initiative, referred to inside the company as "street truthers," have driven more than five million miles, gathering data as they go.[2] Teams of offshore workers have played a critical role in cleaning up the data, massaging together the disparate datasets and correcting errors. Hundreds of employees, many of them in Bangalore, continually key in corrections from user-submitted error reports.

Making and updating an HD map requires costly human time and labor, which increases the likelihood that in the future the marketplace will be controlled by private sector companies that have deep pockets. In many nations, all levels of the government diligently collect and maintain massive troves of raw data, documenting the location of traffic lights or making detailed topographic maps of mountain ranges. However, most of that data is not readily available. It's true (at least in the United States) that a person armed with lots of time and Freedom of Information Act applications could visit individual cities, states, and federal agencies and eventually pull together an impressive dataset. However, such an undertaking would be inefficient and time consuming, particularly since the collected data would need to be cleaned up and placed into a standard format in order to be usable.

The future market for HD maps could be a diverse and lucrative one. One potential client might be city motor-vehicle departments that need to keep track of the surface condition of their local streets and roads and monitor the erosion of lane markers. Police departments might find it useful to know which stretches of roads cause driverless cars to abruptly brake or maneuver in an unsafe manner.

Well-heeled corporate clients could include insurance companies and tech companies that make driverless-car software. The more detailed a car's built-in digital map, the safer the car, and the greater its market value to potential buyers. Consumers of the future will pay a premium for a car whose HD map contains intimate knowledge of a region's streets—for example, which roadside shoulders are safe for pulling over.

As long as HD maps are costly to create and maintain, they'll have market value, since any company considering entering the marketplace will face a high barrier to entry. In the long term, however, HD maps will become a commodity. Two forces will drive this transition. First, as digital cameras and deep-learning software continue to improve, the balance of reliance on a car's operating system will shift from stored map data to real-time scene recognition. Driverless cars' maps will become a less crucial component of a car's visual intelligence.

The second force will be, ironically, automation. Once cars are capable of driving themselves around, they can automatically update and enhance the level of detail in their own on-board HD digital maps. When human labor costs are removed from the equation, the once-prohibitive costs of making highly detailed digital maps will drop precipitously. Driverless cars will be top-notch map updaters thanks to their own robotic energy, patience, and hive minds.

ROBOT, AUTOMATE THYSELF

One of the fascinating side effects of applying deep-learning software to driving is that while the proficiency of the guiding software improves slowly at first, once it reaches a critical tipping point, its performance continues to improve at an increasingly accelerated rate. In other words, the more data that driverless cars collect, the better drivers they become. One way to sum up this virtuous cycle would be that training data begets machine-learning software, whose performance continues to improve as it consumes yet more data, eventually enabling the fully automated collection of even more training data.

This virtuous cycle would work as follows. Initially, human drivers will be needed to train a car's deep-learning software. At some point, the deep-learning software will reach the point where it can guide a driverless car on its own, enabling the car to drive alone and collect a steady stream of new training data as it goes. The new data will be applied to train the deep-learning software to reach even higher levels of accuracy in recognizing objects, further improving its performance. As cars' guiding software becomes even more capable, more driverless cars can be dispatched to the streets, collecting yet more training data.

Driverless cars will work in fleets, adding another multiplier to the equation. Fleets of driverless cars equipped with cameras and deep-learning software will record the details of every tree, every wall, every trash can, and every feature of the landscape. At the end of the day, each car will upload its visual data to a central database so other cars can tap into it. As thousands—perhaps millions—of contributing driverless cars update their software from this rich pool of fresh training data, the performance of their deep-learning software will improve at an exponential rate.

Fleet learning will accelerate the performance improvement of driverless cars in another way. When several cars record the same visual environment, the overlapping data can be cross-checked. As error-checking software checks in new data from multiple cars, it can conduct a simple statistical cross-check to validate data accuracy. If a thousand cars each report seeing a fallen tree branch lying next to the road and their sightings are consistent over time and from several different angles, the likelihood that the reported object is indeed a fallen tree is quite high.

The ability of deep-learning software to ultimately improve upon itself is reminiscent of an intriguing automated process that enables mobile robots to improve the accuracy of their own maps. This map-building process is known as *simultaneous localization and mapping,* or SLAM. The student who devised this approach initially called the algorithm *simultaneous mapping and localization,* a name whose unfortunate acronym would be SMAL.

Figure 11.1

A 3-D map built using a process of simultaneous localization and mapping (SLAM).
Source: Jakob Engel, Jorg Stuckler, and Daniel Cremers, "Large-Scale Direct Slam with Stereo Cameras," in *2015 IEEE International Conference on Intelligent Robots and Systems (IROS)*, pp. 1935–1942. IEEE, 2015; Andreas Geiger, Philip Lenz, and Raquel Urtasun, "Are We Ready for Autonomous Driving? The KITTI Vision Benchmark Suite," in *2012 IEEE Conference on Computer Vision and Pattern Recognition (CVPR)*, pp. 3354–3361, IEEE, 2012.

(Fortunately, his PhD adviser convinced him to rearrange the words, and the powerful acronym SLAM was born.)

SLAM is essentially a map bootstrapping process in which a mobile robot rapidly builds up its knowledge of a new environment by starting out with knowledge of a single point, and going forward from there. The process begins with the robot selecting a starting position. Next, it records the positions of every object its visual sensors can "see" from that initial vantage point. The captured visual data is recorded onto a blank starting map.

Next, the robot inches forward and repeats the scan, creating a second map of its surroundings as seen from the new vantage point. If the robot did not move very far between the two maps, it is very likely that a large portion of the objects seen from the previous position will also be visible from the new vantage point. The overlap between the two partial maps allows the robot to align the two maps and merge them into a single, larger, and more accurate map. This new fused map is then used to triangulate where exactly the robot is located relative to the objects it has seen, and what unknown frontier of the map it should explore next.

As the robot repeats the SLAM process again and again and again, in fairly short order it is able to build up a complete and accurate map of a particular area. We've seen research robots use SLAM to rapidly learn their way around a building. The robot starts out with a blank map and after roaming the hallways for a few hours, manages to generate a detailed map of the entire accessible space.

SLAM enables a robot to improve the accuracy of its own maps. As a mobile robot uses the SLAM process to collect sensory information, the quality of the robot's stored maps continues to improve. Thus begins a virtuous cycle. As the robot's stored maps reach new levels of detail and accuracy, the robot becomes an even better navigator and is able to venture forth and collect yet more data to update its maps.

Today SLAM is used by mobile robots everywhere in applications that range from military reconnaissance to domestic vacuum-cleaning robots that map out the floor of their house. Similar to fleet learning, there's *group SLAM*, a process in which several robots work together by combining their visual data. Another variant is *3-D SLAM*, a technique used by autonomous submarines to map out the ocean's floor and airborne drones to map the insides of caves.

Someday fleets of driverless cars will bootstrap the accuracy of their own HD maps and deep-learning software. They will use a process similar to group SLAM and 3-D SLAM to repeatedly film every street scene and scrutinize every crack, bump, and lane marker on the surface of the world's roads. As a steady stream of fresh data is fed into the car's software, the result will be an ever-improving digital model of pedestrian behavior and the surface details of a region's streets and roads. When fleets of cars pool their individual driving experiences into a collective robotic mind, their combined experience will equal that of a human driver who has spent thousands of years behind the wheel.

PREDICTING TRAFFIC

As future driverless cars go about their business, their location, speed, and chosen route will yield a useful byproduct: traffic data. Today we get by with primitive route-planning software that provides limited guidance on how to beat traffic. Most of us have a cell phone with a simple app that guides us to a particular destination. Some more sophisticated versions of these apps factor traffic information into their calculation.

Driverless cars will contain sophisticated predictive traffic analytics software that uses machine-learning software to learn from real-time and historic traffic data. By studying traffic patterns from previous hours, weeks, and years, machine-learning software will learn to recognize factors that cause road congestion, such as accidents or the presence of road construction. Other events that affect traffic include holidays, school breaks, sports games, and social events. Weather and winter storms are another hugely disruptive factor.

Traffic prediction and planning software will follow a performance improvement curve similar to that of deep-learning software. The more traffic data available, the more accurate the traffic prediction machine-learning models will become. The more a car drives and the more traffic situations it experiences—similar to a human driver who knows which route to take during rush hour—the better its traffic prediction software gets at finding the best route.

A few decades from now the state of traffic prediction software could reach new levels we can only dream about today. When driverless cars analyze years of traffic data, we may discover that their prediction software uncovers complex dependencies between distant, seemingly unrelated traffic situations. City planners will find that one traffic situation will indirectly trigger another in what's known as a *butterfly effect;* for example, a seemingly trivial road closing will cause severe traffic delays on several distant roads ten hours later.

Route-planning and traffic-prediction software will do more than just plan a route, predict traffic congestion, and guide the car to avoid it. Route-planning software will take a big picture view of the traffic patterns of an entire city. Occasionally, however, a situation will call for a micro-level view, in which a very short route is planned in a similarly short time frame. When planning the best way to reach a destination that's nearby, a driverless car will create a rapid series of short-term predictive models as it "thinks" about the most efficient route. For example, if you're in a driverless car headed to the grocery store and have some flexibility in where you shop, your car could consider only nearby traffic patterns and steer you to the grocery store that's the currently easiest to get to.

Traffic systems are a classic example of what scientists call a *nonlinear system*, a system made up of a combination of multiple codependent effects that affect one another in ways that are difficult to predict. Identifying the subtle and complex codependent network effects in a nonlinear system is an active area of research for scientists and engineers in many disciplines. Stock markets are complex systems whose dynamics are in a continual state of flux, pulled off-center by market forces, and in rampaging human investors. The ecological fluctuations in a rainforest are similarly complex, involving hundreds of dependent and independent variables that act on one another in unpredictable ways.

You have probably experienced the effects of "traffic nonlinearity" each time you are confronted with the morning commute paradox: Leave before 8 am, and you get to the office half an hour early; on the other hand, leave half an hour later, and you get to the office an hour too late. Somewhere in between leaving too early and too late there is a sweet spot, but finding that optimal departure time is challenging. It's difficult to correctly time a morning commute because the departure time that will get you to the office exactly at 9 am keeps shifting since it's influenced by multiple competing factors.

One reason traffic patterns are nonlinear is that human group behavior determines which route people choose. When someone sitting in her car hears about a traffic delay on the radio she thinks, "Wait, if everyone else is redirected to the alternative route, then I'd be better off continuing to drive to where the accident is." Driverless cars will also be notified about traffic delays, but unlike humans, they'll react in a more rational and obedient manner. Their advanced route-planning software will quickly model several different future traffic situations by playing out 'what if" scenarios. As driverless cars inform one another of their chosen route-plan, overseeing software will distribute cars along several different routes, making the journey more efficient for everybody.

As driverless cars become more common, the amount of available traffic data will increase and the machine-learning models will continue to improve. As a result, route-planning software will be able to predict and manage complex traffic patterns hours and even days in advance. One unresolved issue for policymakers and car manufacturers of the future will be defining how accurate the software that makes traffic predictions will need to be.

Driverless cars carrying human passengers will not be the only vehicles to benefit from powerful route-planning and traffic-prediction software. Autonomous commercial freight and delivery vehicles will, too. Planning optimal routes for commercial delivery vehicles is much more complicated than planning optimal routes for the family car. Several additional logistical factors significantly increase the complexity of the problem.

A fleet of autonomous delivery vehicles that drive daily to every neighborhood in a large city and make multiple stops along the way poses a path-planning problem as thorny and complex as the process of modeling weather patterns. One complicating factor is that trucks and delivery vehicles have a longer time window for route planning. Most personal car trips are short, less than thirty miles.[3] In contrast, delivery vehicles drive continuously all day long. Route-planning software for autonomous delivery vehicles must plan multiple stops over the course of an entire day, or perhaps even a week.

The complexity continues. If a driverless delivery truck needs to make a dozen stops at several different locations, there are almost half a billion possible permutations of routes it could take. Figuring out the optimal order of delivery drop-offs is a classic *order of operations* problem in complex systems research. Finding the best route requires not just finding the shortest path, but finding the best order in which deliveries should be dropped off on that particular day.

Route-planning machine-learning software will prove to be a skilled driver. When driverless cars and trucks are the norm, HD digital maps will contain information of the exact location, status, and growth rate of every detail on the road's surface. Combine this intimate knowledge of the road with the big picture intelligence of route-planning analytics, and the level of mastery driverless cars have over the roadways increases even more.

With human drivers out of the equation, roads will no longer require physical signs. Instead, streets will be virtually "marked" by being depicted in a car's digital 3-D model. Driverless cars will know exactly what the speed limit is without having to look at a road-side sign. Their software will keep track of details of dangerous spots—for example, a particular bridge that becomes icy when temperatures plummet. When driverless cars are the norm, today's one-size-fits-all speed limits can be replaced by flexible, adaptive speed limits that factor in road and traffic conditions, as well as a particular driverless vehicle's unique capabilities.

Some of the benefits of driverless cars will kick in only when most of the vehicular traffic on the roads is fully autonomous. One such benefit would be the implementation of an automated "traffic priority" system that would ease commutes and help emergency vehicles more quickly ferry their ailing passengers to the hospital. Such a tiered traffic prioritization system would require that all cars be fully autonomous since human drivers don't always have the self-discipline or the big-picture view to follow route-planning instructions appropriately.

In an automated traffic priority system, different modes of traffic would be placed into priority tiers. The highest-priority traffic, of course, would be emergency vehicles, or passengers in some kind of distress. Next could be underage children unaccompanied by their parents. The next tier could be adult commuters on their way to work or running routine errands. The lowest tier would be commercial delivery vehicles that could be routed onto slower and less efficient side routes to clear the streets for higher-priority traffic. One potentially controversial possibility would be that city planners set up a "priority free market" where people buy and sell traffic priority, similar to the way airlines offer passengers more money if they give up their seats on an overbooked flight.

PRIVACY

Another regulatory challenge that will need to be solved with driverless cars is that of passenger privacy. Smart phones and social media have already introduced a whole new host of ethical challenges involving privacy. Driverless cars will be just as problematic. Ideally, the same regulation and consumer watchdog groups that strive to protect people against government surveillance and corporate data brokers will extend their future efforts to driverless cars as well.

Driverless cars will have unique privacy problems. Cars are mobile, and once they're equipped with several high-definition video cameras plus super-human perception and recognition ability, they could morph into ubiquitous robotic spies. The potential for abuse is high. Driverless cars could photograph their passengers or pedestrians walking by the side of the road and run those photos through face-recognition software. Their face-recognition software could send updates to the government about the people it spots. Less sinister but more annoying, car software could send data describing the garb, travel patterns, or other habits of their passengers to marketing departments of corporations eager for insight into how fashion trends play out by age-group, or where people like to eat lunch.

Both pedestrians and passengers who ride in driverless cars will need some sort of privacy protections or, at least, transparent rules of engagement. Everyone who owns a driverless car should know what data is being collected and who can access it. If the companies that make driverless-car software plan to sell their customer's data to third-party brokers, their customers should have a say in whether or not they want their personal data to be brokered.

If the future of personal mobility is on-demand driverless pods, the companies that manage fleets of pods will need to operate under strict data privacy guidelines. Given the high volumes of passengers and journeys they handle, driverless taxis will be a potential gold mine for data brokers, intrusive government surveillance, and garden-variety snoops. Passengers should be in control of whether they wish to permit their driverless taxi to collect and share data about their journey. Perhaps some taxi passengers might agree to a full data share, but only if they receive a discounted taxi fare in exchange.

Privacy is related to another sort of safety challenge, that of software vulnerabilities. Any software operating system is vulnerable to simple malfunction and malevolent hacks. As we discussed in previous chapters, both hardware and software systems contain potential security vulnerabilities. A car's CAN bus is an unguarded entry point for a would-be hacker. On the software level, a driverless car's operating system will need to be designed so it's redundant, so should a reliability problem occur, the back-up system can quickly take the wheel.

If the car is reliant on external data, delays in data transmission—be they malicious or benign—could be a safety hazard. GPS spoofing could become a new form of criminal sabotage. HD digital maps could be another target. The data channels that provide map updates must be secure, and their data source authenticated and certified. A car's route-planning and traffic-prediction software stays informed by sending data on a car's destination to the broader traffic system, representing another potential target for a security breach.

ETHICS

Data privacy and safety are one sort of ethical challenge raised by driverless cars that must be addressed. Another is how the car responds to an emergency. When faced with a hazardous situation, driverless cars use data and software—not human instinct—to calculate how best to respond. In order to design a car that reacts appropriately, a human programmer has to make difficult decisions about the value of human life and property by quantifying its value.

When software drives the car, a human driver will no longer be in place to make the grisly calculation of "who to kill" at the time of a crash. Instead, the logic of the decision will be made in advance, by the human programming the car's software. Driverless-car software will be designed to calculate how to respond to an accident in such a way that yields an optimal outcome with minimal collateral damage. However, in order to create such software, we as a society must first define what constitutes "optimal," and in the process, consciously articulate how we value human life and property.

The practice of assigning value to human life and property raises uncomfortable questions about what these values should be, and who gets to set them. Passengers inside the car will have an assigned value, as will pedestrians. Possible outcomes associated with car accidents—for example, property damage, or damage to the car—will also be quantified. If a driverless car is programmed with the generic goal of "reducing damage to property" in the case of an accident, it's not clear exactly how what that response should look like.

When we give talks to audiences about the value and potential impact of driverless cars, inevitably someone at the back of the room will raise his hand and ask a variation of this question: "If faced with a fatal situation, how will a driverless car decide between whether it will kill two babies next to the roadside, or all five adult passengers inside the car?" While raised in a new context, this ethical choice question is actually an old chestnut, a variant of the well-known *Trolley Problem*[4] that students in philosophy classes have discussed for decades.

The Trolley Problem, conceived by Philippa Foot in 1967, describes the ethical conundrum of "a driver of a runaway tram [who] can steer only from one narrow track onto another; five men are working on one track and one man on the other; anyone on the track he enters is bound to be killed." Most people will do the simple utilitarian calculation that five lives are worth more than one, and consider this a no-brainer. But the Trolley Problem case then continues to get more complicated with other morbid choices that lead, eventually, to paradoxical dilemmas.

The Trolley Problem is not unique to driverless cars. Recently, in downtown Ithaca in upstate New York, we witnessed a tragic demonstration of the Trolley Problem. One sunny Friday afternoon while driving down the steep hill that leads into Ithaca's bustling downtown, a truck driver became aware that his brakes had given out. He was forced to make the painful decision about which way to aim his deadly, out of control two-ton truck. The driver elected to steer his truck away from a group of construction workers and instead, aimed his truck into a nearby café, accidentally killing Amanda Bush, 27, a young mother spending that summer afternoon earning extra money as a bartender.

One researcher writing about ethics articulates a common concern as follows. "One major disadvantage of automated vehicles during crashes is that unlike a human driver who can decide how to crash in real-time, an automated vehicle's decision of how to crash was defined by a programmer ahead of time."[5] Statements such as this make us question why it is considered acceptable for a human driver to "decide how to crash in real-time," yet it's considered an ethical problem if a vehicle's crash reaction was "defined by a programmer ahead of time." For one, driverless vehicles will actually conduct a more rational and rapid risk/ benefit analysis than could a drunk, selfish, or tired human. Second, driverless cars will have 360-degree sensory perception to inform them.

It seems that the perceived "ethical" problem of driverless cars is not based on the fact that driving (no matter who's behind the wheel) involves an ongoing series of calculations in which the cost of risk is weighed against its benefits. Instead, the so-called ethical problem of driverless cars lies in the fact that these calculations will be performed with cold precision by artificial intelligence. The issue at stake is not whether driverless cars will be "ethical." The real ethical challenge is defining what the precrash logic should look like.

Every human driver performs some kind of risk/benefit calculation when faced with danger. One person might decide that the best way to reduce damages would be to react in such a way that the car does the least possible harm to the driver, even though that decision means the car will run over several people. Another person might react by steering the car away from the people near the road, at the cost of totaling the car and killing himself.

Most experienced human drivers know that when they drive, they are making a continual stream of decisions that involve assigning a value to different types of life and property. This process is usually subconscious. More than once one of us has had to perform an emergency maneuver to avoid hitting a "minor" life form, a squirrel running across the road. My rational brain does not ask myself whether my swerve was "worth it." Yet, the fact that I elected to swerve to avoid the squirrel means that I did the calculation and decided that the value of the life of the squirrel is worth more than the tiny risk to myself and my car should my swerve cause me to lose control of my vehicle and crash.

My calculation of risk could grow very complex. If I had three children in the back seat of my car, I might have chosen to not swerve and to let the squirrel take his chances. If the roads were icy and crowded with pedestrians, my moral calculation would likely have been that the value of the human lives inside and outside the car was higher than that of the squirrel. In that case, I would have opted not to swerve. My calculation could grow even more complex were the hypothetical squirrel be replaced by a dog, then an old person on crutches, and so on.

Those of us fortunate enough never to have had a severe traffic accident have not had to perform the uncomfortable task of publicly articulating why we reacted the way we did when faced with an unavoidable traffic tragedy. Driverless cars stir up consternation since they force us to publicly reveal this calculation. Even more challenging, driverless cars will require that, as a society, we agree on a uniform set of ethical codes that will guide the decision-making process of artificial-intelligence software when faced with an emergency.

Driverless cars will require us to agree on a set of cultural moral codes to guide an automated vehicle's decision-making process in an emergency. In a fair and democratic society, the standards of this set of codes would be agreed upon by the general public and adhered to by the companies that make driverless cars. Not only should the calculus of tragedy be publicly agreed upon, if disaster strikes, a car's disaster response "rule book" should be made open, transparent, and verifiable after an accident. Similar to the steps aviation officials take after a plane crash, after a car accident a driverless car's guiding software, its "black box," should be made available to insurance investigators and law enforcement officials so they can analyze what steps, exactly, the car's software went through.

As these moral codes are translated into law, the result will be new forms of ethical lapses and crime. Imagine if an analysis of a car's black box were to reveal that a driverless-car company sold cars bearing illegal "guardian software" designed to place a high value on only the lives of the people inside the car and zero value on those in other cars. Or imagine that after an accident, a car's black box revealed that a misguided mechanic had tinkered with a car's software to in order to minimize physical damage to the car, no matter what the cost to other people nearby.

Self-driving vehicles will challenge how we define privacy and liability, and will transform driving into an activity guided not by human instincts, but by data. The geography of cities will undergo another wave of change as parking lots vanish and data-driven cars plan optimal routes, easing the pain of car travel. When driverless cars become commonplace, autonomous transportation will give us new choices in where we live, and how we work. Some jobs will disappear. New jobs will emerge, created by business models made possible by removing human drivers from the cost equation.

12

THE RIPPLE EFFECTS

Now that we've nearly reached the end of this book, we would like to bring up an issue that any in-depth exploration of driverless cars would be incomplete if it did not address: the topic of hype. In recent years, driverless cars have been the subject of a great deal of attention from the media. However, if there's one lesson the long and colorful history of hands-free, feet-free driving should have taught us, it's that even as people long for autonomous vehicles, desire is no guarantee that such a vehicle will actually appear.

Veterans of the tech industry may recall a two-wheeled go-cart called the Segway. In the year 2001, the Segway was launched with great fanfare. A few days before the launch, an article in *Time* magazine described the clouds of hype that accompanied the Segway's secretive development process.[1] According to the article, in a leaked book proposal about the technology, Steve Jobs predicted the Segway would be as "big as the PC" and legendary venture capitalist John Doerr pondered whether the Segway could be "maybe bigger than the Internet." Turns out nearly everybody was wrong. Today, the Segway enjoys a quiet existence as a niche transportation solution, enabling warehouse workers and mail delivery personnel to roll short distances.

The swift rise and fall of emerging technologies such as the Segway raise an interesting question: why do some promising new technologies eventually disrupt entire industries, while others fail to live up to their hype? Like many others, we have pondered this question at length. Over the years, we've developed a useful little test we call the *Zero Principle* to assess the long-term potential of new technologies.

Here's how the Zero Principle works. Emerging technologies that disrupt established industries share a common trait: their introduction dramatically reduces one or more production costs to nearly zero. In fact, once technologies that follow the Zero Principle have been in use for a few years, their effect on their industry is so disruptive that the eventual result is an industrial revolution.

Let's look at some historical examples, beginning with the steam engine. If you were a technology observer in England during the late 1700s, would you have invested in the newly commercialized steam engine? If you had pondered this new contraption in the context of the Zero Principle, you would have immediately seen its potential.

The steam engine dramatically reduced the cost of keeping industrial machinery running. Before the invention of steam power, factories and mills were powered by sources that introduced either direct costs or indirect costs in the form of operating constraints. Factories fueled by running water had to be located in regions that boasted fast-running streams or waterfalls. Animal power was location-independent, but animals were not as powerful as the force of running water, plus they tired rapidly and had to be tended and fed.

When the commercial steam engine was introduced to industry, both the direct and indirect costs of powering industrial machinery nearly evaporated, transforming the manufacturing process and eventually bringing about an industrial revolution. Steam power made it cost-effective to produce steel, which triggered another cascade of downstream innovation. The availability of cheap, robust steel, in turn, gave birth to several downstream industries such as rail transportation and the construction of "ironclads," naval vessels lined with steel to protect them against cannon fire.

Nearly two centuries later, another profoundly disruptive technology appeared: the computer. The computer, like the steam engine, was destined to shake up established industries since it reduced another once-formidable cost factor to nearly zero, the cost of numerical calculation. For most of human history, making mathematical calculations has been a slow, expensive, and (depending on the person) inaccurate process. Even the most highly trained expert humans armed with the best tools could make only a few hundred calculations per hour.

As computing technology matured in the 1950s, the cost of calculation began to drop precipitously. In the decades that followed, silicon chips replaced analog technologies, making computers faster and more reliable and affordable. Small businesses gained the capacity to carry out once-costly calculations quickly, accurately, and tirelessly. By the end of the twentieth century, cheap calculation enabled the emergence of a massive global market for productivity software and video games as regular people bought their own personal computer or gaming console.

History reveals that two very different technologies—the steam engine and the computer—shared an underlying trait in common. Their introduction to industry removed a once-major cost barrier, changing business practices in many different industry sectors and dramatically reshaping how people lived and worked. Today, driverless-car technology continues to develop by leaps and bounds. Only the passage of time will reveal whether we're currently on the cusp of another period of sweeping social change, or whether we'll eventually dismiss driverless cars as just another over-hyped emerging technology that failed to bear fruit.

Let's apply the Zero Principle to driverless cars and examine the direct and indirect costs they reduce. One of the most significant monetary and social costs that driverless cars will reduce is that of harm from traffic-related accidents. Another cost that's eradicated is the cost of time spent driving. For regular people, time spent driving is an indirect opportunity cost; for transportation companies, the cost of a human driver's time is direct in the form of salary, a major cost component that defines how goods are moved from one place to another. Finally, since driverless cars remove accident-prone humans from the wheel, cars and delivery trucks will no longer need to be weighty and environmentally unfriendly, reducing the cost of fuel and enabling the introduction of a wide variety of vehicle body shapes and sizes.

Four core costs are reduced to nearly zero by autonomous vehicle technology.

1. Toward zero harm Driving is a high-risk activity. Driverless cars will greatly reduce the direct and indirect costs that result from car accidents. They greatly reduce the annual cost of traffic-related hospital bills (an estimated price tag of $18 billion a year in the United States) and the associated cost of lost wages ($33 billion a year).[2] Industries that rely on revenue from car accidents—medical, insurance, organ donor—will lose a major source of revenue.

2. Toward zero skill Driverless cars remove a major cost of transporting people or goods: salaries. A truck driver's salary is a significant cost element of moving goods and merchandise. Most of the cost of using a taxi is associated with paying the driver's salary.

3. Toward zero time Driverless cars reduce the indirect cost of time spent driving. The average person in the United States spends about three hours a day driving[3] and a total of sixty-three hours a year stuck in traffic.[4] The opportunity cost of time formerly spent driving will be replaced by productive work time or enjoyable personal time.

4. Toward zero size Human-driven cars are large and bulky as a result of safety-related design constraints. Driverless cars will be much less likely to have accidents, so their body size can be smaller and more lightweight. Delivery vehicles without a human driver will need to be only as large as the object they're delivering.

Figure 12.1
GM's Electric Networked-Vehicle (EN-V) Concept pod, an autonomous two-seater codeveloped with Segway for short trips in cities.
Source: General Motors

JOBS

The direct and indirect costs of human-driven vehicles have defined business models for nearly a century. As driverless cars reduce or even remove these costs, the result will be that some businesses will no longer be viable. As some businesses close up shop and jobs disappear, new businesses and professions will emerge.

The first job likely to go will be that of driving a truck, a stable, well-paying blue-collar job that has been largely immune from the effects of offshoring and automation. According to the 2010 U.S. Census, there are nearly 3.5 million truckers in the United States. In fact, driving a truck is the twenty-ninth most common job category in the nation. If driverless trucks become a viable way to transport merchandise from place to place, in a few short years automation may finally be coming to claim trucking jobs as well.

Figure 12.2

The most common job in most U.S. states in 2014 was truck driving.
Source: National Public Radio

Truckers won't be the only ones whose jobs are taken by driverless vehicles. Taxi drivers and chauffeurs will also find themselves out of work. The profession of taxi driving has already been disrupted by the growing popularity of services such as Uber and Lyft, where anybody with a car can become a cabby. Driverless cars will sound the final death knell to the jobs of roughly 233,700 cabbies and chauffeurs employed in the United States.[5]

Uber's CEO, Travis Kalanick, believes that the biggest cost component of running a taxi service is paying the car's driver. In a talk at a conference, Kalanick said, "When there's no other dude in the car, the cost of taking an Uber anywhere becomes cheaper than owning a vehicle."[6] To develop a car that can drive without a "dude" behind the wheel, Uber has invested $5.5 million to develop driverless-car technology, hiring dozens of robotics researchers from Carnegie Mellon University's National Robotics Engineering Center (NREC).[7]

Driverless cars will transform other jobs in the gigantic economic value chain that supports the buying, selling, and maintaining of the automobile. We recently brought our car to the dealer for a routine service. While waiting in the service center's waiting room, sipping free coffee from a Styrofoam cup and reading old, sticky magazines, we overheard a muffled argument between employees over their next week's work schedules. The two employees were arguing about who would take the weekend shift. Little do they know that in a decade or two, clocking in on a Saturday may become a common occurrence.

When cars become capable of driving themselves, human passengers will no longer need to visit a car dealer's service center during business hours. Cars will drive themselves to the dealership when they need service. Since most people won't want their car to disappear at an inconvenient time, they ll ask their car to go for service at 3 am and be home by morning. The 739,900 employees in the United States who currently work as automotive service technicians might argue about who's going to take the 3 am shift, but no one will be there to overhear them.[8]

As jobs disappear, whether or not new jobs will appear in their place remains an open question. In the 1940s economist Joseph Schumpeter coined the term *creative destruction* to describe the restructuring process that follows the introduction of a disruptive technology. While this restructuring process touches several major parts of the economy, including equipment used and regulatory structures, its most visible and controversial manifestation is in the destruction of jobs.

Economists who are Schumpeterians take a positive view of the cycle of creative destruction. They believe that the net long-term effect of disruptive technology is job creation. Although a disruptive technology may displace an entire sector of workers, Schumpeterian thinking would argue that the long-term effect will be the creation of more and better jobs, as new industries spring out of the ashes of the old one.

Proponents of creative destruction point out that as technology destroys old industries, new industries emerge. Countless examples of creative destruction abound. Desktop-publishing software eliminated typesetting jobs, but it created new market opportunities for creative people and small firms who finally had their own tools to design and publish their own brochures, books, and newsletters. In the travel industry, web sites such as Expedia led to the near-elimination of the occupation of travel agents. Yet when travelers gained the ability to make their own travel arrangements, Expedia also helped spark the creation of a much larger and more active global tourism industry.

As artificial-intelligence software and robots become increasingly sophisticated and skilled, however, the notion that the process of creative destruction ushers in newer and better jobs for displaced workers is falling under greater scrutiny. In the previous two centuries, human workers displaced by a new technology could (at least in theory) find jobs in the industries spawned by the new technology. In contrast, in recent years as the automation of jobs climbs the skill ladder from manual factory jobs to white-collar analytical jobs, it's harder to find uses for the human workers automation displaces. Because of the efficiencies enabled by modern information technologies, when old jobs go away, frequently the number of new jobs created is far fewer and these new jobs are poorly paid.

As more and more future work will be handled by intelligent software and robots, two key questions will determine whether the process of creative destruction winds up eventually being truly creative, or whether its long-term impact will be merely destructive. The first question is whether new jobs are better than the old ones, meaning as secure, interesting, and well paid. The second question involves the length of the period of displacement. Will displaced workers be unemployed for just a few months, or will their displacement stretch on for years? Ideally, displaced workers would be retrained and quickly rehired. However, in the worst-case scenario, workers displaced by technology would be forced to sit outside of the workforce for years, perhaps even a lifetime.

As machines take away human jobs, one potentially devastating effect will be to further exacerbate the trend toward income inequality, a growing global problem. Research published by anti-poverty charity Oxfam shows that the world's rich are getting richer. The percentage of the world's wealth that's owned by the wealthiest 1 percent of the global population has increased from 44 percent in 2009 to 48 percent in 2014 and is expected to continue until, in the next couple of years, the wealthiest 1 percent will own more than half of the world's assets and resources.[9]

An in-depth analysis of creative destruction is beyond the scope of this book. We introduce the concept here to demonstrate what could happen when driverless cars—like other disruptive technologies before them—rearrange the structure of several industries and take away millions of jobs. The worst-case scenario would be that as driverless cars disrupt industries and remove the need for human drivers, the already widening gap between rich and poor will only grow larger. On the other hand, a more positive outcome could be that driverless cars create economic growth and high-quality jobs for people at all levels of society.

THE WAGES OF ACCIDENTS

Let's examine some industries whose profitability will be dented by driverless cars. As the old saying goes, one man's gain is another man's loss. While driverless cars will save lives, fuel, and time, the losers will be the companies whose business models rely on the morbid profits generated by car accidents. These morbid merchants include a broad array of businesses, from car insurers to personal-injury lawyers, from body shops to part suppliers, from highway-patrol officers to defensive-driving instructors, from organ-donation organizations to emergency-room operators, and from traffic courts to jails.

In the United States, each year the total population spends a total of one million days in the hospital as a result of injuries from car accidents.[10] Approximately 20 percent of organ transplants in the United States originate from victims of fatal traffic accidents.[11] Even prisons rely on the weakness of human drivers. In 1997, 7 percent of jail inmates and 14 percent of probationers were in for driving while intoxicated (DWI).[12]

Car-related foibles earn cities billions of dollars each year from collected fines. An unpleasant truth about law and parking enforcement is that tickets are sometimes given not as a matter of public safety, but in order to maintain a municipality's coffers. If humans were no longer speeding or parking badly, an important source of revenue for many municipalities would disappear.

In the United States alone, an estimated $6 billion of revenue is generated from speeding tickets each year.[13] In an average year, New York City collects more than $600 million from parking tickets.[14] A world of driverless cars that obey the law perfectly and have recorded data to prove it would disrupt revenue sources on which cities and states have come to rely.

Another industry that will need to be revamped is the business of selling car insurance. The jury is still out on how, exactly, the $200 billion-a-year auto insurance industry will be affected. One the one hand, insurance companies might see a boom in their profits as driverless cars have fewer accidents, costing less money in claims. On the other hand, if car accidents become exceedingly rare, people who own driverless cars might pressure companies to lower their insurance rates. In the United States, since car insurance is regulated at the state level, consumers could pressure their state governments to eventually eliminate mandatory car insurance requirements altogether.

Driverless cars will force the law and insurance companies to reconsider how fault is assigned in car accidents. Insurance legal scholar Robert Peterson writes that insurance and tort law (the law of who's at fault) are like fraternal twins: not identical, but a reflection of one another. Peterson states that as autonomous vehicles gain popularity, "an increasing amount of liability for injuries is likely to bypass drivers and alight on the sellers and manufacturers of the vehicle."[15]

If the burden of liability is passed from individual human driver to driverless vehicle, insurance companies will be forced to change how they structure the cost of insurance. Traditional vehicle insurance premiums hinge on the human driver's risk profile. If the age, gender, and driving record of a car owner are no longer relevant in the calculation of insurance premiums, traditional ways to assess a driver's risk will no longer apply.

If driverless cars were to be insured in the same way that products are, the manufacturers of the vehicles would be legally required to assume liability in the case of an accident. The cost of insuring a driverless car would be based on the potential risk the car represents as a product. New ways to assess a car s risk profile would have to be invented, perhaps the humansafe rating of the car's operating system we discussed earlier, or the total number of deep-learning miles the car's "fleet mind" has collectively driven.

If insurance companies held car manufacturers responsible for passengers' safety, a tremendous amount of work would have to be done to legally clarify exactly which manufacturer was at fault in the case of a driverless car accident. The two primary manufacturers in question would likely be those that provide the car's operating system and those that provide the car's mechanical body. Given the complexity of a driverless car's operating system and the tight integration of hardware and software, however, deciding which manufacturer is ultimately at fault will a difficult process, particularly in cases where misuse or hazardous road conditions are involved.

Another area that will need further exploration in assigning liability is the issue of car maintenance. If the owner of a driverless car or taxi were to fail to obtain regular software and hardware updates for his vehicle, it would no longer be an open-and-shut case that the car's manufacturer was at fault. A good corporate lawyer could argue that if a mechanic tampered with a car's operating system or broke a critical hardware sensor, the mechanic—not the manufacturing company or the car's owner—should be responsible for paying damages resulting from an accident.

One solution to the problem of car insurance would be for taxi companies to offer "per ride" insurance as part of the car's software guarantee. Before hopping into a driverless taxi, a passenger would be asked to agree to accept whatever harmful consequences might arise as a result of riding in the car. Today we buy our computers with a click-through license. Perhaps someday, as we clamber into a driverless taxi pod, we may find ourselves squinting at a 200-page click-through license that asks us to agree to waive our right to seek retribution if our taxi winds up in a car crash.

THE NEW CAR BODY

We predict that driverless cars will look different, both inside and outside. The steering wheel will disappear, the dashboard will become flexible workspace, and the car's cabin will contain whatever people need for their on-board leisure and work activities. Outside, cars won't need side mirrors or tail lights.

As we described in chapter 3, our prediction is that the car industry of the future will divide itself into two broad categories: companies that make standard-issue utilitarian transportation pods, and companies that produce special-purpose cars for consumers, ranging from tiny one-person custom pods to large, luxurious mobiles for sleeping or work. Most of the new cars will be sold to transportation companies rather than directly to consumers. While the market for special-purpose, privately owned cars will be relatively small, it will need skilled car designers.

One positive side effect of driverless cars will be that consumer car design will enjoy a renaissance, a new golden age of automobiles. In the 1950s and 1960s, car designers created cars with showy large fins, painted in unapologetically cheerful colors. Driverless car designers will specialize in shamelessly luxurious or cleverly designed multipurpose flexible interiors that enable people to sleep, eat, and work inside their cars.

As safety becomes less of a concern, perhaps consumers will design their own car bodies with the help of intelligent, automated design software. New car buyers, even those who know nothing of car design, will browse through virtual showrooms online. As their eyes alight on a pleasing design, their computer will note the

Figure 12.3
Passengers relax with electronics n this driverless concept mockup.
Source: Rinspeed AG; image © Rinspeed Inc.

dilation of their pupils and show them several additional iterations. Of course consumer's car designs would be subject to some
restrictions in order to obey the laws of aerodynamics. To be
considered "street legal," consumer's designs would also have to
meet other established basic safety guidelines in order to be
manufactured.

The buyer and software would follow an iterative design process, going back and forth several times to refine the new car's
shape and styling. Once a buyer settled on a design, the car would
take a week to manufacture. Its body panels and chassis would be
3-D printed out of carbon fiber, creating a frame as light and strong
as a bird's bones. The freshly printed car would be sent on its way
and programmed to text its new owners when it was an hour away
from their home. Upon arrival, the new custom car would glide
into the driveway, unlock its doors, and present itself to its new
owner/passengers.

In an era of driverless vehicles, some automotive jobs will be
quite specialized. A new high-paying specialty will emerge, that

of software mechanic. Software mechanics will be automotive engineers who specialize in a particular aspect of a car's operating system, either low-, mid-, or high-level controls. Some software mechanics will be reliability specialists who advise car buyers on the merits of different humansafe ratings.

Another specialty will be noise and vibration cancellation. Anyone who has tried to sleep in a rocking, rattling bed in an RV that's in motion has experienced the discomforts of sleeping in a moving vehicle. Acoustic dampening, vibration cancellation, and motion compensation have long been an area of engineering expertise in many other fields. Automotive engineers who specialize in predictive signal processing (the same technology used by noise canceling headphones) will be able to make driverless cars smoother and quieter.

THE NEW MARKETING

Another side effect of driverless cars that we foresee will be that the process of marketing products gains a new physical dimension. Driverless-car software will become the site of a new marketing battleground: route bidding. Today's traditional static maps point out local "points of interest," notable landmarks that could be anything from restaurants to tourist attractions to parks to shopping malls to museums.

In a driverless future, businesses will pay the companies that make HD maps to be presented as a "point of interest." When a passenger hails a driverless taxi and asks to get to her destination, the pod's operating system will ask whether she wants to stop at a few, specially chosen, destinations. Passengers who agree will get 25 percent off on every store they stop at along the way.

The idea that merchants can influence a customer's experience in return for free or discounted prices is not new. Even now, people enjoy reading content on free websites whose business model is based on online advertising. Most of us accepted this new kind of "free" tradeoff long ago. We permit companies to mine the contents of our emails and our text messages in exchange for free email services and cheap phones.

Driverless car passengers will negotiate their terms as well. Savvy passengers will know how to exchange their physical presence at a "point of interest" destination for reduction in taxi fare, or if they own the driverless car, to receive cheaper fuel. Restaurants will agree to split the cost of the gas for a family's road trip if their digital profile indicates that each time this family dines out, they spend $200. Some passengers will trade the value of their time. In exchange for a slightly longer and less convenient route, they'll get cheaper taxi fare.

THE NEW RETAIL

Business and restaurants that skillfully find ways to route customers their way will benefit from driverless cars. Another industry that will change is the retail business. Driverless cars will be the latest disruption in an industry that's already been transformed several times over the past century, first by the introduction of mass production, then malls, then big box discount stores, then online retail.

In ancient times, rare spices were transported in camel caravans from the Far East to European markets. Today, tankers carry mass-produced goods to ports all over the world where gigantic containers are loaded onto trucks and carried to the loading dock of the store. Regardless of the nature of the product, transportation costs factor into its price. For physical products, transportation costs account for approximately 14 percent of the price of agricultural goods, and 9 percent of the price of manufactured goods.[16]

The cost of transporting goods to the buyer has always been a key element in determining a retailer's business strategy. Driverless cars will remove one major competitive advantage enjoyed by large companies, economies of scale. As the once-prohibitive costs of transporting cottage goods to market shrink,

Figure 12.4
Autonomous delivery method.
Source: Image courtesy Starship Technologies

small companies will be able to compete on price with larger companies.

One retail industry that's poised for disruption is that of locally grown and organic food. Consumers happily pay top dollar for fresh, locally produced, farm-to-table food. Consumers also like the idea of supporting a diverse agricultural economy made up of several small regional farms. Despite the appeal of locally grown food, however, most of us still wind up buying factory farmed produce in the grocery store. Since they grow and transport food in high volumes, industrial-scale corporate farms can survive with smaller profit margins on individual products, and therefore are able to offer consumers lower-priced food in chain grocery stores.

Driverless trucks will enable artisan food producers to compete with corporate factory farms. Our friends in upstate New York own a sheep farm where they enjoy a peaceful life in the countryside growing organic vegetables and tending their animals. The most expensive and onerous part of their go-to-market strategy is their biweekly drives to the city where they sell their fresh merchandise in urban farmer's markets.

Twice a week during the summer months, their market day begins at 1 am. The drive to New York City takes four hours, leaving them one hour to rest and another two to set up before the market opens at 7 am. At the end of a long day of selling their wares, they drive back in the dark. Imagine if they could buy a driverless truck and spend the journey sleeping soundly in the back. Even better, they could broaden their commercial reach by sending some of their produce off in a driverless vehicle to other regional markets where a colleague could sell their products on commission.

Small farms are just one of millions of regional-scale manufacturers whose business model is burdened by transportation overhead. Any company that produces small runs of perishable lower-margin commodities needs an efficient distribution network to remain profitable. Networks of efficient driverless transportation vehicles will enable small firms to sell their wares at regional points of retail at prices that are competitive with those of mass-produced, corporate products.

One of the major components in the cost of transporting goods has been the salary of the human driver. Companies deal with the high cost of salaries by delivering goods to retail outlets using one large truck rather than two or three small ones. Cost-conscious shipping companies aggregate several individual shipments into a single, large delivery vehicle. This approach has led to the widespread use of an inefficient "hub and spoke" transportation model that delays delivery and causes vehicles to drive additional miles. In a hub-and-spoke model, individual shipments must first journey to the nearest hub, or distribution center, where they are aggregated with other small shipments into a single, larger one before being finally dispatched to their final destination. When the cost of the human driver is removed from the equation, a shipment can take a more direct route to its buyer.

When autonomous delivery vehicles deliver merchandise directly to stores or customer s doorsteps, their size and shape will reflect the physical dimensions of the products they deliver. Today's delivery vehicles have to account for the fact that there's a human driver on board, therefore a substantial portion of their size is dedicated to the driver's comfort and safety. For example, a human-driven vehicle that delivers pizza weighs more than a ton, even though the pizza being delivered weighs only a few pounds. In contrast, an autonomous delivery vehicle would not need airbags or a heavy, crash-resistant frame, spare tire, dashboard, or air-conditioning. It would be compact, lightweight, and cheap and just a little bit larger than its on-board merchandise.

Online shopping already has made inroads into traditional forms of in-store retail and each year, the number of goods that people buy online continues to increase. According to the NPD group, a market research firm that tracks sales instances across 165,000 stores worldwide, brick-and-mortar retailers have been experiencing a gradual drop in "buying visits," visits where a buyer walks out of the store with a product in hand.[17] Between the years 2012 and 2014, brick-and-mortar buying visits dropped by 13 percent, while online buying visits rose by 21 percent. Although in-person buying visits are still almost four times more common than online buying visits, as time passes, eventually online shopping will dominate.

Online shopping changes the trade-offs that consumers have to make. According to conventional retail wisdom, most people make their purchasing decisions based on "3 Cs": Cost, Quality, and Convenience. For most of history, consumers had to choose two of these three ideal qualities. Convenient, high-quality goods were not cheap, whereas easily accessible cheap goods usually involved a compromise on quality. E-commerce, however, has changed the rule of the 3 C's. As online retailers continuously accelerate the speed of their shipping methods and offer high quality products at low prices, the trend toward buying online is likely to continue.

Driverless delivery vehicles will increase the appeal of online shopping even more. Some enterprising retailers will take advantage of the low cost of driverless pods to bring the physical store to

Figure 12.5
Autonomous delivery truck.
Source: Inage courtesy IDEO

the customer. For example, if a customer of the future wants to buy a new pair of shoes, she'll order half a dozen candidate pairs of shoes online. A driverless pod will deliver several pairs of shoes to her home so she can try them on in private, test them out for size and comfort, and pack the unwanted pairs back into the delivery pod to take back to the store.

Driverless delivery vehicles will usher in a new era of e-commerce. Today, online retailers in urban areas already compete over who can deliver purchases more quickly. In population-dense cities, same-day delivery, even two-hour delivery, is becoming an increasingly popular option. Nearly instantaneous delivery by a swift, fuel-efficient pod will erode one of the few remaining benefits offered by brick-and-mortar stores, the ability to receive products immediately.

CRIME AND (ADULT) ENTERTAINMENT

No analysis of a new technology would be complete without acknowledging one of its potential dark sides: criminal activity. Many of us have already experienced the dark side of computer crime in the form of malevolent data breaches and identify theft.

Driverless cars will also appeal to ambitious and intelligent criminals who have a taste for high-tech crime.

Some hackers will apply their talents to stealing and compromising data from driverless car sensors, digital maps, and operating systems. Another type of attack that will require a less brainy perpetrator will be that of *robojacking*, or hijacking a driverless car by walking in front of it while it is stopped at an intersection. Robojacking will be a particular problem in countries that are already plagued today by crimes of kidnapping and ransom.

Robojackers will take advantage of the fact that driverless cars will be programmed to spare the lives of a human whenever possible. To stop a two-ton driverless vehicle in its tracks, all a gang of robojackers would have to do would be to exploit the vehicle's built-in safety features. If a few robojackers stood firmly in front and behind a driverless car, it would be frozen in place, unable to move.

Most robojacking assaults would be made on vehicles carrying lucrative, high-value cargo. Occasionally, however, a passenger car would be captured. With no "manual override" to force the stalled driverless vehicle to speed away to safety, the terrified passenger would be a sitting duck, trapped in a bizarre AI nightmare.

Another new form of mischief might be that human drivers bully driverless cars by driving erratically near them. A human-driven vehicle zigzagging down the highway, weaving in and out of a driverless platoon, would create mayhem. Over time, this sort of disruption, however, would eventually die out. As the car's on-board machine-learning software learns to share the road with vehicles exhibiting erratic driving patterns, human troublemakers would have to come up with some other new form of unpredictable behavior.

Speaking of potential mischief and unpredictable behavior, what will regular people do in driverless cars, once they no longer have to worry about driving? According to a survey conducted by Carnegie Mellon University, the most popular pastime for passengers in a driverless car will be using their mobile devices. Next on the list will be eating then reading, watching movies, and, finally, working.[18]

Once people no longer have to worry about driving, they'll find new ways to entertain themselves while they travel. Today most ease the tedium of driving by listening to the car radio. In fact, surveys show that nearly half of the time people spend listening to the radio is while they're in the car.[19] When people are no longer limited to hearing only their in-car entertainment, radio consumption will plummet while consumption of visual entertainment such as movies and video games will increase.

The crude, poorly designed in-car infotainment systems of today's vehicles will no longer exist. Privately owned luxury mobile offices or commuting vehicles will boast their own entertainment devices. In contrast to their luxurious cousins, driverless taxis will be stripped-down, no-nonsense affairs. Passengers will spend their time watching media on their own private devices and socializing online over the car's on-board wireless network.

For those lucky few who own their own mobile, driverless luxury vehicles, drive-time will also become time to indulge in their vice of choice, be it sex, drugs, or alcohol. We've learned from direct experience that many people have a strong interest in the future of vice. Every time we speak about driverless cars, someone approaches us privately afterward to ask "offline" whether we have thought about these three taboo "elephants," the topics that everybody thinks about but no one wants to mention out loud. In a nutshell, our answer is "yes." People will use driverless cars to indulge in all of these three popular vices.

There's one caveat, however. Since it's illegal to consume drugs in general, and against the law to consume alcohol inside a vehicle, if driverless cars are equipped with a camera that faces inside the cabin, some interesting things could happen. Deep-learning software could learn to detect the presence of people using drugs or imbibing alcohol in the car. If cities are struggling to make up for the lost revenue that used to come from parking and speeding tickets, one way they could revitalize their bottom lines could be to require that the car "report" on its passengers' wrongdoings.

Sex in a driverless car, however, would likely not be illegal (as long it's between two, unpaid consenting adults). One new line of driverless cars could be a "bed bus" model, complete with shaded windows for privacy. Over the past few decades, the consumption of pornography has been an accelerating force in the development of technologies like the VHS video player, streaming video, and the internet. Driverless cars could offer a comfortable new viewing environment for fans of pornography to immerse themselves in, particularly as virtual-reality goggles like the Oculus Rift make the experience even more intense.

THE ROAD AHEAD

What lies ahead? Robotics technologies are reaching a critical tipping point and driverless cars are finally showing real promise in becoming a safe and viable mode of transportation. I sometimes find myself wondering what it will be like to someday explain to younger generations how the act of driving used to be equated with adulthood and freedom. I imagine them snickering in disbelief when I mention that in high school, we studied driving for an entire semester.

Those of us old enough to remember what it felt like to drive will miss human-driven cars in the same way people once claimed they missed using a manual typewriter when word processors became available. Intelligent autonomous vehicles will swiftly seduce us with their efficiency and ease of use. Yet, I suspect that some of us will insist that we miss the feeling of our hands on the steering wheel and feet on the brakes, our memory of the hassles of driving cloaked by a fond haze of nostalgia.

Perhaps someday when driverless cars make travel nearly painless, people will find themselves craving a new form of entertainment: driving ranges. These future driving ranges won't be for playing golf; they'll be for driving old-fashioned cars around a track, a retro form of entertainment popular with the older generation and a few youngsters savoring the pleasures of being ironic. Maybe one of those people drawn to the driving range will be me.

A few decades from now when I'm retired and find myself with time on my hands, I may surprise myself and buy a membership in a driving range, let's call it U-Drive. Like a temperamental writer of yore letting off steam by banging hard on the keys of an old manual typewriter, when I'm craving speed or need some meditative time behind the steering wheel, I'll grab my protective driving helmet and ask my driverless car to take me to U-Drive.

Once I get there, I'll hurry to the check-in desk in hopes of getting my hands on one of the more sought-after vehicles, an ambulance or a police car. Nothing like speeding around a race track to the accompaniment of a wailing siren! As I slide behind the old, familiar steering wheel, it will feel like coming home. I'll sing along loudly to the antique radio inside the car. I'll honk the horn until the other human drivers make rude gestures at me.

Some days, this future me might drive without a helmet, even without wearing a seatbelt if I'm feeling particularly bold. I'll press my car's gas pedal as hard as I can, gleefully ignoring the rusty antique speed-limit signs posted at regular intervals next to the driving range's track. Regardless of how wild my fellow human drivers and I become, one thing is certain: the company that owns U-Drive will know how to handle us. U-Drive's owners won't tell customers this, but at the first hint of real trouble, their old-fashioned cars will shift immediately into driverless mode and their steering wheels and brakes will become useless.

Afterword: The Cambrian Explosion

Before the Cambrian explosion, the evolutionary event during which most major animal phyla appeared, life-forms were simple. Over the next few million years, the rate of diversification accelerated and life-forms began to resemble the multicellular organisms that make up the animal kingdom we are familiar with today. Some of these organisms, like the spinous slug Wiwaxia and the five-eyed Opabinia, look nothing like anything we would recognize, and would make a good template for an alien horror movie. But most of the fossils from that era are recognizable ancestors of the rich and diversified phylogeny of life-forms roaming the earth today.

In his 1989 book *Wonderful Life*, Steven Jay Gould popularized the notion of the Cambrian explosion and explored answers to the puzzle of its origin. Why did all modern animals appear in such a relatively brief period of time? The sudden diversification seemed to be contradictory to the gradual and continuous improvement process suggested by Darwinian evolution. Darwin himself, in *The Origin of Species*, noted that the sudden appearance of species with no apparent antecedents is "undoubtedly of the gravest nature" in objections to his burgeoning theory of natural selection.

The Cambrian puzzle led Gould and contemporaries like Harry Whittington and Niles Eldredge to propose the modern view of evolutionary theory, a theory of punctuated equilibria. In this view, evolution is composed of "long intervals of near-stasis punctuated by short periods of rapid change."[1]

EVOLUTIONARY ROBOTICS

Indeed, when we ran our own experiments in robot evolution, progress typically was not steady. The branch of robotics known as *evolutionary robotics* involves simulating Darwinian evolutionary processes in a computer by applying generations of variation and selection to populations of robots. In our experiments, we let the computer randomly put together robot components—mechanical joints, rigid links, motors, wires, and neurons—to make virtual machines. We then programmed the computer to select the fastest of these robots, mutate and recombine them into "offspring," place those offspring back into the population, and repeat. We then stood back and watched what happened.

In the first generation, all robots were nothing but static piles of junk, not moving at all. For at least a hundred generations thereafter, robots remained static, and it seemed as if we would never see anything interesting come out of this experiment. At around the 120th generation, the wires, motors, joints, and links were arranged by chance in such a way that caused them to vibrate and move a tiny amount. While that motion was minuscule, it was infinitely better than in the other piles of junk, which did not move at all. And so, vibrating piles of junk took over our virtual world. That "discovery of vibration," as we can retrospectively call it,

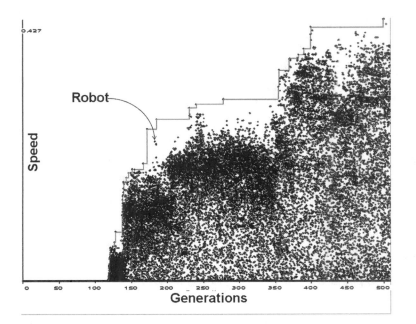

Figure 13.1
Progress of robots over hundreds of generations.

caused an abrupt "punctuated" improvement in performance of our entire simulated robot world. A few hundred generations later, some other discovery was made, and performance once again visibly improved in a large step. The process continued. After hundreds of generations we began to see beautifully working robots, some totally alien, but others with somewhat recognizable forms.

THE QUEEN OF SENSORS

While synthetic evolution of robots in the lab leaves a perfect digital record, biological evolution leaves few traces. What gave rise to the Cambrian explosion remains a mystery. Some attribute this sudden prehistoric diversification to the discovery of multicellularity itself. Others attribute it to an abundance of resources like oxygen, to the improvement of habitable conditions on earth, or to adaptive radiations following mass extinctions. Some ascribe part of it to the "discovery" of certain "enabling technologies" that unleashed a wealth of new possibilities that were not feasible before.

One of the key "technologies" that appeared during the Cambrian explosion is eyesight. There is no evidence of eyes in any fossil record before the Cambrian era, but a wide diversity of eye organs followed it. In the Burgess Shale of the Middle Cambrian and even more in later shales, there are different types of eyes, adapted to the various conditions of the organisms that bore them—eyes with different acuity, different sensitivities to light levels, different wavelengths and differences in the ability to detect motion and color.

As we noted in chapter 1, according to Andrew Parker's "light switch" theory, the appearance of eyesight "technology" changed the nature of predator-prey encounters[2] as well as chances of mating. Before eyesight, hunting and evading relied on close-range senses like smell, taste, vibration, and touch. But when predators could sense their prey from a distance using sight, new defensive and offensive strategies were needed, leading to a coevolutionary arms race. As the predator could see better, the pray needed to learn how to hide, how to run faster, how to camouflage or develop spines, each of these "new technologies" leading to further morphological diversification.

Whether or not eyesight played a key role in the Cambrian diversification we will never know for sure, but we can suggest one more hypothesis here: it was more than the eye itself that led to diversification, it was the development of the cognitive capacity that followed it.

Unlike touch, taste, and smell, visual information is "high bandwidth," in spatial resolution as well as in temporal flow, leading to data rates that are substantially higher than other sensors. Because eyesight is also a long-distance sensor, it covers a broad swath of the world outside the organism, requiring new cognitive apparatuses for scene segmentation, spatial modeling, and an expanded world understanding. Perhaps the firehose of data that suddenly flooded early brains with eyes gave an advantage to those individuals with a slightly better cognitive capacity. With that extended cognitive capacity came numerous new opportunities: new predator-prey tactics, new mate finding strategies, and access to new resources.

The machinery that makes sense of the visual information dominates our brain. Each eye contains 150 million light sensors, whereas an average ear contains just 30,000 sound-sensitive neurons. Neurons devoted to processing visual information account for 30 percent of the cortex, compared to 8 percent for touch and 3 percent for hearing.[3]

Eyesight no doubt involved the gradual coevolution of the optical eye side-by-side with the evolution of the visual cortex. The neural apparatus involved in interpreting the visual scene probably quickly found new "applications," leading to a cascade of biological innovations. First, eyesight may have contributed to cooperative evolution like symbiosis between organisms, such as the cooperation between bees and flowering plants. It may also have helped individuals find mates more easily from a distance.

Initially, this advanced mate-finding sensor may have been used just to identify individuals of the same species. But as vision acuity improved, there was an advantage to distinguishing between more desirable and less desirable mates, probably leading to eventual behaviors involving sexual selection and other forms of social communication.

The analogy between the Cambrian explosion of biological life and the imminent explosion of robotic life is hard to miss. As Gill Pratt, former director of the DARPA robotics program, who was appointed head of Toyota's autonomous vehicle division in 2015, writes:

> Today, technological developments on several fronts are fomenting a similar explosion in the diversification and applicability of robotics. Many of the base hardware technologies on which robots depend—particularly computing, data storage, and communications—have been improving at exponential growth rates. Two newly blossoming technologies—"Cloud Robotics" and "Deep Learning"—could leverage these base technologies in a virtuous cycle of explosive growth.[4]

Indeed, a number of base technologies that are key to robotics are improving rapidly, and these technologies are enabling a potential and imminent diversification of forms of autonomous robotics.

1. Exponential improvement in power storage and efficiency Autonomous robots need to be autonomous in power. Over the last few decades, battery technology has improved substantially, from the lead-acid batteries of the 1950s to three-fold improvement seen in lithium polymer technology today.[5] Battery capacity aside, even greater power gains are obtained from improved power efficiency of robot technologies, such as the exponential improvement of computing cycles per watt of power, and the improvement in motor efficiency. The combination of improving energy storage and improving energy efficiency led to the acceleration of total energy performance of autonomous systems.

Robots with better power performance can spend more time doing and learning, and less time charging or looking for power.

2. Exponential improvement in computational power As Moore's law predicted, the amount of computing power available per dollar continues to double every eighteen months or so. While transistor miniaturization has slowed down in recent years as a result of physical limitations, computing power per dollar continues to grow through other means such as parallelization of multiple cores. Computing power is essential to an autonomous system that needs to process streaming data locally and make decisions in real time. Faster processing allows robots to roam around in less structured environments, and to learn faster from their experiences.

3. Exponential improvement in sensor technology Across a range of technologies from lidar to sonar, sensors are becoming more precise, higher in bandwidth, and cheaper. One of the most rapidly improving sensors along all these dimensions is the video camera. Driven by mobile devices, camera technology has improved performance and price at an exponential rate. The cost, size, power, and performance of optics and sensors allow multiple cameras to be mounted on a single robot. Multiple data streams allow for better cognitive performance, because more reliable scene understanding can be obtained from multiple viewpoints (e.g., depth perception and velocity perception from super-stereo vision), as well as more physical robustness to damage or temporary sensory blinding.

4. Exponential improvement in data storage The ability to store data is improving at an exponential rate. This improvement affects not just how many bytes can be stored per dollar, but also the speed and reliability of data storage and retrieval, the energy per transaction, and the physical weight of memory (bytes per kilogram). When robots can efficiently store lots of data locally, they can recall and reuse prior experiences, extract new knowledge from past stored experiences, and store and use maps and other high-definition information about the world.

5. Exponential improvement in communication band-width Both short-range and long range bandwidth have been improving exponentially over the last few decades. Just a few decades ago sending information was slow, difficult, expensive, and unreliable. Today we send terabytes across the planet and we don't think twice about whether the information will arrive intact. The ability to communicate long distance and reliably allows robots to share data and the results of its local analysis with other robots, leading to a combined shared intelligence known as *cloud robotics*.

THE KING OF EXPONENTIALS—ALGORITHMS

It is tempting to point at these hardware improvements in computation, communication, and sensing as the underlying root to the exponential takeoff of robotics technology, but all too often we forget the improvements resulting from the discovery and invention of new algorithmic techniques themselves.

Among computer scientists and electrical engineers there is a saying that whatever improvements hardware engineers will come up with, software engineers will waste away immediately (the actual wording is a bit spicier, but not fit for print). We all know that no matter how fast computers have become, their operating system software always runs too slowly. But the truth is quite the contrary.

Unlike processing speed per year or megapixels per dollar, algorithm improvement is difficult to quantify over long periods of time because algorithms are so diverse in the tasks they perform, and their goals are a rapidly moving target. But to take just one example, consider algorithms for solving differential equations. Such mathematical algorithms are a key component of any robot that needs to predict and control motion over time. Between 1945 and 1985, the algorithms for performing this fundamental task have improved by a factor of 30,000, or an average of 29 percent per year.[6] This improvement rate is on a par with that of the underlying hardware during the same period.

Another example is the improvement of algorithms for data analysis. The classical fast Fourier transform (FFT) algorithm that is used ubiquitously in any sign-processing system has led to orders of magnitude of speedup in performance compared to the original algorithm. By exactly how much did the algorithm improve speed? It turns out that the factor of improvement depends largely on the size of the dataset to be analyzed. For small datasets the improvement is small, but for large datasets, the improvement is so substantial that it would take decades of hardware improvements to catch up.[7] Because of algorithmic improvements we can now analyze data in a way that otherwise would not have been feasible even if Moore's law kept on going for a hundred years.

Unlike hardware improvements that seem to be relatively smooth exponentials, improvements in algorithms are more similar to the "punctuated equilibria" observed or conjectured for evolutionary systems. Algorithms do not improve smoothly; they improve by fits and starts. Like biological ecosystems, an algorithmic improvement needs to take hold in a market of competing algorithms. Some algorithms get invented and then die in academic obscurity. Other algorithms make it big only to become extinct shortly after, when a better algorithm eats their lunch, or when a problem they solve is no longer relevant. An algorithm may need to be reinvented multiple times by different people, until it finally makes its way, by fortuitous circumstances, to global recognition.

Artificial-intelligence algorithms have been no exception to this trend. In fits and starts over a century, AI algorithms have improved and regressed, come into fashion and gone out of vogue. But regardless of whatever camp of artificial intelligence is currently in the lead, AI algorithms have improved dramatically over the decades. We know that no amount of processor speed, data storage, or camera resolution would allow Rosenblatt's original Perceptron to reliably differentiate between a cat and a dog. We now know that no amount of computation would allow even a

1990s standard two-layer neural network to succeed reliably in that task, or a support vector machine from 2010, either. It took an ecology of competing algorithms in the Large Scale Visual Recognition Challenge to eventually allow one particular algorithm to rise to the top. Like mammalian critters hiding between the rocks, convolutional neural networks eventually rose to outperform the traditional AI dinosaurs.

The jolt felt in the AI community as deep-learning algorithms demonstrated their prowess was a visceral instance of a punctuated evolutionary process making one of its step transitions. Perhaps the automotive industry felt a similar jolt as the industry transitioned from hardware to software.

THE CASCADE OF IMPROVING ALGORITHMS

We will never know what role the eye played in catalyzing the development of the brain, but we do know that intelligence spread far beyond the visual cortex—from recognizing predators, prey, and potential mates, to the full-blown communication and self-awareness you are using to read this book. Similarly, we do know that the deep-learning algorithms that were initially developed for visual perception are now finding their way into many other areas of AI, from speech recognition to language generation and even artistic creativity. And we can only assume that this trend will continue.

How far this trend can continue and what is its endpoint is a topic for both science fiction writers and philosophers to speculate on. If we try to use raw hardware power as a baseline to predict AI progress, then predictions seem to converge on the 2020s as the decade when computing power meets the calculation power of the brain.[8] To us, however, that prediction always remained somewhat unsatisfying. We really wanted to know when computers will be as smart as humans in their behavior, not in their raw computing power. The problem is that this kind of prediction is much harder to make.

The ability of computers to develop something akin to self-awareness, or consciousness, is not just a matter of better hardware—it requires a different kind of algorithm. And while we don't know exactly what self-awareness is, we do know that it is more amorphous than the ability to play chess or drive a car, and therefore it is unlikely to be directly programmed by a genius software developer, as most sci-fi movies like to portray.

Instead, self-aware machines well develop slowly and gradually. What is self-awareness? Let's take the practical definition, that it is "merely" the ability to "simulate oneself"—to predict the future consequence of current actions, without having to perform those actions in physical reality. Can you imagine yourself walking on the beach tomorrow? Can you smell the ocean and feel the sand? Is this feeling good enough to for you to consider action? If so, you are self-aware. One can argue that even sentient emotions, like fear and joy, are mere projections of future consequences onto our current state, based on learned past experiences. For example, while "pain" may signify current damage, "fear" may signify a high likelihood of grave imminent damage, whereas "worry" may reflect a less severe and more distant negative consequence predicted by the internal self-model.

If a robot is able to predict what it will sense in the future based on actions it takes now, and then use that predictive model to plan its future actions, then to some degree it is also self-aware. In 2006, we demonstrated a robot that was able to construct an image of itself—a sort of primitive stick-figure that was not very accurate, but was good enough to learn how to walk with no physical trials or external programming. But our robot's self-image hit the limit of perception and the prediction algorithms available at the time.

Perhaps, as deep-learning algorithms worm their way into all AI applications, we will begin to see new generations of robots that form increasingly accurate models of themselves and their surroundings, gradually approaching self-awareness.

A self-aware car will not meet you in the driveway and joke about the road conditions. Nor will it be genuinely interested in your feelings. But a self-aware car will have an increasingly accurate model of how it drives, and how you would like it to drive—what it can and can't do, and what the risks and benefits of each of its possible actions are. And just as our own self-awareness extends beyond ourselves to ascribe feelings and intentions to others, a future driverless car may be able to predict what other cars on the road are likely to be planning.

Let's estimate that visual perception appeared about 50 million years after multicellularity, and *Homo sapiens* appeared 500 million years later, all using the same "hardware" infrastructure. We can attempt to draw an analogy: if it took fifty years to discover perception from the early blind robots of the 1950s, perhaps human-level self-awareness AI will take another 500 years. Hardware evolution will accelerate this this trend, but algorithm evolution has to go through its punctuated fits and starts.

Whether 2020 or 2500, that's just a blip in human evolution.

* * *

The human race has been enamored of the quest to make life out of matter. Early alchemists tried and tested numerous ways to breathe life into clay. Mythical potions came and went, and over the years alchemists were replaced by their modern ancestors, roboticists. Today, we roboticists have better tools, deeper understanding, and a little more funding. But ultimately, we are still trying to breathe life into inanimate machines.

Notes

Chapter 1

1. Andrew Parker, "In the Blink of an Eye: How Vision Sparked the Big Bang of Evolution" (Cambridge, Mass.: Perseus, 2003).

2. Kirsten Korosec, "Elon Musk Says Tesla Vehicles Will Drive Themselves in Two Years," Fotune.com, December 21, 2015, at http://fortune.com/2015/12/21/elon-musk-interview

3. Gary Silberg, "Self-Driving Cars: Are We Ready?" KPMG whitepaper, October 2013.

4. Boston Consulting Group, "Revolution in the Driver's Seat: The Road to Autonomous Vehicles," April 2014.

5. "The Driverless Debate: Equal Percentages of Americans See Self-Driving Cars as the 'Wave of the Future' Yet Would Never Consider Purchasing One," The Harris Poll #18, March 24, 2015.

6. Mike Van Nieuwkuyk, "Autonomous Driving Update," talk presented as part of a panel session, Societal Issues and Non-Technical Challenges, at the annual Automated Vehicles Symposium, Burlingame, California, July 2014.

7. National Center for Statistics and Analysis, *Distracted Driving: 2013 Data*, in *Traffic Safety Research Notes*, DOT HS 812 132, April 2015, National Highway Traffic Safety Administration, Washington, D.C.

8. World Health Organization, Fact Sheet no. 310, "The Top Ten Causes of Death," updated May 2014, retrieved online at http://www.who.int/mediacentre/factsheets/fs310/en/ Administration, Washington, D.C.

9. *World Report on Violence and Health: Summary* (Geneva: World Health Organization, 2002).

10. United Nations Office on Drugs and Crime, *World Drug Report 2014* (United Nations publication, Sales No. E. 14.XI.7).

11. Daniel Fagnant and Kara Kockelman, "Preparing a National for Autonomous Vehicles: Opportunities, Barriers and Policy Recommendations," Eno Center for Transportation. October 2013.

12. Todd Litman, "Autonomous Vehicle Implementation Predictions: Implications for Transport Planning," Victoria Transport Policy Institute, December 2015.

13. National Highway Traffic Safety Administration, Department of Transportation (US). Traffic Safety Facts 2012: Older Population, Washington, D.C.: NHTSA; 2012.

14. IHS Automotive report, *Autonomous Driving: Question Is When, Not If,* 2015.

15. Litman, "Autonomous Vehicle Implementation Predictions."

16. Ravi Shanker et al., "Autonomous Cars: Self-Driving the New Auto Industry Paradigm," Morgan Stanley report, November 2013.

Chapter 2

1. *The Economist,* "From Horseless to Driverless," in *The World If,* August 2015, http://worldif.economist.com/article/11/what-if-autonomous-vehicles -rule-the-world-from-horseless-to-driverless

2. Luis Martinez, "Urban Mobility System Upgrade: How Shared Self-Driving Cars Could Change City Traffic," International Transport Forum report, 2015, http://www.internationaltransportforum.org/Pub/pdf/15CPB _Self-drivingcars.pdf

3. Brandon Schoettle and Michael Sivak, "Potential Impact of Self-Driving Vehicles on Household Vehicle Demand and Usage," UMTRI-2015-3, University of Michigan Transportation Research Institute, February 2015.

4. U.S. Energy Information Administration, "Frequently Asked Questions: How Much Carbon Dioxide Is Produced by Burning Gasoline and Diesel Fuel?" http://www.eia.gov/tools/faqs/faq.cfm?id=307, last updated 4/18/13, accessed 3/19/16.

5. Kenneth Rapoza, "In Auto Market, China Steps on the Gas," *Forbes,* May 6, 2013.

6. China Association of Automobile Manufacturers, "The Passenger Cars Exceeded 20 Million for the First Time," January 20, 2016, http://www.caam .org.cn/AutomotivesStatistics/20160120/1305184265.html

7. David Schrank, Bill Eisele, Tim Lomax, and Jim Bak, "2015 Urban Mobility Scorecard," Texas A&M Transportation Institute, August 2015, http://mobility.tamu.edu/ums/report/ .

8. Rodney Stiles, Lindsey Siegel, Jeffrey Garber, Hillary Neger, and Asm Ullah, "2014 Taxicab Fact Book," NYC Taxi and Limousine Commission, http://www.nyc.gov/html/tlc/downloads/pdf/2014_taxicab_fact_book.pdf

9. James Manyika, Michael Chui, Jacques Bughin, Richard Dobbs, Peter Bisson, and Alex Marrs, "Disruptive Technologies: Advances That Will Transform Life, Business, and the Global Economy," McKinsey Global Institute, McKinsey & Company, May 2013, http://www.mckinsey.com/business -functions/business-technology/our-insights/disruptive-technologies

10. Christopher MacKechnie, "How Long Do Buses (and Other Transit Vehicles) Last?" About.com Transit Vehicles section, 3.22.16, http://publictransport.about.com/od/Transit_Vehicles/a/How-Long-Do-Buses-And-Ohter-Transit-Vehicles-Last.htm

11. Samuel Barradas, "Facts About Trucks—Everything You Want to Know About Eighteen Wheelers," Truckers Report, June 2013, http://www.thetruckersreport.com/facts-about-trucks/

12. Daniel J. Fagnant and Kara Kockelman, "Preparing a Nation for Autonomous Vehicles: Opportunities, Barriers and Policy Recommendations for Capitalizing on Self-Driven Vehicles," Transportation Research Part A 77: 167–181, 2015.

13. Manyika, Chui, Bughin, Dobbs, Bisson, and Marrs, "Disruptive Technologies."

14. Donald Shoup, "Cruising for Parking," Transport Policy 13 (2006): 479–486.

15. Alain Bertaud, "Self-Driving Cars in the Evolving Urban Landscape," Marron Institute Conference on Self-Driving Vehicles, August 25, 2015, http://marroninstitute.nyu.edu/uploads/content/Self_Driving_Vehicles_in_the_Evolving_Urban_Landscape_(Marron).pdf

16. Paul Barter, "Cars Are Parked 95% of the Time; Let's check!" Reinventing Parking, February 22, 2013, http://www.reinventingparking.org/2013/02/cars-are-parked-95-of-time-lets-check.html

17. John R. Meyer, John F. Kain, and Martin Wohl, The Urban Transportation Problem (Cambridge, Mass.: Harvard University Press, 1965).

18. Jeffrey R. Kenworthy and Felix B. Laube, An International Sourcebook of Automobile Dependence in Cities 1960-1990, chapter 3 (Boulder: University Press of Colorado, 1999).

19. Donald Shoup, The High Cost of Free Parking (Chicago: American Planning Association Press, 2011), p. 160.

20. Ibid.

21. Liewen Jiang, Malea Hoepf Young, and Karen Hardee, "Population, Urbanization, and the Environment," World Watch 21, no. 5 (2008): 34–39, Academic Search Premier, Web, 23 November 2015.

22. Brian McKenzie and Melanie Rapino, "Commuting in the United States: 2009," September 2011, American Community Survey Reports, https://www.census.gov/prod/2011pubs/acs-15.pdf

23. Lawrence Burns, William Jordan, and Bonnie Scarborough, "Transforming Personal Mobility," The Earth Institute, Columbia University, January 27, 2013.

24. Alex Williams, "Friends of a Certain Age," *New York Times*, July 13, 2012, http://www.nytimes.com/2012/07/15/fashion/the-challenge-of-making-friends-as-an-adult.html

25. Martha De Lacey, "Mum's Taxi Service: Average Mother Drives Children around for 1,248 Miles Each Year," *Daily Mail*, 29 August 2013 (BoostApak study), http://www.dailymail.co.uk/femail/article-2405436/Mums-taxi-service-Average-mother-drives-children-1-248-miles-EACH-YEAR--London-Zurich-round-trip.html

Chapter 3

1. "What's the Difference between Fully Self-Driving Cars and Driver Assistance?" Google driverless car project website, Frequently Asked Questions, https://www.google.com/selfdrivingcar/faq/#q1

2. Ina Fried, "Apple's Jeff Williams: The Car Is the Ultimate Mobile Device," at a re/code Conference, May 27, 2015, http://recode.net/2015/05/27/apples-jeff-williams-the-car-is-the-ultimate-mobile-device/

3. Automotive research facilities in Silicon Valley, Auto News website interactive map, http://www.autonews.com/section/map502

4. Mike Ramsey, "Ford, Mercedes-Benz Set Up Shop in Silicon Valley," *Wall Street Journal*, March 27, 2015, http://www.wsj.com/articles/ford-mercedes-set-up-shop-in-silicon-valley-1427475558

5. "Autonomous Vehicles: Self-Driving—the New Auto Industry Paradigm," *Morgan Stanley Research,* December 6, 2013.

6. Industrial Robot Statistics, World Robotics 2015, March 19, 2016, http://www.ifr.org/industrial-robots/statistics/

7. Scott Corwin, Joe Vitale, Eamonn Kelly, and Elizabeth Cathles, "The Future of Mobility," Deloitte Report, September 24, 2015, http://dupress.com/articles/future-of-mobility-transportation-technology

8. Adrienne LaFrance, "The High-Stakes Race to Rid the World of Human Drivers," *Atlantic*, December 1, 2015, http://www.theatlantic.com/technology/archive/2015/12/driverless-cars-are-this-centurys-space-race/417672/

9. Deloitte Report.

10. Lee Iacocca, with William Novak, *Iacocca: An Autobiography* (New York: Bantam Books, 1984), p. 226.

11. Deloitte Report

12. "How Many Parts Is Each Car Made Of?" Toyota Web site, http://www.toyota.co.jp/en/kids/faq/d/01/04/

13. Ibid.

14. The U.S. Department of Transportation's National Highway Traffic Safety Administration (NHTSA) is the federal agency tasked with driving policy to improve vehicle and highway safety. For example, the NHTSA is responsible for decisions such as mandating where the gas tank should be placed, or defining seat belt laws. On May 30, 2013, the U.S. Department of Transportation's National Highway Traffic Safety Administration (NHTSA) decided to define five levels of vehicle autonomy. The definitions are as follows:

• NHSTA Autonomy Level 0: No-Automation: The driver is in complete and sole control of the primary vehicle controls—brake, steering, throttle, and motive power—at all times.

• NHSTA Autonomy Level 1: Function-specific Automation: Automation at this level involves one or more specific control functions. Examples include electronic stability control or pre-charged brakes, where the vehicle automatically assists with braking to enable the driver to regain control of the vehicle or stop faster than possible by acting alone.

• NHSTA Autonomy Level 2: Combined Function Automation: This level involves automation of at least two primary control functions designed to work in unison to relieve the driver of control of those functions. An example of combined functions enabling a Level 2 system is adaptive cruise control in combination with lane centering.

• NHSTA Autonomy Level 3: Limited Self-Driving Automation: Vehicles at this level of automation enable the driver to cede full control of all safety-critical functions under certain traffic or environmental conditions and in those conditions to rely heavily on the vehicle to monitor for changes in those conditions requiring transition back to driver control. The driver is expected to be available for occasional control, but with sufficiently comfortable transition time. The Google car is an example of limited self-driving automation.

• NHSTA Autonomy Level 4: Full Self-Driving Automation: The vehicle is designed to perform all safety-critical driving functions and monitor roadway conditions for an entire trip. Such a design anticipates that the driver will provide destination or navigation input, but is not expected to be available for control at any time during the trip. This includes both occupied and unoccupied vehicles.

To add to the confusion, six months later—in January of 2014— the Society for Automotive Engineers (SAE), perhaps the largest vehicle expert industry association, kicked it up a notch by announcing its own set of six, not five, levels of automation. Here are the SAE levels (quoted verbatim):

• SAE Autonomy Level 0: No Automation. The full-time performance by the human driver of all aspects of the dynamic driving task, even when enhanced by warning or intervention systems

• SAE Autonomy Level 1: Driver Assistance: The driving mode-specific execution by a driver assistance system of either steering or acceleration/ deceleration using information about the driving environment and with the expectation that the human driver perform all remaining aspects of the dynamic driving task

• SAE Autonomy Level 2: Partial Automation. The driving mode-specific execution by one or more driver assistance systems of both steering and acceleration/deceleration using information about the driving environment and with the expectation that the human driver perform all remaining aspects of the dynamic driving task Automated driving system ("system") monitors the driving environment

• SAE Autonomy Level 3: Conditional Automation: The driving mode-specific performance by an automated driving system of all aspects of the dynamic driving task with the expectation that the human driver will respond appropriately to a request to intervene.

• SAE Autonomy Level 4: High Automation. The driving mode-specific performance by an automated driving system of all aspects of the dynamic driving task, even if a human driver does not respond appropriately to a request to intervene.

• SAE Autonomy Level 5: Full Automation. The full-time performance by an automated driving system of all aspects of the dynamic driving task under all roadway and environmental conditions that can be managed by a human driver.

15. David Mindell, *Our Robots, Ourselves: Robotics and the Myths of Autonomy* (New York: Viking Press, 2015), p. 201.

16. Google Self-Driving Car Project Monthly Report, October 2015, http:// static.googleusercontent.com/media/www.google.com/en//selfdrivingcar/files/ reports/report-1015.pdf

17. S. G. Klauer, F. Guo, J. Sudweeks, and T. A. Dingus, "An Analysis of Driver Inattention Using a Case-Crossover Approach on 100-Car Data" (Report DOT-HS-811-334) (Washington, D.C.: National Highway Traffic Safety Administration, 2010).

18. Catherine C. McDonald and Marilyn S. Sommers, "Teen Drivers' Perceptions of Inattention and Cell Phone Use While Driving," *Traffic Injury Prevention* 16 (supp. 2) (2015): S52. DOI: 10.1080/15389558.2015.1062886

19. Quote comes from Google Self-Driving Car Project Monthly Report, October 2015, https://static.googleusercontent.com/media/www.google.com/en//selfdrivingcar/files/reports/report-1015.pdf

20. Description of the bus incident here, https://static.googleusercontent.com/media/www.google.com/en//selfdrivingcar/files/reports/report-0216.pdf

21. Kevin Root, "Self Driving Cars, Autonomous Vehicles, and Shared Mobility," Slideshare, http://www.slideshare.net/traveler138/self-driving-cars-v11

Chapter 4

1. "Car Balk," updated from the archive, Snopes.com, October 14, 2010, www.snopes.com/humor/jokes/autos.asp

2. Hans Moravec, *Mind Children: The Future of Robot and Human Intelligence* (Cambridge, Mass.: Harvard University Press, 1988), p. 15.

3. Ferris Jabr, "How Humans Ended Up with Freakishly Huge Brains," *Wired*, November 28, 2015, http://www.wired.com/2015/11/how-humans-ended-up-with-freakishly-huge-brains/

4. B. F. Miessner, *Radiodynamics* 1916.

Chapter 5

1. Ashlee Vance, "The First Person to Hack the iPhone Built a Self-Driving Car. In His Garage," *Bloomberg Business,* December 16, 2015; Tesla Motors, "Correction to article: The First Person to Hack the iPhone Built a Self-Driving Car,"https://www.teslamotors.com/support/correction-article-first-person-hack-iphone-built-self-driving-car

2. "Right-of-Way Rules," *California Driver Handbook— Laws and Rules of the Road,* California DMV, https://www.dmv.ca.gov/portal/dmv/detail/pubs/hdbk/right_of_way

3. Luke Fletcher, Seth Teller, Edwin Olson, David Moore, Yoshiaki Kuwata, Jonathan How, John Leonard, Isaac Miller, Mark Campbell, Dan Huttenlocher, Aaron Nathan, and Frank-Robert Kline, "The MIT–Cornell Collision and Why It Happened," *Springer Tracts in Advanced Robotics* 56:509–548.

4. A. Chou, J. Yang. B. Chelf, S. Hallem, and D. Engler, "An Empirical Study of Operating System Errors," *Proc. 18th ACM Symp. On Operating Syst. Prin.*, ACM, 2001, pp. 73–88.

5. "2013 Motor Vehicle Crashes: Overview," Research Note, US Department of Transportation National Highway Traffic Safety Administration, December 2014, http://www-nrd.nhtsa.dot.gov/Pubs/812101.pdf

6. "The Latest Chapter for the Self-Driving Car: Mastering City Street Driving," Google Official Blog, April 28, 2014, https://googleblog.blogspot.com/2014/04/the-latest-chapter-for-self-driving-car.html

7. "Statistical Summary of Commercial Jet Airplane Accidents Worldwide Operations, 1959–2013," Aviation Safety Boeing Commercial Airplanes, August 2014, http://asndata.aviation-safety.net/industry-reports/Boeing-Statistical-Summary-1959-2013.pdf

8. Andrew Tanenbaum, Jorrit Herder, and Herbert Bos, "Can We Make Operating Systems Reliable and Secure?" *Computer* 39, no. 5:44–51, http://cs.furman.edu/~chealy/cs75/important%20papers/secure%20computer-2006a.pdf

Chapter 6

1. Wikipedia, "Futurama (New York World's Fair)," retrieved March 24, 2016, http://en.wikipedia.org/wiki/Futurama_(New_York_World's_Fair)

2. Robert W. Rydell, *World of Fairs* (Chicago: University of Chicago Press, 1993), pp. 135–141.

3. Normal Bel Geddes, *Magic Motorways,* https://archive.org/details/horizons00geddrich

4. Ibid.

5. Ibid., p. 295.

6. Laura J. Nelson, "Digital Projection Has Drive-in Theaters Reeling," *Los Angeles Times*, January 19, 2013, http://www.latimes.com/entertainment/envelope/cotown/la-et-ct-drive-ins-digital-20130120,0,5280624,full.story

7. Advertisement, Central Power and Light Company, displayed in the *Victoria Advocate*, Sunday, March 24, 1957.

8. "The IBM 700 Series: Computing Comes to Business," IBM 100's Icons of Progress, IBM, http://www-03.ibm.com/ibm/history/ibm100/us/en/icons/ibm700series/impacts/

9. V. K. Zworykin and L. Flory, "Electronic Control of Motor Vehicles on the Highway," Proceedings of the Thirty-Seventh Annual Meeting of the Highway Research Board, Washington, D.C., January 6–10, 1958.

10. Ibid.

11. Ibid.

12. Full text of "Town Topics (Princeton), June 12–18, 1960," http://www
.archive.org/stream/towntopicsprince1514unse/towntopicsprince1514unse
_djvu.txt

13. Ibid.

14. Ibid.

15. The Pavilion Guide, 1964 New York World's Fair, 1964-65, nywf64.com.

16. Gijsbert-Paul Berk, "Self-Drive Cars and You: A History Longer than
You Think," *Velocetoday*, August 5, 2014, http://www.velocetoday.com/self
-drive-cars-and-you-a-history-longer-than-you-think/

17. Alain L. Kornhauser, "Smart Driving Cars: Where Are We Going? Why
Are We Going? Where Are We Now? What Is in It for Whom? How Might We
Get There? Where Might We End Up?" presented at the 2013 TransAction
Conference, Atlantic City, N.J.

18. Robert E. Fenton and Karl W. Olson, "The Electronic Highway," *IEEE
Spectrum,* July 1969.

19. Ibid.

20. National Technical Information Service (NTIS), Report on 1960–63
Corvair Safety, FB 211-014.

21. Kenneth T. Jackson, *Crabgrass Frontier: The Suburbanization of the
United States* (New York: Oxford University Press, 1985).

22. Daniel Yergin, *The Prize: The Epic Quest for Oil, Money, and Power* (New
York: Simon and Schuster, 2008), p. 587.

Chapter 7

1. Susan Zimmerman, Nelsie Alcoser, David Hooper, Crystal Huggins,
Amber Keyser, Nancy Santucci, Terence Lam, Josh Ormond, Amy Rosewarne,
and Elizabeth Wood, "Intelligent Transportation Systems: Vehicle-to-
Infrastructure Technologies Expected to Offer Benefits, but Deployment
Challenges Exist," United States Government Accountability Office Report,
September 2015, http://www.gao.gov/assets/680/672548.pdf

2. "Vehicle-to-Vehicle Communications for Safety," NHSTA Official page,
http://www.nhtsa.gov/Research/Crash+Avoidance/Vehicle-to-Vehicle
+Communications+for+Safety

3. Vehicle-to-Vehicle Communications: Readiness of V2V Technology for
Application. August 2014. NHTSA Report DOT HS 812 014.

4. "National Automated Highway Systems Program," chapter 1, Transportation Research Board, ISTEA Part E, Section 6054(b), http://onlinepubs.trb
.org/onlinepubs/sr/sr253/sr25301.pdf

5. Ibid.

6. "Request for Applications Number DTFH61-94-X-0001 to Establish a National Automated Highway System Consortium," Federal Highway Administration, Washington, D.C., December 1993.

7. Jameson M. Wetmore, "Driving the Dream: The History and Motivations behind 60 Years of Automated Highway Systems in America," Consortium for Science, Policy & Outcomes, *Automotive History Review*, Summer 2003, pp. 4–19.

8. Sanghyun Cheon, "An Overview of Automated Highway Systems (AHS) and the Social and Institutional Challenges They Face," University of California Transportation Center, 2003.

9. Federal Highway Administration, "Demo '97: Proving AHS Works," *Public Roads Magazine* 61, no. 1 (July/August 1997), https://www.fhwa.dot.gov/publications/publicroads/97july/demo97.cfm

10. "Proposed Rules," *Federal Register* 79, no. 161 (Wednesday, August 20, 2014).

11. Susan Zimmerman, Nelsie Alcoser, David Hooper, Crystal Huggins, Amber Keyser, Nancy Santucci, Terence Lam, Josh Ormond, Amy Rosewarne, and Elizabeth Wood, GAO Report.

12. Pedro Hernandez, "Smart Cities Will Drive IoT Device Demand in 2016: Gartner," Datamation.com, http://www.datamation.com/cloud-computing/smart-cities-will-drive-iot-device-demand-in-2016-gartner.html?google_editors_picks=true

13. Tsz-Chiu Au, Shun Zhang, and Peter Stone, "Autonomous Intersection Management for Semi-Autonomous Vehicles," *Handbook of Transportation,* ed. Dušan Teodorović (New York: Routledge 2015).

14. Daimler Press Release, "AUDI AG, BMW Group and Daimler AG agree with Nokia Corporation on Joint Acquisition of HERE Digital Mapping Business," August 3, 2015, http://media.daimler.com/dcmedia/0-921-656186-1-1836824-1-0-0-0-0-0-0-0-0-0-0-0-0-0.html

15. "Volvo Car Group tests road magnets for accurate positioning of self-driving cars," Volvo Car Group Press Release, March 11, 2014, https://www.media.volvocars.com/global/en-gb/media/pressreleases/140760/volvo-car-group-tests-road-magnets-for-accurate-positioning-of-self-driving-cars

16. Bill Vlasic, "U.S. Proposes Spending $4 Billion on Self-Driving Cars," *New York Times,* January 14, 2016, http://www.nytimes.com/2016/01/15/business/us-proposes-spending-4-billion-on-self-driving-cars.html?_r=0

17. Brad Templeton "California DMV Regulations May Kill the State's Robocar Lead," 4brad.com, December 17, 2015, http://ideas.4brad.com/california-dmv-regulations-may-kill-states-robocar-lead

18. Grace Meng, "H.R.3876—Autonomous Vehicle Privacy Protection Act of 2015," Congress.gov, https://www.congress.gov/bill/114th-congress/house-bill/3876/text

Chapter 8

1. Marsha Walton, "Robots Fail to Complete Grand Challenge," CNN.com, May 6, 2004,http://www.cnn.com/2004/TECH.ptech/03/14/darpa.race/index.html

2. Sebastian Thrun (interview). "Google's Original X-Man," *Foreign Affairs* 92, no. 6 (November/December 2013), http://www.foreignaffairs.com/discussions/interviews/googles-original-x-man

3. Luke Fletcher, Seth Teller, Edwin Olson, David Moore, Yoshiaki Kuwata, Jonathan How, John Leonard, Isaac Miller, Mark Campbell, Dan Huttenlocher, Aaron Nathan, and Frank-Robert Kline, "The MIT–Cornell Collision and Why It Happened," *Springer Tracts in Advanced Robotics* 56:509–548.

4. Michael Belfiore, "Three Teams out of the Running at Auto-Bot Race," *Danger Room,* November 3, 2007, from Wired.com, archived from the original on November 6, 2007.

5. Daniel K, "What Is Machine Learning?" Stack Overflow, http://stackoverflow.com/questions/2620843/what-is-machine-learning

6. "Kasparov Wins," *TIME Magazine,* Monday, February 19, 1996.

7. Erik Brynjolfsson and Andrew McAfee, *The Second Machine Age: Work, Progress and Prosperity in a Time of Brilliant Technologies* (New York: W.W. Norton & Co., 2014).

8. During the 1980s and 1990s, several pioneering researchers devised self-driving car prototypes that could drive short stretches without a human. In 1977, Tsukuba Mechanical Engineering Lab in Japan developed a computerized driverless car that achieved speeds of up to 20 mph by using machine vision to follow white street markers. Ernst Dickmanns's VaMoRs Mercedes van tested three generations of systems between 1986 and 2003. One system installed in a Mercedes sedan would cover thousands of miles, including even some lane changing in traffic. In 1996, as part of the European PROMETHEUS project, the ARGO team drove their Lancia 1200 miles around Italy, 94 percent of the time autonomously. At Carnegie Mellon University in Pittsburg, a series of outdoor self-driving field robots spanned

thirty years of research, from the 1984 Terregator through the NavLab 1 (1986) and NavLab 2 (1992).

9. Yoshimasa Goto and Anthony Tentz, "Mobile Robot Navigation: The CMU System," IEEE Expert 1987.

10. DARPA award contract issued to Cornell University.

11. Chris Urmson et al., "Autonomous Driving in Urban Environments: Boss and the Urban Challenge," *Journal of Field Robotics* 25 (9) (2008): 426–464.

12. "Autonomous Cars: Self-Driving the New Auto Industry Paradigm," Morgan Stanley Blue Paper, November 6, 2013.

13. Google Official Blog, "The Latest Chapter for the Self-Driving Car: Mastering City Street Driving," April 28, 2014, https://googleblog.blogspot .nl/2014/04/the-latest-chapter-for-self-driving-car.html

14. Google Annual Report, 2007.

15. Burkhard Bilger, "Has the Self-Driving Car at Last Arrived?" *New Yorker*, November 25, 2013, http://www.newyorker.com/reporting/2013/11/25/ 131125fa_fact_bilger?currentPage=all

16. Mark Harris "The Unknown Start-up That Built Google's First Self-Driving Car," IEEE Spectrum Online, November 19, 2014, http://spectrum .ieee.org/robotics/artificial-intelligence/the-unknown-startup-that-built -googles-first-selfdriving-car

Chapter 9

1. Cadie Thompson, "There's One Big Difference between Google and Tesla's Self-Driving Car Technology," TechInsider.com, December 5, 2015, http:// www.techinsider.io/difference-between-google-and-tesla-driverless-cars -2015-12

2. "GPS Accuracy," GPS.gov Official U.S. Government information about the Global Positioning System (GPS), http://www.gps.gov/systems/gps/ performance/accuracy/

3. McWilliams, "Re: How Fast Does an Eye Blink?" University of Missouri– St. Louis, MadSci Network, retrieved April 28, 2013 (via Wikipedia, http:// en.wikipedia.org/wiki/Blink)

4. Adam Levin "How Hackers Can Hijack Your Car," Today.com, August 29, 2013, http://www.today.com/money/how-hackers-can-hijack-your -car-8C11034118

5. Dash, https://dash.by/

Chapter 10

1. Warren S. McCulloch and Pitts Walter, "A Logical Calculus of the Ideas Immanent in Nervous Activity," *Bulletin of Mathematical Biophysics* 5 (1943): 115–133.

2. Charles C. Tappert, "Rosenblatt's Contributions," The Michael L. Gargano 9th Annual Research Day, Friday, May 6, 2011, http://csis.pace.edu/~ctappert/srd2011/rosenblatt-contributions.htm

3. Kunihiko Fukushima, "Neocognitron: A Self-Organizing Neural Network Model for a Mechanism of Pattern Recognition Unaffected by Shift in Position," *Biological Cybernetics* 36, no. 4 (1980): 193–202.

4. Yann LeCun, Léon Bottou, Yoshua Bengio, and Patrick Haffner, "Gradient-Based Learning Applied to Document Recognition," *Proceedings of the IEEE* 86, no. 11 (1998): 2278–2324, doi:10.1109/5.726791.

5. "What Happens on the Internet in 60 Seconds," BuzzFeed Videos, https://www.youtube.com/watch?v=Uiy-ETbymqk

6. Fei-Fei Li, TED Talk, "How We're Teaching Computers to Understand Pictures," March 23, 2015, https://www.ted.com/talks/fei_fei_li_how_we_re_teaching_computers_to_understand_pictures?language=en

7. ImageNet Large Scale Visual Recognition Challenge 2010 results, http://www.image-net.org/challenges/LSVRC/2010/results

8. ImageNet Large Scale Visual Recognition Challenge 2011 results, http://www.image-net.org/challenges/LSVRC/2011/results

9. ImageNet Large Scale Visual Recognition Challenge 2012 results, http://www.image-net.org/challenges/LSVRC/2012/results

10. ImageNet Large Scale Visual Recognition Challenge 2013 results, http://www.image-net.org/challenges/LSVRC/2013/results

11. ImageNet Large Scale Visual Recognition Challenge 2014 results, http://www.image-net.org/challenges/LSVRC/2014/results

12. ImageNet Large Scale Visual Recognition Challenge 2015 results, http://www.image-net.org/challenges/LSVRC/2015/results

13. Kaiming He, Xiangyu Zhang, Shaoqing Ren, and Jian Sun,. "Deep Residual Learning for Image Recognition," *arXiv*:1512.03385v1, submitted December 2015.

14. D. H. Hubel and T. N. Wiesel. "Receptive Fields of Single Neurons in the Cat's Striate Cortex," *Journal of Physiology* 148, no. 3 (October 1959): 574–591.

Chapter 11

1. Henry Miller and Shih-lung Shaw, *Geographic Information Systems for Transportation: Principles and Applications* (New York: Oxford University Press, 2001).

2. Alexis Madrigal, "How Google Builds Its Maps and What It Means for the Future," *The Atlantic,* September 2012.

3. "Summary of Travel Trends 2009," National Household Travel Survey, http://nhts.ornl.gov/2009/pub/stt.pdf

4. Philippa Foot, *The Problem of Abortion and the Doctrine of the Double Effect in Virtues and Vices* (Oxford: Basil Blackwell, 1978) (originally appeared in the *Oxford Review*, no. 5, 1967).

5. Noah J. Goodall, "Ethical Decision Making during Automated Vehicle Crashes," *Transportation Research Record: Journal of the Transportation Research Board*, 2014.

Chapter 12

1. John Heilemann, "Reinventing the Wheel," *TIME Magazine,* Sunday, December 2, 2001.

2. L. Blincoe, A. Seay, E. Zaloshnja, T. Miller, E. Romano, S. Luchter, and R. Spicer, "The Economic Impact of Motor Vehicle Crashes 2000," Plans and Policy, National Highway Traffic safety Administration, Washington, D.C., May 2002.

3. U.S. Department of Transportation Federal Highway Administration, "Average Annual Miles per Driver by Age Group," http://www.fhwa.dot.gov/ohim/onh00/bar8.htm

4. "National Congestion Tables," *2015 Urban Mobility Scorecard,* Texas A&M Mobility research, http://d2dtl5nnlpfr0r.cloudfront.net/tti.tamu.edu/documents/ums/congestion-data/national/national-table1.pdf

5. Bureau of Labor Statistics, "Taxi Drivers and Chauffeurs," http://www.bls.gov/ooh/transportation-and-material-moving/taxi-drivers-and-chauffeurs.htm

6. Casey Newton, "Uber Will Eventually Replace All Its Drivers with Self-Driving Cars," TheVerge.com, May 28, 2014, http://www.theverge.com/2014/5/28/5758734/uber-will-eventually-replace-all-its-drivers-with-self-driving-cars

7. Adrienne LaFrance, "The High-Stakes Race to Rid the World of Human Drivers," *The Atlantic*, December 1, 2015, http://www.theatlantic.com/

technology/archive/2015/12/driverless-cars-are-this-centurys-space-race/
417672/

8. Bureau of Labor Statistics, U.S. Department of Labor, *Occupational Outlook Handbook, 2016-17 Edition*, Automotive Service Technicians and Mechanics.

9. OXFAM, "An Economy for the 1%: How Privilege and Power in the Economy Drive Extreme InEquality and How This Can Be Stopped," 210 OXFAM Briefing Paper, January 18, 2016.

10. U.S. Center for Disease Control and Prevention, "Motor Vehicle Crash Injuries," http://www.cdc.gov/vitalsigns/crash-injuries/index.html

11. Stacy Dickert-Conlin, Todd E. Elder, and Brian Moore, "Donorcycles: Motorcycle Helmet Laws and the Supply of Organ Donors" (September 4, 2009), available at SSRN: http://ssrn.com/abstract=1471982 or http://dx.doi.org/10.2139/ssrn.1471982, https://www.msu.edu/~telder/donorcycles _current.pdf

12. Laura M. Maruschak, "DWI Offenders under Correctional Supervision," U.S. Department of Justice, Office of Justice Programs Bureau of Justice Statistics Special Report,http://www.bjs.gov/content/pub/pdf/dwiocs.pdf

13. "Parking Ticket Statistics," StatisticBrain.com Data Source: Radar Detector, Department of Motor Vehicles, August 25, 2015, http://www .statisticbrain.com/parking-ticket-statistics/

14. Lawrence Berezin, "NYC Parking Ticket Statistics That Will Shock and Awe You," December 23, 2008 (data from THE City Room of the New York Times), http://newyorkparkingticket.com/some-shocking-nyc-parking-ticket -statistics/

15. Robert W. Peterson, "New Technology, Old Law: Autonomous Vehicles and California's Insurance Framework," *Santa Clara Law Review* 52 (2012).

16. U.S. Federal Highway Administration "The Economic Costs of Freight Transportation," http://ops.fhwa.dot.gov/freight/freight_analysis/ freight_story/costs.htm

17. "Driving Change without a Driver: How the Driverless Car Will Alter Retail Forever," National Purchase Diary NPD.com, https://www.npd.com/ wps/portal/npd/us/news/tips-trends-takeaways/driving-change-without-a -driver-how-the-driverless-car-will-alter-retail-forever/

18. Survey conducted by the College of Engineering at Carnegie Mellon University, January, 2015, http://engineering.cmu.edu/media/press/2015/01 _22_autonomous_vehicle_survey.html

19. "Radio Facts and Figures," compiled from 2016 Nielsen Audio Today; Pew State of the News Media 2015, News Generation, http://www .newsgeneration.com/broadcast-resources/radio-facts-and-figures/

Afterword

1. Wikipedia, "The Cambrian Explosion," https://en.wikipedia.org/wiki/ Cambrian_explosion

2. Andres Parker, *In the Blink of an Eye* (Cambridge, Mass.: Perseus Books), 2003.

3. Denise Grady, "The Vision Thing: Mainly in the Brain," *Discover Magazine*, June 1, 1993, http://discovermagazine.com/1993/jun/thevisionthingma227

4. Gill A. Pratt, "Is a Cambrian Explosion Coming for Robotics?" *Journal of Economic Perspectives* 29, no. 3 (2015): 51–60.

5. Battery University, "What's the Best Battery?"http://batteryuniversity .com/learn/article/whats_the_best_battery

6. Jon Bentley, "Programming Pearls," *Comm. ACM* 27, no. 11 (November 1984): 1087–1092.

7. Gary A. Shaw and Mark A. Richards, "Sustaining the Exponential Growth of Embedded Digital Signal Processing Capability," ADM001742, HPEC-7, vol. 1, Proceedings of the Eighth Annual High Performance Embedded, Computing (HPEC) Workshops, September 28–30, 2004,https://www.ll.mit.edu/ HPEC/agendas/proc04/abstracts/shaw_gary.pdf

8. Hans Moravec, "When Will Computer Hardware Match the Human Brain?" *Journal of Evolution and Technology* 1 (1998), http://www .transhumanist.com/volume1/moravec.htm

INDEX

A* algorithm, 82

Actuators, 47, 191–192

Adoption timeline, 18–21

Adult recreation, 275, 276

AI winters, 207, 208

AlexNet. *See* Deep learning

Artificial intelligence
  Data-driven AI. *See* Machine
    learning
  Rule-based AI, 7, 76
  Rule-based AI, limitations of, 7,
    8, 76, 88, 91–93, 154, 155
  Symbolic AI. *See* rule-based AI
  See also Artificial perception;
    Deep learning; Machine
    learning; Neural networks

Artificial perception
  Challenges with automating, 6,
    85–88, 91, 92
  Importance of, 7, 47, 85, 86,
    95
  Template-based perception, 91
  See also Artificial Intelligence;
    Machine vision; Mid-level
    controls; Moravec's paradox;
    Object recognition;
    SuperVision

Automation bias, 56

Automotive control software. *See*
  Controls engineering

Automotive industry
  Competition with software
    companies, 46–55, 63
  Driverless car impact on, 47,
    52–55
  Future of car design, 266–268
  Incremental approach, 45,
    49–51

Industry insularity, 49–51
Possible strategies, 52–55

Automotive operating system
  Challenges of creating, 55–63,
    68–75, 87–93, 98–102
  Overview of, 47, 66, 67
  See also Controls engineering;
    High-level controls; Low-level
    controls; Mid-level controls

AUVSI conference, 47

Aviation operating systems,
  103–105

Backprop algorithm. *See* Error
  backpropogation

Bar detectors. *See* Edge detectors

Bel Geddes, Norman, 110, 111

Bengio, Yoshua, 224

Business models, 263–272

Butterfly effect, 244

Caltech-101, 219

Cambrian Explosion, 9, 283

CAN bus, 192–195

Car industry. *See* Automotive
  industry

Carnegie Mellon University (CMU),
  68–72, 151, 157, 166, 274. *See
  also* NREC

CHIMP, 69–71

Cities. *See* Downtowns

Closed world, 5

Cloud robotics, 235

CMU. *See* Carnegie Mellon
  University

CNNs. *See* Convolutional Neural
  Networks

Commuting, 38–40

Computer operating systems
    Operating system failure,
        98–100, 104
Cone of uncertainty, 95–97. *See also*
    Mid-level controls
Consumer acceptance, 11–13
Controls engineering
    Overview of, 47, 75–77
    See also Low-level controls;
        Mid-level controls; High-level
        controls
Convolutional neural networks
    (CNNs), 214–218
Corner cases, 4, 5, 89, 154
Creative destruction, 261–263
Crime, 273, 274

DARPA Challenges, 149, 150
DARPA Grand Challenge 2004,
    150
DARPA Grand Challenge 2005, 151,
    152
DARPA Urban Challenge 2007,
    156–158
Data
    CAN bus protocol, 193, 194
    Data collection, 239, 240
    Training data for deep learning,
        218–220
    See also Machine learning;
        Route-planning software;
        Traffic prediction software
Deep learning
    History of, 197, 199–202, 219,
        223–226
    How deep learning works, 7, 8,
        226–231
    See also ImageNet competition;
        Neocognitron; Perceptron;
        SuperVision

Demo 97, 134, 135
Digital cameras, 173–175
Disney Hall, Los Angeles, 36,
    37
Disney's Magic Highway U.S.A.,
    115
Dog of War, 79
Downtowns, 32–37
Drive by wire191–194
Driver assist, 55–58. *See also*
    Human in the loop
Driverless-car reliability, 98–104,
    195–196
Drive-PX 225

E-commerce, 271, 272
Edge detectors 229
Electronic Highway
    History of, 116–120
    Reasons for demise, 123, 124
    See also General Motors
        Corporation (GM)
Environment. *See* Platooning;
    Traffic congestion; Traffic
    prediction software; Vehicular
    lifespan
Error backpropagation. 211–213
Ethics, 249–253
Exponential technologies, 183, 255.
    See also Moore's law

Face recognition, 233
Federal Highway Administration
    (FHA), 129, 132, 133,
    134
Federal policy on autonomous
        vehicles
    History of, 131–135
    Overview of, 102, 103, 127,
        128

Recommendations for,
143–147
See also Humansafe ratings;
Intelligent Transportation
Systems; U.S. Department
of Transportation (USDOT);
V2X
FHA. *See* Federal Highway
Administration
Firebird, 121–122
Fleet learning, 102, 240
Fuel efficiency, 29, 30
Fukushima, Kunihiko, 214
Futurama, 107–110

General Motors Corporation (GM),
107–110, 116–120
Global positioning system (GPS), 10,
185–187
GM. *See* General Motors
Corporation
Google
Google's car accidents, 62, 63
Google's Chauffeur project, 48,
58, 62, 102, 168–169
Google's HD maps, 237, 238
Google's self-driving prototype,
45, 77
Government oversight. *See* Federal
policy on autonomous
vehicles)
GPS. *See* Global positioning system
GPUs. *See* Graphics processing
units
Graphic processing units (GPUs),
221, 222

Hackers, 99, 195, 249, 274
Handoff problem, *See also* Human in
the loop, 57, 58, 62, 63

Hardware sensors, 171–185. *See
also* Digital cameras; High-
definition digital maps; IMU;
LIDAR; Radar sensor
Hebb, Donald, 201
Hebbian learning, 201
Herculano-Houzel, Suzana, 73
High-definition digital maps, 11,
171–173, 238, 239
High-level controls, 75, 76, 81, 82
Highway infrastructure
Dumb highways, 141–143
See also Electronic Highways
Hinton, Geoffrey, 224
Hubel, David, 229
Human in the loop, 55–62
Humansafe rating, 102–104

ILSVRC. *See* ImageNet Large Scale
Visual Recognition
Competition
ImageNet, 219, 220
ImageNet Large Scale Visual
Recognition Competition
(ILSVRC), 223–225
IMU. *See* Internal measurement
unit
Industrial revolution. *See* Zero
Principle
Insurance, 264, 265
Intelligent Transportation Systems,
131–135
Internal measurement unit (IMU),
187–191
Invariant representation, 89

Jobs, 259, 260

Kornhauser Alain, 138
Krizhevsky, Alex, 224

LeCun, Yann, 224
Li, Fei-Fei, 219
Lidar, 177–180
Loneliness, 40–43
Low-level controls, 75, 76, 78–80

Machine decision-making. *See* Ethics
Machine intelligence. *See* Artificial intelligence
Machine learning
  Driving, applying machine-learning to, 152–153, 166
  History of, 158–163, 202–219
  How machine learning works, 161–164
  See also Deep learning
Machine vision
  Challenges with automating, 6, 72–75, 85–88, 91–92
  History of, 6, 7
  See also Artificial perception
Marketing, 268, 269
Mean distance between failures, 101. *See also* Humansafe rating
Mean time between failures (MTBF), 101. *See also* Humansafe rating
Mid-level controls, 86–87, 93–98
Mid-level software. *See* Mid-level controls
Minsky, Marvin, 208–210
Moore's Law, 10, 166
Moravec's paradox, 72–74
Mortality rates from automobiles, 14
Municipal zoning, 33–35

Musk, Elon, 11, 85–86
Myths, 16–18

National Automated Highway System Consortium (NAHSC), 133–135. *See also* Intelligent Transportation Systems
National Highway Transportation and Safety Administration (NHTSA), 128
Neocognitron, 214–216
Neural networks, 199
  Academic politics, 198, 199, 208–210
  History of neural networks, 201–203, 210–213
  How neural networks work, 199–201
  See also Perceptron
Ng, Andrew, 224
NHTSA. *See* National Highway Transportation and Safety Administration
1964 World's Fair, 121
1939 World's Fair, 107–110
NREC, 68–72
NVIDIA, 225

Object recognition, 87–90. *See also* Artificial perception
Occupancy grid, 11, 93–95. *See also* Mid-level controls
Operating systems. *See* Artificial Intelligence; Automotive operating system; Controls engineering; Robotic operating system

Parking lots, 32–37
Perceptron, 202–206, 208, 209

Platooning, 30
Precision agriculture, 74
Pratt, Gill, 183
Privacy, 247, 248, 249
Public transportation, 40, 41, 42

Qualia, 231–233

Radar, 181–184
RCA, 116–120
Reactive controls. See Low-level
    controls
Rebound effect, 25
Recombinant innovation, 166
Reliability, 67, 98–104, 195. See also
    Humansafe ratings
Residual learning 228
Retail, 269–272
Road capacity, 30
Robotic density, 48
Robotic operating system
    Challenges of creating, 71–74
    Overview of, 63, 67
    See also CHIMP; Controls
    engineering
Robot morality. See Ethics
Rosenblatt, Frank, 202, 203,
    206–209
Route-planning software, 245, 246

Safety
    Death rates from car accidents,
    13, 14
    Defining acceptable levels of
    safety, 102–104
    Hackers, 99, 195, 274
    See also CAN bus; Humansafe
    ratings
Scene understanding, 89. See also
    Moravec's paradox

Seven delaying myths, 16, 17, 18
Sex. See Adult recreation
Shakey the robot, 90, 91
Short-term trajectory planner, See
    also Mid-level controls, 97
Simultaneous Localization and
    Mapping (SLAM), 240–243
SLAM. See Simultaneous
    Localization and Mapping
Software companies versus car
    companies, 46–55, 63
State space, 76, 165
Sun, Jian, 225
SuperVision, 224–227. See also Deep
    learning
Sutskever, Ilya, 224

Taxi drivers, 260
Template-based perception, 91,
    229, 230. See also Shakey the
    robot
Templeton, Brad, 142–146
Thrun, Sebastian, 152, 168
Traffic congestion, 25–28
Traffic prediction software,
    243–247
Trolley problem. See Ethics
Truckers, 259–263

Uber, 68, 260
Unemployment. See Jobs
U.S. Department of Transportation
    (USDOT), 128–132

V2I. See V2X
V2V. See V2X
V2X
    Drawbacks of, 136–140
    Overview of, 129, 130, 136
Vehicular lifespan, 28, 29

Werbos, Paul, 210, 213
"Who to kill." *See* Ethics
Wiesel, Torsten, 229
World's Fair (New York, 1939),
        107–110
World's Fair (New York, 1964), 121

XOR problem, 208

Yosinski, Jason, 232

Zero Principle, 255–258. *See also*
        Business models